SUCCEED

REVISION GUIDE

AQA GCSE

Religious Studies A (9–1)

Christianity & Islam

Marianne Fleming
Peter Smith
Harriet Power

OXFORD
UNIVERSITY PRESS

OXFORD
UNIVERSITY PRESS

Great Clarendon Street, Oxford, OX2 6DP, United Kingdom

Oxford University Press is a department of the University of Oxford. It furthers the University's objective of excellence in research, scholarship, and education by publishing worldwide. Oxford is a registered trade mark of Oxford University Press in the UK and in certain other countries

First published in 2018

British Library Cataloguing in Publication Data
Data available

978-138-207366-0

10 9 8 7 6 5 4 3 2 1

Paper used in the production of this book is a natural, recyclable product made from wood grown in sustainable forests. The manufacturing process conforms to the environmental regulations of the country of origin.

Printed in China by Shanghai Offset Printing Products Ltd

Please note that the Practice Questions in this book allow students a genuine attempt at practising exam skills, but they are not intended to replicate examination papers.

The manufacturer's authorised representative in the EU for product safety is Oxford University Press España S.A. of El Parque Empresarial San Fernando de Henares, Avenida de Castilla, 2 – 28830 Madrid (www.oup.es/en or product.safety@oup.com). OUP España S.A. also acts as importer into Spain of products made by the manufacturer.

MIX
Paper | Supporting responsible forestry
FSC www.fsc.org FSC® C109093

Acknowledgements

The publisher and authors would like to thank the following for permission to use photographs and other copyright material:

Cover(t): Image Source/Getty Images; **Cover(b):** Ground Picture/ Shutterstock.

Photos: p16: Renata Sedmakova/Shutterstock; **p17:** GrahamMoore999/iStock/Getty Images; **p46:** MuMuV/DigitalVision Vectors/Getty Images; **p53:** afby71/iStock; **p64:** JOAT/Shutterstock; **p88:** mshch/iStock/Getty Images; **p93:** zendograph/Shutterstock; **p111:** CARL DE SOUZA/AFP/Getty Images; **p134:** Yuriy Boyko/ Shutterstock; **p138(t):** Nick Savage/Alamy Stock Photo; **p138(b):** wong yu liang/Shutterstock.

Artwork by Jason Ramasami, and QBS Learning.

We are grateful to the authors and publishers for use of extracts from their titles and in particular for the following:

Scripture quotations [marked NIV] taken from the **Holy Bible, New International Version Anglicised** Copyright © 1979, 1984, 2011 Biblica. Used by permission of Hodder & Stoughton Ltd, an Hachette UK company. All rights reserved. 'NIV' is a registered trademark of Biblica UK trademark number 1448790. Excerpts from **The Qur'an OWC** translated by M. A. S. Abdel Haleem (Oxford University Press, 2008). © M. A. S. Abdel Haleem 2004, 2005. Reproduced with permission of the Licensor through PLSclear. **Alliance of Religions and Conservation:** *Assisi Declarations on Nature*, http://www.arcworld.org/faiths.asp?pageID=179 (ARC, 1986). Reproduced with permission from Alliance of Religions and Conservation. **Anglican Pacifists:** *Anglican Pacifist Fellowship (APF)'s Pledge*, http://anglicanpeacemaker.org.uk/wp-content/uploads/2015/11/TAP-Oct-2015.pdf (Anglican Pacifist Fellowship, 2015). Reproduced with permission from Anglican Pacifist Fellowship. **AQA:** *Paper 1A: Specimen question paper*, (AQA 2017). Reproduced with permission from AQA. **AQA:** *Paper 1A: Additional specimen question paper*, (AQA 2017). Reproduced with permission from AQA. **Christian Aid:** *Refugee Crisis Appeal*, http://www.christianaid.org.uk/emergencies/areas-of-concern/refugee-crisis.aspx Christian Aid, 2016). Reproduced with permission from Christian Aid. **The Church of England:** Lines from the *Creeds*, the *Lord's Prayer*, the *marriage rite*, and the *baptism rite*. (The Archbishops' Council, 2017). © The Archbishops' Council. Reproduced with permission from The Archbishops' Council. **The Church of England:** *The Lambeth Conference: Resolutions Archive from 1930*, (Anglican Communion Office, 2005). © The Archbishops' Council. Reproduced with permission from The Archbishops' Council. **S. Hucklesby**: 'Mutual cooperation, not mutual destruction' say Churches, The Methodist Church in Britain website, 23rd May 2015. http://www.methodist.org.uk/news-and-events/news-releases/mutual-cooperation-not-mutual-destruction-say-churches (The Methodist Church in Britain, 2015). Reproduced with permission from The Methodist Church in Britain. **Pope Francis:** quote from speech at the Pontifical Academy of Sciences, October 2014. (The Vatican, 2014). © Libreria Editrice Vaticana. Reproduced with permission from The Vatican. **Pope Paul VI:** *Humanae Vitae*, (The Vatican, 1968). © Libreria Editrice Vaticana. Reproduced with permission from The Vatican. **The United Nations:** *The Universal Declaration of Human Rights*, (UDHR) (United Nations, 1948). Reproduced with permission from United Nations. **The Vatican:** *Catechism of the Catholic Church*, (The Vatican 1993). © Libreria Editrice Vaticana. Reproduced with permission from The Vatican.

We have made every effort to trace and contact all copyright holders before publication, but if notified of any errors or omissions, the publisher will be happy to rectify these at the earliest opportunity.

Contents

How exam-ready are you?

Introduction

What will the exam be like?

For your GCSE Religious Studies exam, you will sit two papers.

- **Paper 1 will cover the study of religions.** You will need to answer questions on the beliefs and teachings, and practices, of **two** world religions. There will be separate question and answer booklets for each religion. Chapters 1 and 2 of this revision guide will help you to answer questions on Christianity for Paper 1. Chapters 3 and 4 will help you to answer questions on Islam.
- **Paper 2 will cover thematic studies.** There are six themes on the paper. You will need to **choose four themes**, and answer all the questions for each chosen theme. You will need to know about religious beliefs and viewpoints on themes and issues. Except in those questions where the main religious tradition of Great Britain is asked for, you can use beliefs from any religion in your answer. For example, you might want to focus on Christianity, including viewpoints from different traditions within Christianity, such as Catholic or Protestant views. Or you might want to include beliefs across six religions, including Christian, Buddhist, Hindu, Muslim, Jewish or Sikh viewpoints. Chapters 5 to 10 of this revision guide cover the six themes, focusing on a Christian and Muslim perspective.

If you are studying **St Mark's Gospel**, then the six themes will appear in Section A of Paper 2. You will need to choose **two themes**. You will then also need to answer the **two questions on St Mark's Gospel** from Section B.

TIP

Each paper is 1 hour and 45 minutes long, and you'll need to answer four full questions. Aim to spend 25 minutes on each question.

What kind of questions will be on the exam?

Each question on the exam will be split into five parts, worth 1, 1, 4, 6 and 12 marks.

The 1 mark multiple-choice question

The 1 mark **multiple-choice question** tests knowledge and understanding.

It always has four answers to choose from. It will usually include the command words: '**Which one of the following...**'

Which **one** of the following is the idea that God is three-in-one?

Put a tick (✔) in the box next to the correct answer.

A	Atonement	☐
B	Incarnation	☐
C	Salvation	☐
D	Trinity	☐

[1 mark]

How is it marked?

1 mark is awarded for a correct answer.

The 1 mark question

The 1 mark question tests knowledge and understanding.

It always begins with the command words '**Give one...**' or '**Name one...**'

> Give **one** way in which religious believers help victims of war.
>
> **[1 mark]**

How is it marked?

1 mark is awarded for 1 correct point.

TIP

The examiner is expecting one simple point, not a detailed explanation. You would get 1 mark if you answered "Praying for victims". You don't need to waste time by writing a full sentence and giving a long explanation.

The 4 mark question

The 4 mark question tests knowledge and understanding.

It always begins with the command words '**Explain two...**'

It might test your knowledge of how a religion influences individuals, communities and societies. Or it might ask for similarities or differences within or between religions.

> Explain **two** different ways in which Holy Communion is celebrated in Christianity.
>
> **[4 marks]**

How is it marked?

For the first way or belief:

- 1 mark is awarded for a simple explanation
- 2 marks are awarded for a detailed explanation.

For the second similar/different way or belief:

- 1 mark is awarded for a simple explanation
- 2 marks are awarded for a detailed explanation.

So for the full 4 marks, the examiner is looking for two ways/beliefs and for you to give detailed explanations of both. The examiner is expecting you to write in full sentences.

What is a detailed explanation?

An easy way to remember what you need to do for the four mark question is:

Make one point → **Develop it**

Make a second point → **Develop it**

TIP

One point you might make to answer this question is to say "Catholics celebrate Holy Communion by receiving offerings of bread and wine." This would get you 1 mark. For a second mark you could develop the point by giving further information: "During the service they believe the bread and wine become the body and blood of Jesus Christ." There is more you could probably say, but as you'd get 2 marks for this, it would be better to turn your attention to thinking about a second different way in which Holy Communion is celebrated, and then developing that second point.

But how do you develop a point? You might do this by:

- giving more information
- giving an example
- referring to a religious teaching or quotation.

The 'Great Britain' question

Sometimes there may be additional wording to the 4 mark question, asking you to '**Refer to the main religious tradition of Great Britain and one or more other religious traditions.**'

> Explain **two** different religious beliefs about contraception.
>
> In your answer you should refer to the main religious tradition of Great Britain and one or more other religious traditions.
>
> **[4 marks]**

The main religious tradition of Great Britain is Christianity, so in your answer **you must refer to Christianity**. You can refer to **two different denominations within Christianity**, or you can compare **a Christian belief with that from another religion,** such as Buddhism, Hinduism, Islam, Judaism or Sikhism.

For theme C: The existence of God and revelation, the wording will say: 'In your answer you should refer to the main religious tradition of Great Britain **and non-religious beliefs.**' You must refer to Christianity and a non-religious belief.

This type of question will only be asked about certain topics. We point them out in this Revision Guide using this feature:

> You might be asked to compare beliefs on contraception between Christianity (the main religious tradition in Great Britain) and another religious tradition.

TIP

You can't, for example, refer to two different groups within Buddhism, or compare Buddhism and Islam. There must be a reference to Christianity or you won't get full marks for this question however detailed your answer is.

The 6 mark question

The 6 mark question tests knowledge and understanding.

Like the 4 mark question, it always begins with the command words '**Explain two...**' In addition it will also ask you to '**Refer to sacred writings or another source of religious/Christian belief and teaching in your answer.**'

> Explain **two** reasons why Christians pray.
>
> Refer to sacred writings or another source of Christian belief and teaching in your answer.
>
> **[6 marks]**

How is it marked?

For the first belief/teaching/practice:

- 1 mark is awarded for a simple explanation
- 2 marks are awarded for a detailed explanation.

For the second belief/teaching/practice:

- 1 mark is awarded for a simple explanation
- 2 marks are awarded for a detailed explanation.

Plus 1 mark for a relevant reference to sacred writings or another source of religious belief and teaching.

Plus 1 mark for applying the reference to sacred writings or another source of religious belief and teaching to the question.

So for the full 6 marks, the examiner is looking for two beliefs/teachings/practices and for you to give detailed explanations of both, just like the 4 mark question. **For the fifth and sixth marks, you need to refer to a writing or teaching that is considered holy or authoritative by a religion, and apply it to the question.** The examiner is expecting you to write in full sentences. You might aim to write six sentences.

What counts as 'sacred writings or another source of religious belief and teaching'?

Sacred writings or religious beliefs and teachings might include:

- a quotation from a holy book, for example the Bible or the Qur'an
- a statement of religious belief such as the Apostles' Creed or Shahadah
- a prayer such as the Lord's Prayer
- a statement made by a religious leader, for example the Pope
- a quotation from a religious text such as the Catechism of the Catholic Church or Hadith.

TIP

Try to quote exact phrases if you can, but if you can't then it's fine to paraphrase. It's also ok if you can't remember the exact verse that a quotation is from, but it would be helpful to name the holy book, for example to specify that it is a teaching from the Bible.

The 12 mark question

The 12 mark question tests analytical and evaluative skills. It will always begin with a statement, and then ask you to **evaluate the statement**. There will be bullet points guiding you through what the examiner expects you to provide in your answer.

From Paper 1:

'The Bible tells Christians all they need to know about God's creation.'

Evaluate this statement. In your answer you should:

- refer to Christian teaching
- give reasoned arguments to support this statement
- give reasoned arguments to support a different point of view
- reach a justified conclusion.

[12 marks]

[+3 SPaG marks]

TIP

The examiners are not just giving marks for what you know, but for your ability to weigh up different sides of an argument, making judgements on how convincing or weak you think they are. The examiner will also be looking for your ability to connect your arguments logically.

From Paper 2:

'War is never right'.

Evaluate this statement. In your answer you:

- should give reasoned arguments in support of this statement
- should give reasoned arguments to support a different point of view
- should refer to religious arguments
- may refer to non-religious arguments
- should reach a justified conclusion.

[12 marks]
[+3 SPaG marks]

TIP For Paper 2, on thematic issues, you can use different views from one or more religions, and you can also use non-religious views.

How is it marked?

Level	What the examiner is looking for	Marks
4	A well-argued response with two different points of view, both developed to show a logical chain of reasoning that leads to judgements supported by relevant knowledge and understanding. ***References to religion applied to the issue.***	10–12 marks
3	Two different points of view, both developed through a logical chain of reasoning that draws on relevant knowledge and understanding. ***Clear reference to religion.***	7–9 marks
2	One point of view developed through a logical chain of reasoning that draws on relevant knowledge and understanding. OR Two different points of view with supporting reasons. ***Students cannot move above Level 2 if they don't include a reference to religion, or only give one viewpoint.***	4–6 marks
1	One point of view with supporting reasons. OR Two different points of view, simply expressed.	1–3 marks

TIP This question is worth the same amount of marks as the 1, 1, 4 and 6 mark questions combined. Try to aim for at least a full page of writing, and spend 12 minutes or more on this question.

Tips for answering the 12 mark question

- **Remember to focus your answer on the statement you've been given**, for example 'War is never right.'
- **Include different viewpoints, one supporting the statement, one arguing against it** – for example one viewpoint to support the idea that war is *never* right, and an alternative viewpoint to suggest that war is sometimes necessary.
- **Develop both arguments showing a logical chain of reasoning** – draw widely on your knowledge and understanding of the subject of war, and try to make **connections** between ideas. Write a detailed answer and use evidence to support your arguments.
- **Be sure to include religious arguments** – a top level answer will explain how religious teaching is relevant to the argument.
- **Include evaluation** – you can make judgements on the strength of arguments throughout, and you should finish with a justified conclusion. If you want to, you can give your own opinion.
- **Write persuasively** – **use a minimum of three paragraphs** (one giving arguments for the statement, one for a different point of view and a final conclusion). The examiner will expect to see extended writing and full sentences.

Spelling, punctuation and grammar

Additional marks for **SPaG – spelling, punctuation and grammar** will be awarded on the 12 mark question.

A maximum of 3 marks will be awarded if:

- your spelling and punctuation are consistently accurate
- you use grammar properly to control the meaning of what you are trying to say
- you use specialist and religious terminology appropriately. For example, if you use appropriately the term 'resurrection' rather than just 'rising from the dead'.

In Paper 1, SPaG will be awarded on the Beliefs question for each religion.

In Paper 2, SPaG will be assessed on each 12 mark question, and the examiner will pick your best mark to add to the total.

TIP

Always try to use your best written English in the long 12 mark questions. It could be a chance to pick up extra marks for SPaG.

How to revise using this book

This Revision Guide takes a three-step approach to help with your revision.

RECAP	This is an overview of the key information. It is not a substitute for the full student book, or your class notes. It should prompt you to recall more in-depth information. Diagrams and images are included to help make the information more memorable.
APPLY	Once you've recapped the key information, you can practise applying it to help embed the information. There are two questions after each Recap section. The first question will help you rehearse some key skills that you need for the questions on the exam that test your knowledge (the 1, 1, 4 and 6 mark questions). The second question will help you rehearse some key skills that you will need for the 12 mark question, which tests your evaluative skills. There are suggested answers to the Apply activities at the back of the book.
REVIEW	At the end of each chapter you will then have a chance to review what you've revised. The exam practice pages contain exam-style questions for each question type. For the 4, 6 and 12 mark questions, there are writing frames that you can use to structure your answer, and to remind yourself of what it is that the examiner is looking for. When you've answered the questions you can use the mark schemes at the back of the book to see how you've done. You might identify some areas that you need to revise in more detail. And you can turn back to the pages here for guidance on how to answer the exam questions.

The revision guide is designed so that alongside revising *what* you need to know, you can practise *how* to apply this knowledge in your exam. There are regular opportunities to try out exam practice questions, and mark schemes so you can see how you are doing. Keep recapping, applying and reviewing, particularly going over those areas that you feel unsure about, and hopefully you will build in skills and confidence for the final exam.

Good luck!

1 Christianity: Beliefs and teachings

1.1 The nature of God

RECAP

Essential information:

- [ ] Christianity is the main religion in Great Britain.
- [ ] Christianity has three main traditions: Catholic, Protestant and Orthodox.
- [ ] Christianity is **monotheistic**, meaning that Christians believe in one Supreme Being, **God**.

Different branches of Christianity

CHRISTIANITY

- **Catholic** – based in Rome and led by the Pope.
- **Orthodox** – split from Catholic Christianity in 1054 CE and practised in Eastern Europe.
- **Protestant** – split from Catholic Christianity in the 16th century and branched out into different **denominations** (distinct groups), e.g. Baptist, Pentecostal, Methodist, United Reformed Churches. Protestants agree that the Bible is the only authority for Christians.

TIP

If you are asked about similarities and differences in a religion, try to remember that even though Christianity has different denominations, they all share the same belief in God.

What do Christians believe about God?

- There is only one God:

> “We believe in one God”
> *The Nicene Creed*

- God is the creator and sustainer of all that exists.
- God works throughout history and inspires people to do God's will.
- People can have a relationship with God through prayer.
- God is spirit (John 4:24) – neither male nor female – but has qualities of both.
- God is **holy** (set apart for a special purpose and worthy of worship).
- Jesus is God's son – the true representation of God on earth (Hebrews 1:3).

TIP

See page 13 for more Christian beliefs about God.

APPLY

A Christians believe that there is only one God. Refer to scripture or another Christian source of authority to support this idea.

B 'Christianity is a major influence on people's lives.'

Write a paragraph to **support this statement**.

1.2 God as omnipotent, loving and just

RECAP

Essential information:

Christians believe:

- ☐ God is **omnipotent**, almighty, having unlimited power.
- ☐ God is **benevolent**, all-loving and all-good.
- ☐ God is **just**, the perfect judge of human behaviour who will bring about what is right and fair or who will make up for a wrong that has been committed.

Some qualities of God

Omnipotent	Benevolent	Just

• God is the Supreme Being who is all-powerful. • God has unlimited authority.	• God uses his power to do good. • God shows his love by creating humans and caring for them. • God showed his love by sending God's Son, Jesus, to earth.	• God is a just judge of humankind. • God will never support injustice, ill-treatment, prejudice or oppression.

The problems of evil and suffering

The problems of evil and suffering challenge belief in these qualities of God:

- If God is benevolent, **why does God allow people to suffer**, and to hurt others?
- If God is omnipotent, **why does God not prevent evil and suffering**, such as the suffering caused by natural disasters?
- If God is just, **why does God allow injustice** to take place?

Christians believe a just God treats people fairly, so they trust God even when things seem to be going wrong.

TIP

See page 101 for more arguments in response to these challenges to belief in God.

APPLY

A Give **one** way in which Christians believe God shows his benevolence.

B Write the response a Christian would make to someone who said that a loving God would not allow suffering. Think of **two** arguments and develop them.

TIP

In the 12 mark exam answer, using the key terms 'omnipotent', 'benevolent' and 'just' where appropriate, and spelling them correctly, may gain you more marks for SPaG.

1.3 The Oneness of God and the Trinity

RECAP

Essential information:

- [ ] Christians believe there are three persons in the one God: Father, Son and Holy Spirit. This belief is called the **Trinity**.
- [ ] Each person of the Trinity is fully God.
- [ ] The persons of the Trinity are not the same.

TIP
The Apostles' Creed and/or the Nicene Creed, Christian statements of belief, are useful to know when discussing the Trinity. They begin 'I/We believe in one God' and include references to 'the Father Almighty', 'the Son' and 'the Holy Spirit'.

The Trinity

- God is understood by Christians as a relationship of love between Father, Son and Holy Spirit.
- In describing God as Trinity, 'person' does not mean a physical being, although Jesus did have a physical presence in history.

God the Father, the creator of all life, acts as a good father towards his children. He is all powerful (omnipotent), all loving (omnibenevolent), all knowing (omniscient) and present everywhere (omnipresent).

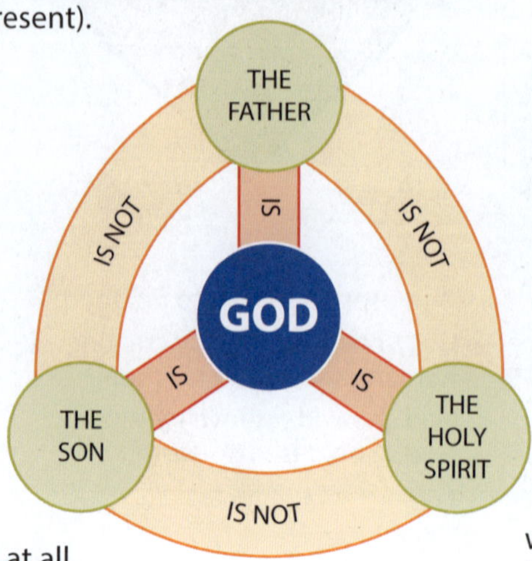

God the Son became incarnate through Jesus who was both fully human while on earth and fully God at all times. Jesus is called the **Son of God** to show his special relationship to God the Father.

God the Holy Spirit is the unseen power of God at work in the world, who influences, guides and sustains life on earth.

APPLY

A Here are **two** Christian beliefs about the Trinity. Develop each point with further explanation or a relevant quotation:

1. *"The Trinity is the Christian belief that there are three persons in the one God."* ______

2. *"One of the persons of the Trinity is God the Father."* ______

B Here are some arguments that could be used to evaluate the statement, 'The Trinity is a helpful way of describing God.' Sort them into arguments in support of the statement, and arguments in support of different views. **Write your own justified conclusion.**

1. The Trinity is a helpful idea because it describes God as a loving relationship of persons.	5. If God is One, then how can God have three persons?
2. The love of God the Son is shown in Jesus' mission and sacrifice.	6. The Holy Spirit is the outpouring of love between Father and Son that encourages Christians to love their neighbour.
3. The Trinity seems contradictory.	7. Jesus was a Jew and believed in the oneness of God.
4. The love of God the Father is shown in his sending his Son to earth to save humankind.	8. The Trinity is not helpful to people of other faiths as they may think that Christians believe in three different Gods.

1.4 Different Christian beliefs about creation

RECAP

Essential information:

- ☐ Christians believe in **creation** by God, the act by which God brought the universe into being.
- ☐ God, the Father, chose to design and create the earth and all life on it.
- ☐ The Holy Spirit was active in the creation (Genesis 1:1–3).
- ☐ The **Word**, God the Son or Jesus, was active in the creation (John 1:1–3).
- ☐ The Trinity, therefore, existed from the beginning and was involved in the creation.

Creation: *Genesis 1:1–3*

> "**In the beginning, God created the heavens and the earth**. Now the earth was formless and empty, darkness was over the surface of the deep, and the Spirit of God was hovering over the waters. And God said, "Let there be light," and there was light."
>
> *Genesis 1: 1–3* [NIV]

- Many Christians believe that the story of the creation in Genesis, while not scientifically accurate, contains religious truth.
- Some Christians believe that God made the world in literally six days.
- God created everything out of choice and created everything 'good'.
- Christians believe that God continues to create new life today.
- Although God the Father is referred to as the creator, the Holy Spirit was active in the creation, according to Genesis.

Creation: *John 1:1–3*

> "In the beginning was the Word, and **the Word was with God, and the Word was God**. He was with God in the beginning. Through him all things were made; without him nothing was made that has been made."
>
> *John 1: 1–3* [NIV]

- In John's gospel, everything was created through the Word, who was both with God and was God.
- The Word refers to the Son of God who entered history as Jesus.
- Christians believe that the Son of God, the Word of God, was involved in the creation.

TIP

See pages 86 and 98–99 for more detail on different Christian beliefs about creation.

APPLY

A Explain **two** ways in which belief in creation by God influences Christians today.

B Here is an argument in support of the statement, 'The Bible is the best source of information about the creation.'

Evaluate the argument. Explain your reasoning.

"The Bible contains the truth about the creation of the world by God. God is omnipotent, so God can just say 'Let there be light' and it happens. The Bible is God's word, so it is true. Other theories about the creation, like evolution and the Big Bang theory, have not been proved."

TIP

Show the examiner that you are aware of different views within Christianity about the way Genesis 1 is interpreted, that is, between those who take the story literally and those who do not.

1.5 The incarnation and Jesus, the Son of God

RECAP

Essential information:

- ☐ Christians believe that Jesus was God in human form, a belief known as the **incarnation** (becoming flesh, taking a human form).
- ☐ Christians believe that Jesus was the Son of God, one of the persons of the Trinity.

The incarnation

> "This is how the birth of Jesus the Messiah came about: His mother Mary was pledged to be married to Joseph, but before they came together, **she was found to be pregnant through the Holy Spirit.**"
>
> *Matthew 1:18* [NIV]

- On separate occasions an angel appeared to Mary and Joseph explaining that it was not an ordinary conception and it was not to be an ordinary child.
- The gospels of Matthew and Luke explain that Mary conceived Jesus without having sex.
- The virgin conception is evidence for the Christian belief that Jesus was the Son of God, part of the Trinity.
- Through the incarnation, God showed himself as a human being (Jesus) for around 30 years.

> "**The Word became flesh** and made his dwelling among us."
>
> *John 1:14* [NIV]

Son of God, Messiah, Christ

- Jesus was fully God and fully human, which helps explain his miracles and **resurrection** (rising from the dead).
- His words, deeds and promises have great authority because they are the word of God.
- Most Jews expected a Messiah who would come to save Israel and establish an age of peace, but do not believe that Jesus was that person.
- Christians believe that Jesus is the Messiah, but a spiritual rather than a political one.
- Gospel writers refer to Jesus as the Christ ('anointed one' or Messiah), but Jesus warned his disciples not to use the term, possibly because his opponents would have him arrested for **blasphemy** (claiming to be God).

Jesus

'The Word'

Christ

Messiah

God the Son, one of the persons in the Trinity

Son of God

APPLY

A Explain **two** Christian beliefs about Jesus' incarnation. **Refer to sacred writings in your answer.**

B **Develop the following argument** to support the statement, 'The stories of the incarnation show that Jesus was the Son of God' by explaining in more detail, adding an example, or referring to a relevant religious teaching or quotation.

"The stories of the incarnation in the gospels of Matthew and Luke show that his mother, Mary, was a virgin. Joseph was not the natural father of Jesus. Jesus' conception was through the Holy Spirit, so really God was his father. That is why he is called the Son of God."

TIP

In a 6 mark question, you need to give a detailed explanation of each belief and then support your answer by quoting from scripture or sacred writings. You must also connect this to the question for full marks. The sacred writings may refer to just one of the beliefs or to both of them.

1.6 The crucifixion

RECAP

Essential information:

- [ ] Jesus was sentenced to death by Pontius Pilate, a death by **crucifixion** (fixed to a cross).
- [ ] Jesus forgave those who crucified him and promised one of the men crucified with him that he would join God in paradise.
- [ ] Jesus' body was buried in a cave-like tomb.

Jesus' crucifixion – what happened?

- Although Jesus was fully God, he was also fully human so suffered pain and horror.
- Jesus' last words before dying were:

> "Father, into your hands I commit my spirit."
> *Luke 23:46* [NIV]

- A Roman centurion acknowledged Jesus was innocent, and said he was the Son of God (Mark 15:39).
- The Roman guards made sure Jesus was dead.
- Joseph of Arimathea was permitted to bury Jesus in a cave-like tomb, rolling a large stone to block the entrance.
- Jesus' burial was rushed because the Sabbath was about to begin.

Jesus' crucifixion – why is it important?

- Jesus' sacrifice on the cross gives hope to Christians that **their sins will be forgiven if they sincerely repent**.
- Christians believe that **God understands human suffering** because Jesus, who is God, experienced it.
- **Christians accept that suffering is part of life**, just as it was a part of Jesus' life.

TIP
See page 23 for more detail on why the crucifixion was important.

APPLY

A Here are two ways in which Jesus' crucifixion influences Christians today:

1) Their sins are forgiven.
2) They have hope when they are suffering.

Develop both points by **explaining in more detail or by adding an example**.

TIP
Keep rereading the statement to make sure you are answering the question asked.

B Read the following response to the statement, 'The crucifixion is the most important belief for Christians.' Underline the **two** best arguments. Explain how this answer could be improved.

"Jesus was arrested in the Garden of Gethsemane and brought to trial, first before the Jewish Council and then before the Roman Governor, Pontius Pilate. In the gospels it says that Pontius Pilate did not think Jesus was guilty of anything, so he didn't want to have him killed. Instead he had him flogged. The Jewish leaders called for Jesus' death, so Pilate gave in to their wishes and sentenced Jesus to death. After about six hours of agony on the cross, Jesus died. A Roman centurion said that because Jesus was innocent, he must surely be the Son of God. When Jesus died, he took the sins of everyone on himself. This is called the atonement. If Jesus had not died, he would not have risen from the dead."

1.7 The resurrection and ascension

RECAP

Essential information:

- ☐ The gospels say that after Jesus died and was buried, he rose from the dead. This event is known as the **resurrection**.
- ☐ The **ascension** of Jesus took place 40 days after his resurrection, when he returned to God the Father in **heaven**.
- ☐ There would be no Christian faith without the resurrection.

The resurrection of Jesus – what happened?

- Early on Sunday morning, some of Jesus' female followers, including Mary Magdalene, visited the tomb to anoint Jesus' body.
- Jesus' body was not there.
- Either a man or two men, who may have been angels, told the women to spread the news that Jesus had risen from the dead.
- Over the next few days, Jesus appeared to several people including Mary Magdalene and his disciples. He told them he had risen from the dead, as he predicted he would before the crucifixion.

> "And if Christ has not been raised, our preaching is useless and so is your faith. But Christ has indeed been raised from the dead… For as in Adam all die, so in Christ all will be made alive."
>
> *1 Corinthians 15:14, 20, 22* [NIV]

TIP

This quote shows that Christianity would not exist without the resurrection. It also shows that the resurrection is important because it is significant evidence for Christians of the divine nature of Jesus.

The ascension of Jesus – what happened?

- After meeting with his disciples and asking them to carry on his work, Jesus left them for the last time, returning to the Father in heaven. This event is called the ascension.

> "While he was blessing them, he left them and was taken up into heaven." *Luke 24:51* [NIV]

The significance of these events for Christians today

The significance of the **resurrection**:

- Shows the power of good over evil and life over death.
- Means Christians' sins will be forgiven if they follow God's laws.
- Means Christians will be resurrected if they accept Jesus, so there is no need to fear death.

The significance of the **ascension**:

- Shows Jesus is with God in heaven.
- Paves the way for God to send the Holy Spirit to provide comfort and guidance.

APPLY

A Give **one** reason why the disciples believed Jesus was alive after his resurrection. (Based on AQA Specimen question paper, 2017)

B 'The resurrection is the most important belief for Christians.'

Develop the following response to the statement, by adding a relevant religious teaching or quotation.

"Without the resurrection, there would be no Christian faith. Jesus' death would have been the end of all the hopes the disciples placed on him. He would have been just like all the other innocent victims put to death for their beliefs."

1.8 Resurrection and life after death

RECAP

Essential information:

- ☐ Jesus' resurrection assures Christians that they too will rise and live on after death.
- ☐ Christians have differing views about what happens when a person who has died is resurrected.
- ☐ Belief in resurrection affects the way Christians live their lives today.

Different Christian views about resurrection

Some Christians believe a person's soul is resurrected **soon after death**.	Other Christians believe the dead will be resurrected at **some time in the future**, when Jesus will return to judge everyone who has ever lived.
Catholic and Orthodox Christians believe in bodily resurrection. This means resurrection is **both spiritual and physical**: the physical body lost at death is restored and transformed into a new, spiritual body.	Some other Christians believe resurrection will **just be spiritual**, not physical as well.

" So will it be with the resurrection of the dead. The body that is sown is perishable, it is raised imperishable; it is sown in dishonour, it is raised in glory; it is sown in weakness, it is raised in power; it is sown a natural body, it is raised a spiritual body. If there is a natural body, there is also a spiritual body. "

1 Corinthians 15:42–44 [NIV]

TIP

This quote explains some of the differences between a living body and a resurrected body. For Catholics and Orthodox Christians, it suggests there is a physical element to resurrection, as it talks about the resurrected body being a 'body', even if it is a spiritual one.

Impact of the belief in resurrection

A belief in resurrection...

- means life after death is real
- gives hope of a future life with Jesus
- gives confidence in the face of death
- shows Christians how much God loves them
- inspires Christians to live life in the way God wants them to, so they can remain in his presence in this life and the next

APPLY

A Explain **two** ways in which a belief in resurrection influences Christians today.

B The table below presents arguments for and against the belief in bodily resurrection. **Write a paragraph** to explain whether you agree or disagree with bodily resurrection, having evaluated both sides of the argument.

For	Against
Jesus rose from the dead and appeared to his disciples.	Science has shown the body decays after death, so there cannot be a physical resurrection.
The gospels insist he was not a ghost, as he ate with them and showed his wounds to them.	Some people are cremated so their bodies no longer exist.
Yet he could appear and disappear suddenly, so it seems that his body was transformed.	Stories of the resurrection appearances may have been exaggerated.
Paul says 'the body that is sown is perishable, it is raised imperishable', suggesting the natural body is raised as a spiritual body, but a body nevertheless.	The disciples may have felt Jesus' presence spiritually rather than seeing him physically.
Catholic and Orthodox Christians believe people's bodies are transformed into a glorified state in which suffering will not exist.	Christians believe in the soul and it is the soul that rises again, not the body.

TIP

If you need to give different points of view in your answer to an evaluation question, you could include different non-religious perspectives as well as religious perspectives.

1.9 The afterlife and judgement

RECAP

Essential information:

- ☐ Christians believe in an **afterlife** (life after death) that depends on faith in God.
- ☐ The afterlife begins at death or at the **Day of Judgement**, when Jesus will come to judge the living and the dead.
- ☐ Judgement will be based on how people have behaved during their lifetimes, as well as their faith in following Jesus. This has an effect on how Christians choose to live their lives today.

The afterlife

Christian beliefs about life after death vary, but many believe that:

- They will be **resurrected** and receive **eternal life** after they die.
- This is a gift from God, and **dependent on faith** in God.
- They will be **judged by God** at some point after they die, and either rewarded by being sent to heaven or punished by being sent to hell.
- This judgement will happen either **very soon after death** or **on the Day of Judgement**. This is a time in the future when the world will end and Christ will come again to judge the living and the dead.

Some of these beliefs about the afterlife are found in the **Apostles' Creed**, which is an important statement of Christian faith:

> "He ascended into heaven, and is seated at the right hand of the Father,
> and he will come to judge the living and the dead:
> I believe in…
> the resurrection of the body;
> and the life everlasting."
>
> *The Apostles' Creed*

Judgement

- Christians believe that after they die, God will judge them on their **behaviour and actions** during their lifetime, as well as their **faith in Jesus** as God's Son.
- In the Bible, Jesus' **parable of the Sheep and the Goats** describes how God will judge people.
- This parable teaches Christians that **in serving others, they are serving Jesus**, so this is the way they should live their lives.

> "For I was hungry and you gave me something to eat, I was thirsty and you gave me something to drink, I was a stranger and you invited me in, I needed clothes and you clothed me, I was ill and you looked after me, I was in prison and you came to visit me."
>
> *Matthew 25:35–36* [NIV]

- Before he died, Jesus told his disciples he would prepare a place for them in heaven with God. He also made it clear that **having faith in him and following his teachings** was essential for being able to enter heaven when he said:

> "I am the way and the truth and the life. No one comes to the Father except through me." *John 14:6* [NIV]

APPLY

A Explain **two** Christian teachings about judgement. **Refer to sacred writings or another source of Christian belief and teaching in your answer.** (Based on AQA Specimen question paper, 2017)

B **Evaluate the statement**, 'The afterlife is a good way to get people to behave themselves and help others.' Present two developed Christian arguments, and two developed non-religious arguments. **Write a justified conclusion.**

TIP

When writing a justified conclusion, do not just repeat everything you have already said. Instead, weigh up the arguments and come to a personal view about their persuasiveness.

1.10 Heaven and hell

RECAP

Essential information:

- [ ] Many Christians believe God's judgement will result in eternal reward or eternal punishment.
- [ ] **Heaven** is the state or place of eternal happiness and peace in the presence of God.
- [ ] **Hell** is the place of eternal suffering or the state of being without God.

What happens after God's judgement?

- After God's judgement, Christians believe they will either **experience eternal happiness in the presence of God** (heaven), or **be unable to experience God's presence** (hell).
- Catholics believe some people might enter an intermediate state, called purgatory, before they enter heaven.
- Knowledge of these states is limited and linked to imagery from the past.

Heaven and purgatory

- **Heaven** is thought to be either a **physical place** or **spiritual state** of peace, joy, freedom from pain and a chance to be with loved ones.
- Traditional images of heaven often show God on a throne with Jesus next to him and angels all around him, or a garden paradise.
- Christians differ in their views about **who is allowed into heaven**, where there may be:
  - only Christians (believers in Jesus)
  - Christians and other religious people who have pleased God by living good lives
  - baptised Christians, regardless of how they lived their lives.
- However, many Christians believe heaven is a reward for **both faith and actions** – not just one of these – as the parable of the Sheep and the Goats seems to show (see page 20).
- **Purgatory** is an intermediate state where souls are cleansed in order to enter heaven. This is a Catholic belief.

Hell

- **Hell** is seen as the opposite of heaven – a state of existence without God.
- It is often pictured as a **place of eternal torment** in a fiery pit ruled by Satan (a name for the Devil), who is the power and source of evil.
- However, many people question whether a loving God would condemn people to eternal torment and pain in hell.
- Christians who believe God would not do this see hell as an **eternal state of mind** of **being cut off from the possibility of God**.
- Hell would then be what awaits someone who did not acknowledge God or follow his teachings during their life.

APPLY

A Give **one** reason why some people do not believe in hell.

B **Make a list of arguments** for and against the idea that heaven and hell were invented to encourage people to behave themselves.

TIP

If this question said 'some Christians', you should offer Christian objections to the idea of hell. 'Some people' means you can give non-religious reasons if you wish.

1.11 Sin and salvation

RECAP

Essential information:

- [ ] **Sin** is any thought or action that separates humans from God.
- [ ] **Original sin** is the in-built tendency to do wrong and disobey God, which Catholics believe all people are born with.
- [ ] The ways Christians can be saved from sin to gain salvation include following God's **law**, receiving God's **grace**, and being guided by the **Holy Spirit**.

The origins and meanings of sin

A sin is any **thought or action that separates humans from God**. Sinful thoughts (such as anger) can lead to sinful actions (such as murder).

- Some sins, like murder or assault, are illegal.
- Other sins, like adultery, are not illegal but are against the laws of God.

Christians believe that all humans commit sins. Some Christians (particularly Catholics) also believe humans are born with an in-built tendency to sin, called **original sin**.

- The idea of original sin comes from Adam and Eve's disobedience of God, when they ate the fruit of the tree of knowledge of good and evil which was forbidden by God. This was the first (original) sin.
- The result of their sin was separation from God, and the introduction of death into the world.

Christians believe **God gave people free will**, but they should use their freedom to make choices God would approve of, otherwise they will separate themselves from God. God provides people with the guidance to make good choices in his law**,** for example the Ten Commandments (Exodus 20:1–19), the Beatitudes (Matthew 5:1–12) and other Christian teachings.

Salvation

- **Salvation** means to be saved from sin and its consequences, and to be granted eternal life with God.
- Salvation **repairs the damage caused by sin**, which has separated people from God.

There are two main Christian ideas about how salvation can come about:

- Through **doing good works** – the Old Testament makes it clear that salvation comes through faith in God and obeying God's law.

> "In the same way, faith by itself, if it is not accompanied by action, is dead."
>
> *James 2:17* [NIV]

- Through **grace** – salvation is given freely by God through faith in Jesus. It is not deserved or earned, but is a free gift of God's love.

> "For it is by grace you have been saved..."
>
> *Ephesians 2:8* [NIV]

- Christians believe it is the **Holy Spirit** who gives grace to Christians and continues to guide them in their daily lives, to help them achieve salvation.

APPLY

A Explain **two** Christian teachings about the means of salvation. **Refer to sacred writings or another source of Christian belief and teaching in your answer.** (Based on AQA Specimen question paper, 2017)

B 'As nobody is perfect, it is impossible not to sin.' **Evaluate the following argument** and explain your reasoning.

"It is perfectly possible to live a good life without sin. Jesus lived his life without sin. Many saints have lived good and courageous lives without acting badly to other people. It is true that nobody is totally perfect, but that's different. Sin separates you from God and goes against God's law, and there are many people who stay close to God and keep his commandments, so I disagree with the statement."

1.12 The role of Christ in salvation

RECAP

Essential information:

- [ ] Christians believe that salvation is offered through the life and teaching of Jesus.
- [ ] Jesus' resurrection shows that God accepted Jesus' sacrifice as **atonement**. This means that through the sacrifice of his death, Jesus restored the relationship between God and humanity that was broken when Adam and Eve sinned.

The role of Jesus in salvation

Christians believe Jesus' life, death and resurrection had a crucial role to play in God's plan for salvation because:

- Jesus' crucifixion **made up for the original sin** of Adam and Eve.
- The death of Jesus, as an innocent man, was necessary to **restore the relationship between God and believers**, to bring them salvation.
- Jesus' resurrection shows the goodness of Jesus defeated the evil of sin. It was proof that God had accepted Jesus' sacrifice on behalf of humankind.
- Jesus' resurrection means humans can now receive forgiveness for their sins.
- Jesus' death and resurrection made it possible for all who follow his teachings to **gain eternal life**.

TIP

This quote shows the Christian belief that death came into the world as a punishment for sin, but salvation is offered through the life and teaching of Jesus.

> "For the wages of sin is death, but the gift of God is eternal life in Christ Jesus our Lord."
>
> *Romans 6:23* [NIV]

Atonement

- Atonement **removes the effects of sin** and allows people to restore their relationship with God.
- Many Christians believe that through the sacrifice of his death, Jesus took the sins of all humanity on himself and paid the debt for them all. He **atoned for the sins of humanity**.
- This sacrifice makes it possible for all who follow Jesus' teachings to **receive eternal life** with God.

> "[…] if anybody does sin, we have an advocate with the Father – Jesus Christ, the Righteous One. He is the atoning sacrifice for our sins, and not only for ours but also for the sins of the whole world."
>
> *1 John 2:1–2* [NIV]

APPLY

A Give **one** reason why the death and resurrection of Jesus is important to Christians.

B Here are some sentences that could be used to evaluate the statement, 'Salvation is God's greatest gift to humans.'

Sort them into arguments in support of the statement, and arguments in support of different views. Try to put them in a logical order. What do you think is missing from these statements to make a top level answer? Explain how the answer could be improved.

1. Atheists do not consider salvation important because they do not think there is a God who saves people.	5. Without salvation, humankind would have to pay the price of human sin.
2. God shows his great love for people by sending his Son to save us.	6. People may doubt the truth of Jesus' resurrection so they don't see the need for a belief in salvation.
3. Even some religious people may think there are greater gifts to humans, such as nature or life itself.	7. Some people may question whether God is loving if God demands the death of his Son in payment for human sin.
4. Everyone needs forgiveness from God.	8. Humans should be grateful every day of their lives for Jesus' sacrifice on their behalf.

TIP

To remember the meaning of 'atonement', think of it as 'at-one-ment', because Jesus' death and resurrection make people at one with God.

REVIEW

1 Exam practice

Test the 1 mark multiple-choice question

1 Which **one** of the following is the idea that God became human in Jesus?

A Atonement B Incarnation C Resurrection D Creation **[1 mark]**

2 Which **one** of the following is the idea that God is loving?

A Omniscient B Omnipotent C Benevolent D Immanent **[1 mark]**

Test the 1 mark question

3 Give **one** way that Christians believe salvation can come about. **[1 mark]**

___

4 Give **one** Christian belief about life after death. **[1 mark]**

___

Test the 4 mark question

5 Explain **two** ways in which a belief in Jesus' crucifixion influences Christians today. **[4 marks]**

• **Explain one way.**	*One way in which a belief in Jesus' crucifixion influences Christians today is that they believe that the crucifixion was a sacrifice Jesus chose to make for them.*
• Develop your explanation with more detail/an example/reference to a religious teaching or quotation.	*He did this in order to give them the opportunity to be granted forgiveness by God, so they can live in confidence that their sins have been forgiven.*
• **Explain a second way.**	*A second way in which a belief in Jesus' crucifixion influences Christians today is that it helps Christians who are suffering because they know Jesus suffered as well.*
• Develop your explanation with more detail/an example/reference to a religious teaching or quotation.	*For example, Christians who are suffering persecution for their faith will be comforted to know that Jesus understands what they are going through because he too was innocent and suffered for his beliefs.*

6 Explain **two** ways in which the belief in creation by God influences Christians today. **[4 marks]**

• **Explain one way.**	
• Develop your explanation with more detail/an example/reference to a religious teaching or quotation.	
• **Explain a second way.**	
• Develop your explanation with more detail/an example/reference to a religious teaching or quotation.	

TIP

The student has explained the influence a belief in Jesus' crucifixion has on a Christian's attitude (their confidence in being forgiven and their comfort in dealing with their own suffering). You could also discuss the influence of this belief on a Christian's life (e.g. it might encourage them to spread the message of Jesus or to make the sign of the cross when they pray to remind themselves of Jesus' sacrifice).

7 Explain **two** ways in which the belief that God is loving influences Christians today. **[4 marks]**

1 Exam practice

Test the 6 mark question

8 Explain **two** Christian beliefs about salvation.
Refer to sacred writings or another source of Christian belief and teaching in your answer. **[6 marks]**

• **Explain one belief.**	*One Christian belief about salvation is that salvation can be gained through good works.*
• Develop your explanation with more detail/an example.	*These good works may be following teachings such as the Ten Commandments, the Golden Rule and 'love your neighbour'. Worshipping and praying regularly also help Christians to earn salvation.*
• **Explain a second belief.**	*A second Christian belief about salvation is that it is gained through grace.*
• Develop your explanation with more detail/an example.	*God gives salvation to people who have faith in Jesus. It is a gift for the faithful.*
• **Add a reference to sacred writings or another source of Christian belief and teaching.** If you prefer, you can add the reference to your first belief instead.	*Paul wrote in his letters that it is through grace, which is a gift from God, that people are saved, not simply through their good works.*
• Apply the reference by explaining how it links to the question.	*This suggests a belief that salvation is achieved through God, not just how a person behaves.*

TIP
The references to scripture here count as development of your first point.

9 Explain **two** Christian teachings about God.
Refer to sacred writings or another source of Christian belief and teaching in your answer. **[6 marks]**

• **Explain one teaching.**	
• Develop your explanation with more detail/an example.	
• **Explain a second teaching.**	
• Develop your explanation with more detail/an example.	
• **Add a reference to sacred writings or another source of Christian belief and teaching.** If you prefer, you can add the reference to your first teaching instead.	
• Apply the reference by explaining how it links to the question.	

TIP
You only need to make one reference to scripture in your answer. It can support either your first or your second point.

10 Explain **two** Christian teachings about atonement.
Refer to sacred writings or another source of Christian belief and teaching in your answer. **[6 marks]**

Test the 12 mark question

11 'The stories of the incarnation prove that Jesus was the Son of God.'

Evaluate this statement. In your answer you should:

- refer to Christian teaching
- give reasoned arguments to support this statement
- give reasoned arguments to support a different point of view
- reach a justified conclusion.

[12 marks]
Plus SPaG 3 marks

REASONED ARGUMENTS IN SUPPORT OF THE STATEMENT • **Explain why some people would agree with the statement.** • Develop your explanation with more detail and examples. • Refer to religious teaching. Use a quote or paraphrase or refer to a religious authority. • **Evaluate the arguments.** Is this a good argument or not? Explain why you think this.	*Christians believe in the incarnation. This means that God took human form in Jesus. The stories of Jesus' birth show he was not conceived in the normal way. The fact he was conceived through the actions of God and born of a virgin proves that he was special and if God was involved it is likely that Jesus was his son. However, even though he was a physical person, he was also God at the same time. John's gospel calls Jesus 'the Son of God' and says he was the Word made flesh, living among us. This supports the idea that Jesus was both God and human.*
REASONED ARGUMENTS SUPPORTING A DIFFERENT VIEW • **Explain why some people would support a different view.** • Develop your explanation with more detail and examples. • Refer to religious teaching. Use a quote or paraphrase or refer to a religious authority. • **Evaluate the arguments.** Is this a good argument or not? Explain why you think this.	*Many people do not agree that Jesus was conceived through the actions of God and believe that Mary, his mother, was not a virgin. If the stories of the incarnation are not correct, they cannot be used as evidence that Jesus was the Son of God although his actions showed he was very special.*
CONCLUSION • **Give a justified conclusion.** • Include your own opinion together with your own reasoning. • **Include evaluation.** Explain why you think one viewpoint is stronger than the other or why they are equally strong. • Do not just repeat arguments you have already used without explaining how they apply to your reasoned opinion/conclusion.	*It may be true that the title 'Son of God' does not mean that there is such a close relationship between Jesus and God. It is possible that he was chosen by God, maybe when he was baptised, to do good works on earth and tell people about Christianity without there being a family relationship between himself and God. If this is true, there is no such thing as incarnation as far as Jesus is concerned.*

TIP

The question is about stories (plural) so it would improve the answer to mention details of Jesus' conception in the gospels of Matthew and Luke.

TIP

This argument could be developed further for more marks. For example, after the sentence that ends 'not a virgin' you might add 'Mary was engaged to Joseph, making it possible that Joseph was Jesus' father.'

TIP

The conclusion shows logical chains of reasoning. It evaluates different interpretations of the title 'Son of God' in relation to the stories of the incarnation. The examiner will want to see that you can link ideas together when developing your argument, and not just repeat what you have said already.

12 'There is no such place as hell.'

Evaluate this statement. In your answer you should:

- refer to Christian teaching
- give reasoned arguments to support this statement
- give reasoned arguments to support a different point of view
- reach a justified conclusion.

TIP

Spelling, punctuation and grammar is assessed on each 12 mark question, so make sure you are careful to use your best written English.

[12 marks]
Plus SPaG 3 marks

REASONED ARGUMENTS IN SUPPORT OF THE STATEMENT • **Explain why some people would agree with the statement.** • Develop your explanation with more detail and examples. • Refer to religious teaching. Use a quote or paraphrase or refer to a religious authority. • **Evaluate the arguments.** Is this a good argument or not? Explain why you think this.	
REASONED ARGUMENTS SUPPORTING A DIFFERENT VIEW • **Explain why some people would support a different view.** • Develop your explanation with more detail and examples. • Refer to religious teaching. Use a quote or paraphrase or refer to a religious authority. • **Evaluate the arguments.** Is this a good argument or not? Explain why you think this.	
CONCLUSION • **Give a justified conclusion.** • Include your own opinion together with your own reasoning. • **Include evaluation.** Explain why you think one viewpoint is stronger than the other or why they are equally strong. • Do not just repeat arguments you have already used without explaining how they apply to your reasoned opinion/conclusion.	

TIP

It's essential to include evaluation because this is the key skill that you are being tested on in the 12 mark question. You can evaluate after each viewpoint, and/or at the end as part of your justified conclusion.

13 'The best way to gain salvation is to obey God's law.'

Evaluate this statement. In your answer you should:

- refer to Christian teaching
- give reasoned arguments to support this statement
- give reasoned arguments to support a different point of view
- reach a justified conclusion.

[12 marks]
Plus SPaG 3 marks

Check your answers using the mark scheme on page 151. How did you do?

To feel more secure in the content you need to remember, re-read pages 12–23.

To remind yourself of what the examiner is looking for, go to pages 6–11.

2 Christianity: Practices

2.1 Worship

RECAP

Essential information:

- ☐ **Worship** is the act of religious praise, honour or devotion. It is a way for Christians to show their deep love and honour to God.
- ☐ Worship can take different forms, including liturgical, non-liturgical and informal worship.
- ☐ **Private worship** is when believers praise or honour God in their own home.

Why do Christians worship?

- To praise and thank God
- To ask for forgiveness
- To seek God's help for themselves or others
- To deepen their relationship with God and strengthen their faith

Different forms of worship

Type of worship	What form does it take?	Examples	Why is it important for Christians?
liturgical worship is a church service that follows a set structure or ritual	• takes place in a church • priest leads the congregation and may perform symbolic actions • formal prayers with set responses • Bible passages are read out, there may be a sermon • music and hymns	the Eucharist for Catholic, Orthodox and Anglican Churches	• worldwide set order for service that is familiar to everyone • ritual passed down through generations gives a sense of tradition • Bible readings follow the Christian calendar and teach Christian history and faith
non-liturgical worship is a service that does not follow a set text or ritual	• takes place in a church • often focused on Bible readings followed by a sermon • may also have prayers and hymns but there is no set order, the number and type can change from week to week	services in non-Conformist churches, e.g. Methodist, Baptist, United Reformed	• services can be planned and ordered to suit a certain theme • non-Conformist churches place an emphasis on the word of God in the Bible
informal worship is a type of non-liturgical worship that is 'spontaneous' or 'charismatic' in nature	• community or house churches meet in private homes and share food • Quaker worship is mainly silent, people speak when moved by God to offer their thoughts or read from the Bible • 'charismatic' worship may involve dancing, clapping, calling out and speaking in tongues	community or house churches, Quaker worship, charismatic ('led by the spirit') worship of the Pentecostal Church	• the style of worship in house churches is similar to the worship of early Christians • people can share readings and prayers and can take an active part in church by calling out or speaking without formal training • service may have an emotional impact with a feeling of personal revelation from God

APPLY

A Going on pilgrimage, celebrating festivals and religious art are also forms of worship. Give **one** more way that Christians worship.

B 'Worship is most powerful when believers follow a set ritual.'

List arguments to support this statement and arguments to support a different point of view.

TIP

The arguments should apply to Christianity. Try to use religious language (see key terms in red).

2.2 Prayer

RECAP

Essential information:

- ☐ **Prayer** is communicating with God, either silently or through words of praise, thanksgiving or confession, or requests for God's help or guidance.
- ☐ Christians may use **set prayers** that have been written down and said more than once by more than one person. An example is **the Lord's Prayer**, which is the prayer Jesus taught to his disciples.
- ☐ Christians may also use **informal prayers** (made up by an individual using his or her own words) to communicate with God. Some Christians find they can express their needs to God more easily by using their own words.

The importance of prayer

The Lord's Prayer

> "Our Father in heaven, hallowed be your name,
> your Kingdom come, your will be done,
> on earth as in heaven.
> Give us today our daily bread.
> Forgive us our sins
> as we forgive those who sin against us.
> Lead us not into temptation, but deliver us from evil.
> For the kingdom, the power, and the glory are yours
> now and for ever. Amen."
>
> *The Lord's Prayer*

- When Jesus' disciples asked him to teach them how to pray, he answered with the Lord's Prayer.
- Christians see it as a **model of good prayer**, as it combines praise to God with asking for one's needs.
- It reminds Christians to **forgive others in order to be forgiven**, since prayer is only effective if people's relationships with others are right.
- It reminds Christians that **God is the Father of the whole Christian community**, and it can create a sense of unity when everyone in the congregation says it together.
- The Lord's Prayer is often used in worship and is nearly always said at Holy Communion, baptisms, marriages and funerals. It is also used in schools and in commemoration services in Britain.

APPLY

A Give **one** reason why the Lord's Prayer is important to Christians.

B 'Private worship has more meaning for a Christian than public worship.' (Based on AQA Specimen question paper, 2017)

Develop the following argument to support the statement by explaining in more detail, adding an example, or referring to a relevant religious teaching or quotation.

"An individual Christian can choose how they want to worship in private, whereas in public worship they have to follow what everyone else is saying and doing. Therefore private worship has more meaning because they can put their heart and soul into it."

TIP

Always analyse the statement carefully. For example, here 'has more meaning' might depend on an individual's reasons for prayer.

2.3 The sacraments: Baptism

RECAP

Essential information:

- ☐ **Sacraments** are holy rituals through which believers receive a special gift of grace (free gift of God's love). Some Christian denominations recognise seven sacraments while others acknowledge fewer.
- ☐ **Baptism** is the ritual through which a person becomes a member of the Church. It involves the use of water to symbolise the washing away of sin.
- ☐ **Infant baptism** is for babies and young children. **Believers' baptism** is for people who are old enough to understand the significance of the ritual.

The sacraments

- **Catholic and Orthodox** Christians recognise **seven** sacraments: baptism, confirmation, Holy Communion, marriage, Holy Orders, reconciliation and the anointing of the sick.
- Many **Protestant** churches recognise **two** sacraments – baptism and Holy Communion – because they believe Jesus taught people to undertake these.
- Some churches that practise believers' baptism consider it to be important but not a 'sacrament'.
- Some churches, like the Quakers or Salvation Army, do not see any ritual or ceremony as being a 'sacrament'.

Baptism

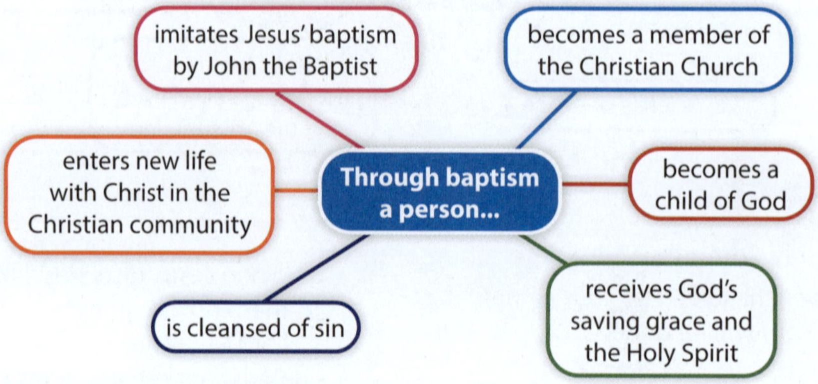

Infant baptism and believers' baptism

	Practised by	Reasons why	What happens
Infant baptism 	Catholic, Orthodox, Anglican, Methodist, and United Reformed Christians	• Removes original sin (Catholic and Orthodox belief). • Allows the child to be welcomed into the Church as soon as possible. • The parents can thank God for their new baby and celebrate with family and friends.	• The priest or minister pours blessed water over the baby's head and says, 'I baptise you in the name of the Father, and of the Son, and of the Holy Spirit.' • Godparents and parents promise to bring up the child as a Christian. • The child is welcomed into the Christian community.
Believers' baptism 	Baptists, Pentecostalists	• People should be old enough to consciously make a mature decision about their faith. • The decision to live a life dedicated to Jesus is what saves a person, rather than the baptism itself.	• The person is fully immersed in a pool which symbolises cleansing from sin and rising to new life in Christ. • When asked whether they are willing to change their lives, the person gives a brief testimony of their faith in Jesus. • The person is baptised 'in the name of the Father, and of the Son, and of the Holy Spirit.'

APPLY

A Explain **two** different ways in which Christians practise baptism and develop each point.

B 'Parents should not have their children baptised if they have no intention of bringing them up as Christians.'

Evaluate this statement.

2.4 The sacraments: Holy Communion

RECAP

Essential information:

- ☐ **Holy Communion** (also known as the Eucharist) is the sacrament that uses bread and wine to celebrate the sacrifice of Jesus on the cross and his resurrection.
- ☐ It recalls the Last Supper of Jesus, using his words and actions.
- ☐ Christians interpret the meaning of Holy Communion in different ways, but all agree that it brings them closer to each other and to God.

The meaning of Holy Communion

Holy Communion is a service which celebrates and gives thanks for the sacrifice of Jesus' death and resurrection (see pages 17–18). It has different meanings for different Christians:

- **Catholics, Orthodox Christians** and **some Anglicans** believe the bread and wine become **the body and blood of Christ**. This means Jesus is fully present in the bread and wine. This is a divine mystery that helps believers share in the saving sacrifice of Jesus' death and resurrection.
- **Protestant Christians** celebrate Holy Communion as a **reminder of the Last Supper**. They do not believe the bread and wine become the body and blood of Christ. Instead, the bread and wine remain **symbols of Jesus' sacrifice**, which helps believers to reflect on its meaning today.

> "For whenever you eat this bread and drink this cup, you proclaim the Lord's death until he comes."
>
> *1 Corinthians 11:26* [NIV]

The impact of Holy Communion

For many Christians, Holy Communion is at the centre of their lives and worship. It affects individuals, local communities and the wider society in a number of ways:

Individuals	Communities	Wider society
• Christians **receive God's grace** by joining in the sacrifice of Jesus. • This helps to strengthen their faith. • They become closer to God.	• Holy Communion **brings the community of believers together** in unity by sharing the bread and wine. • This can provide support and encouragement for those going through a difficult time.	• Holy Communion **acts as a call to love others in practical ways**. • It encourages Christians to work for equality and justice for all. • Many churches collect money during the service to help support those in need, such as people living in poverty or experiencing homelessness.

APPLY

A Explain **two** ways in which Holy Communion has an impact on the lives of believers.

B Use the table below with arguments about the statement, 'It is more important to help people living in poverty than to celebrate Holy Communion.'

TIP
Decide on two ways and explain each. Do not simply list a number of ways without developing any of your points.

Write a paragraph to explain whether you agree or disagree with the statement, having evaluated both sides of the argument.

In support of the statement	Other views
People living in poverty need urgent help, particularly if they are living in low-income countries, so of course it is more important to help them than to receive Holy Communion. Christians are taught to love their neighbour so that must come before their own needs. Remembering Jesus' death and resurrection through Holy Communion is nice, but not very useful to anyone. It's just focusing on the past when people should be thinking about the present.	It doesn't need to be such a stark choice. After all, when Christians break bread together at Holy Communion they remember that people in the world are starving and they try to help them. Many churches collect money for people living in poverty during the service of Holy Communion, so celebrating this sacrament encourages people to care for others, not just themselves. 'Eucharist' means 'thanksgiving', so it makes Christians grateful for God's love and this makes them want to share it.

2.5 Celebrating Holy Communion

RECAP

Essential information:

- In most churches the Holy Communion service has two parts: the ministry of the Word (which focuses on the Bible), and the ministry of Holy Communion (the offering, consecrating and sharing of bread and wine).
- Christians have different practices when it comes to celebrating Holy Communion.

Differences between Holy Communion services

- In the **Orthodox Church**, Holy Communion is called the Divine Liturgy, and is believed to recreate heaven on earth. Much of the service is held at the altar behind the iconostasis, which is a screen that represents the divide between heaven and earth. The priest passes through the iconostasis using the Royal Doors.
- Holy Communion in the **Catholic and Anglican Churches** is very similar. The main difference is that Catholics believe the bread and wine turn into the body and blood of Christ, whereas many Anglicans believe Jesus is only present in a spiritual way when the bread and wine are being eaten.

Further examples of how Holy Communion services differ from each other include the following:

Orthodox Divine Liturgy	Catholic Mass and Anglican Holy Communion	Holy Communion in the United CE Reformed Church
Liturgy of the Word: • There are hymns, prayers and a Bible reading. • The priest comes through the Royal Doors to chant the Gospel. • There may be a sermon. **Liturgy of the Faithful:** • The priest receives wine and bread baked by church members. • Prayers are offered for the church, the local community and the world. • Behind the iconostasis, the priest says the words of Jesus at the Last Supper. • Most of the bread is consecrated as the body and blood of Christ. • The priest distributes holy bread and wine on a spoon. • Prayers of thanksgiving are said. • Unconsecrated pieces of bread are given to people to take home, as a sign of belonging to the Christian community.	**Liturgy of the Word:** • There are three Bible readings, a psalm and a homily. • The Creed is said. • Prayers are said for the Church, the local community, the world, and the sick and the dead. **Liturgy of the Eucharist:** • In the Anglican Holy Communion, people give a sign of peace to each other. • Offerings of bread and wine are brought to the altar. • The priest repeats the words of Jesus at the Last Supper over the bread and the wine. • People say the Lord's Prayer. • In the Catholic Mass, the sign of peace is given at this point. • People receive the bread and wine. • The priest blesses people and sends them out to live the gospel.	• The service begins with a hymn and prayer of praise and thanksgiving. • Bible readings and a sermon are given. • Prayers for the world and the needs of particular people are said. • The minister repeats the words and actions of Jesus at the Last Supper. • There is an 'open table' so anyone who wishes may receive Holy Communion. • Sometimes the bread is cut beforehand, other times it is broken and passed around by the congregation. • Wine is sometimes non-alcoholic and is usually distributed in small cups. • The service ends with a prayer of thanksgiving, a blessing, and an encouragement to go out and serve God.

APPLY

A Explain **two** different ways in which Holy Communion is celebrated in Christianity. (Based on AQA Specimen question paper, 2017)

B **Write a paragraph** in response to the statement, 'Holy Communion services should focus more on the Liturgy of the Word than on the Holy Communion itself.' **Develop your reasons** and include a reference to scripture or religious teaching in your answer.

TIP

Holy Communion services have many similarities. Be sure to choose aspects that are different.

2.6 Pilgrimage

RECAP

Essential information:

- ☐ A **pilgrimage** is a journey made by a believer to a holy site for religious reasons. As well as making a physical journey to a sacred place, the pilgrim also makes a spiritual journey towards God.

- ☐ A pilgrimage gives many opportunities for prayer and worship, and is itself an act of worship and devotion.
- ☐ Two popular pilgrimage sites for Christians are Lourdes (a town in France) and Iona (a Scottish island).

The role and importance of pilgrimage

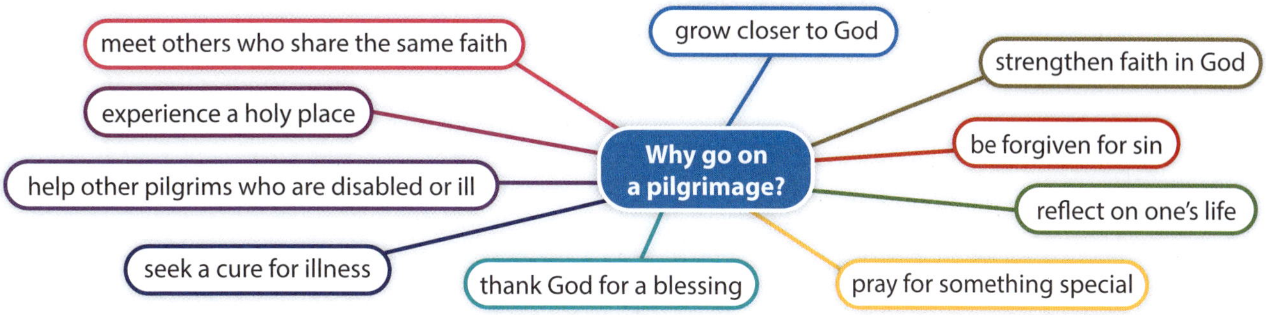

A pilgrimage can impact on a Christian's life in a number of ways. It can:

- give them a better understanding of their faith
- renew their enthusiasm for living a Christian life
- help them to see problems in a new light
- help them to feel cleansed from sin
- help them to feel more connected to the Christian community
- give them a good feeling about helping other pilgrims who are disabled or ill.

Places of Christian pilgrimage

Place	Significance	Activities
Lourdes (a town in France)	• Where Mary is said to have appeared in a number of visions to a young girl called Bernadette. • Mary told Bernadette to dig in the ground, and when she did a spring of water appeared. • The water is believed to have healing properties, and a number of healing miracles are claimed to have taken place here.	• Pilgrims go to Lourdes to bathe in the waters of the spring, or to help other pilgrims who are ill or disabled to bathe in the waters. • Pilgrims also pray for healing or forgiveness. • They may recite the rosary together.
Iona (an island off the coast of Scotland)	• Where St Columba established a monastic community in the 6th century CE. • The community now has an ecumenical centre where pilgrims can stay.	• Because it is quiet, peaceful and a place of natural beauty, pilgrims can spend time praying, reading the Bible, and reflecting or meditating. • Pilgrims can also attend services in the abbey church, take part in workshops, and visit the island's holy or historic sites.

APPLY

A Explain **two** different examples of Christian pilgrimage. (Based on AQA Specimen question paper, 2017)

B 'There is no difference between a pilgrimage and a holiday.'

Develop the following argument against the statement by explaining in more detail, adding an example or referring to Christian teaching.

"Although a pilgrimage can seem a lot like a holiday, especially if you travel abroad, there is a big difference. A pilgrimage is a spiritual journey that people undertake for religious reasons rather than just to sightsee."

TIP

You need to explain why the examples are different, rather than just describing the two places, so be sure to explain the different reasons why pilgrims go there.

2.7 Celebrating festivals

RECAP

Essential information:

- A **festival** is a day or period of celebration for religious reasons.
- Festivals help Christians to remember and celebrate the major events in their religion – particularly the life, death and resurrection of Jesus.
- **Christmas** commemorates the incarnation and the birth of Jesus. Celebrations begin on 25 December and last 12 days, ending with Epiphany (which recalls the visit of the wise men).
- **Easter** celebrates the resurrection of Jesus from the dead. Celebrations begin before Easter Sunday and finish with the feast of Pentecost.

Christmas

Christmas **commemorates the incarnation of Jesus**, which is the belief that God became human in Jesus (see page 16). The celebrations reflect Christian beliefs and teachings in the following ways:

- **lights** represent Jesus as the light coming into the world of darkness
- **nativity scenes** show baby Jesus born into poverty
- **carol services** with Bible readings remind Christians about God's promise of a saviour and the events of Jesus' birth
- **Midnight Mass** reflects the holiness of the night and the joy Christians feel at Jesus' birth
- **Christmas cards and gifts** recall the wise men's gifts to Jesus
- Christians **give to charity** in this time of peace and goodwill because God gave humanity the gift of Jesus, his Son.

Easter

Easter is the most important Christian festival, which **celebrates Jesus' rising from the dead**.

Holy Week (the week before Easter Sunday) remembers the events leading up to Jesus' crucifixion, including his arrest and trial.

On **Good Friday** (the day Jesus was crucified), there are special services and processions led by a person carrying a cross.

- On **Saturday night**, some churches hold a special service to celebrate Christ's resurrection.
- Orthodox Christians walk with candles in procession, then enter the dark church as if going into Jesus' empty tomb.
- The priest announces 'Christ is risen!' to which people answer 'He is risen indeed.'
- Catholics and Anglicans have a vigil that begins in darkness, before the Paschal candle is lit to symbolise the risen Christ. The service ends with Holy Communion.

- On **Easter Sunday**, churches are filled with flowers and special hymns are sung to rejoice at Jesus' resurrection.
- Services are held at sunrise, and shared breakfasts include eggs to symbolise new life.

> "Christ is risen from the dead, trampling down death by death, and upon those in the tombs bestowing life."
> *Traditional Orthodox hymn at the Easter Divine Liturgy*

APPLY

A Give **one** way in which Christians celebrate the festival of Easter.

B 'Christmas is no longer a religious festival.' Evaluate this statement.

RECAP

2.8 The role of the Church in the local community: Food banks

Essential information:

- [ ] **The Church** is the holy people of God, also called the Body of Christ, among whom Christ is present and active.
- [ ] **A church** is a building in which Christians worship.
- [ ] Individual churches and the Church as a whole help the local community in a variety of ways, including the provision of **food banks**. These give food for free to people who cannot afford to buy it.

What does the Church do?

Individual churches and the Church as a whole help the local community in many ways.

Individual churches:

- educate people about Christianity (e.g. Bible study groups)
- are meeting places for prayer and worship
- provide activities for younger people (e.g. youth clubs)
- are places where Christians can socialise and obtain spiritual guidance.

The Church:

- supports local projects such as food banks
- provides social services such as schooling and medical care
- helps those in need
- campaigns for justice.

TIP

You could use this quote in your exam to show that Christians think of the Church as the followers of Jesus, who together are the body of Christ on earth.

> “And God placed all things under his [Jesus'] feet and appointed him to be head over everything for the church, which is his body.”
>
> *Ephesians 1:22–23* [NIV]

Examples of the Church helping the local community

The Trussell Trust and The Oasis Project are two organisations that help the local community by providing food banks and other services. The work of these charities is based on Christian principles (such as the parable of the Sheep and the Goats).

The Trussell Trust

- A charity running over 400 food banks in the UK.
- These provide emergency food, help and support to people in crisis in the UK.
- Non-perishable food is donated by churches, supermarkets, schools, businesses and individuals.
- Doctors, health visitors and social workers identify people in crisis and issue them with a food voucher.
- Their aim is to bring religious and non-religious people together to help end poverty and hunger.

The Oasis Project

- A community hub run by Plymouth Methodist Mission Circuit.
- Provides an internet café, creative courses, a job club, training opportunities, a meeting place and a food bank.
- Spiritual and practical help is given to those in need because of ill health, learning disabilities, domestic violence, substance abuse, low income and housing problems.

TIP

You will not be asked about these particular organisations in your exam, but if you learn what they do, you will be able to give detailed examples of how the Church helps in the local community.

APPLY

A There are **two** meanings of the word 'church'. What are they?

B Below is a response to the statement, 'There will always be a need to feed hungry people in Britain.' Can you improve this answer by including religious beliefs?

"At first this statement appears untrue. No one should be hungry in Britain as there is a welfare state. People who can't work to feed themselves or their families can apply for benefits."

"However, I agree with the statement because people can suddenly be faced with bills they can't pay, or lose their jobs, or become ill so they can't work. It may take many weeks to apply for benefits and be accepted, so what do they do in the meantime? If they don't have much savings they will be really hard up and need the help of food banks."

RECAP

2.9 The role of the Church in the local community: Street Pastors

Essential information:

- ☐ Christians should help others in the local community because Jesus taught that people should show **agape** love (a Biblical word meaning selfless, sacrificial, unconditional love).
- ☐ Christians believe it is important to put their faith into action. They do this through many organisations and projects that help vulnerable people in the community.
- ☐ **Street Pastors** are people who are trained to patrol the streets in urban areas. They help vulnerable people by providing a reassuring presence on the street.

The importance of helping in the local community

- Jesus taught that **Christians should help others by showing agape love** towards them. For example, in the parable of the Sheep and the Goats, Jesus teaches Christians they should give practical help to people in need (see page 20).
- Two examples of Christian organisations that provide practical help to local communities are Street Pastors and Parish Nursing Ministries UK.

> "Faith by itself, if it is not accompanied by action, is dead."
> *James 2:17* [NIV]

TIP

You could use this quote in your exam to show that Christians believe it is very important to take practical action to help others.

Street Pastors and Parish Nursing Ministries UK

Street Pastors	Parish Nursing Ministries UK
• An initiative started in London in 2003, by the Christian charity the Ascension Trust. • Adult volunteers are trained to patrol the streets in urban areas. • The main aim originally was to challenge gang culture and knife crime in London. • The focus then widened to responding to drunkenness, anti-social behaviour and fear of crime. • Street Pastors work closely with police and local councils. • They listen to people's problems, advise on where they might get help, and discourage anti-social behaviour. • A similar group called School Pastors was set up in 2011 to discourage illegal drug use, bullying and anti-social behaviour in schools.	• This Christian charity supports whole-person healthcare through the local church. • They provide churches with registered parish nurses, who promote well-being in body, mind and spirit among the local community. • The nurses help to provide early diagnosis of health problems. • They train and coordinate volunteers to help combat loneliness or provide support during times of crisis. • They give additional help to the NHS. • They encourage people to exercise and have a good diet. • They focus on the whole person, including listening to people and praying with them if asked. They also direct people to specific services if needed.

TIP

When using Christian charities as examples in your answers, focus on their work and why they do it, rather than details about when they were founded and by whom.

APPLY

A Explain **two** ways in which Street Pastors carry out their Christian duty.

B 'All Christians should do something practical to help their community, including praying for their neighbours.'

Develop two religious arguments in support of this statement, and **two** non-religious arguments against it.

2.10 The place of mission and evangelism

RECAP

Essential information:

- [ ] A **mission** is a vocation or calling to spread the faith. The Church has a mission to tell non-believers that Jesus Christ, the Son of God, came into the world as its saviour.
- [ ] Christians spread the faith through **evangelism** (showing faith in Jesus by example or by telling others).
- [ ] They do this to fulfil Jesus' instructions to the disciples to spread his teachings (the **Great Commission**).

The Great Commission

> "Therefore go and make disciples of all nations, baptising them in the name of the Father and of the Son and of the Holy Spirit, and teaching them to obey everything I have commanded you."
>
> *Matthew 28:19–20* [NIV]

TIP

You can use this quote in your exam to show what the Great Commission involves. Jesus instructs his disciples to baptise people and to spread his teachings.

- Jesus gave a Great Commission to his disciples to **spread the gospel** and **make disciples of all nations through baptism**.
- The **Holy Spirit** at Pentecost gave the disciples the gifts and courage needed to carry out the Great Commission.
- All Christians have a duty to spread the gospel and tell others of their faith, but some become **missionaries** or **evangelists** (people who promote Christianity, for example by going to foreign countries to preach or do charitable work).
- The aims of missionary work and evangelism are to **persuade people to accept Jesus as their Saviour**, and to extend the Church to all nations.

Alpha

- Alpha is an **example of evangelism in Britain**.
- It was started in London by an Anglican priest, with the aim of helping church members understand the basics of the Christian faith.
- The course is now used as an **introduction for those interested in learning about Christianity**, by different Christian denominations in Britain and abroad.
- The organisers describe it as 'an opportunity to explore the meaning of life' through talks and discussions.
- Courses are held in homes, workplaces, universities and prisons as well as in churches.

APPLY

A Give **one** way in which the Church tries to fulfil its mission.

B **Unscramble the arguments** in the table below referring to the statement, 'Every Christian should be an evangelist.' Decide which arguments could be used to support the statement and which could be used against it.

Write a paragraph to explain whether you agree or disagree with the statement, having evaluated both sides of the argument.

1. If Christians don't help to spread the faith, it might die out.	4. Not every Christian should be an evangelist because some people are just too shy.
2. Some Christians live in countries where they are persecuted, so if they spoke in public about their faith they would be risking death or imprisonment.	5. All Christians have received the Great Commission from Jesus to preach to all nations.
3. Evangelism can happen in small ways, for example Christians can spread their faith to people they meet in everyday life or just give a good example of loving their neighbours.	6. Christians who go around evangelising can annoy people, so it does not help their cause.

2.11 Church growth

RECAP

Essential information:

- ☐ Up to a third of the world's population claim to be Christian (including people who rarely attend church), and around 80,000 people become Christians each day.
- ☐ The Church expects new Christians to help spread the faith as part of their commitment to Jesus.
- ☐ Christ for all Nations is an example of a Christian organisation that promotes evangelism.

The growth of the Church

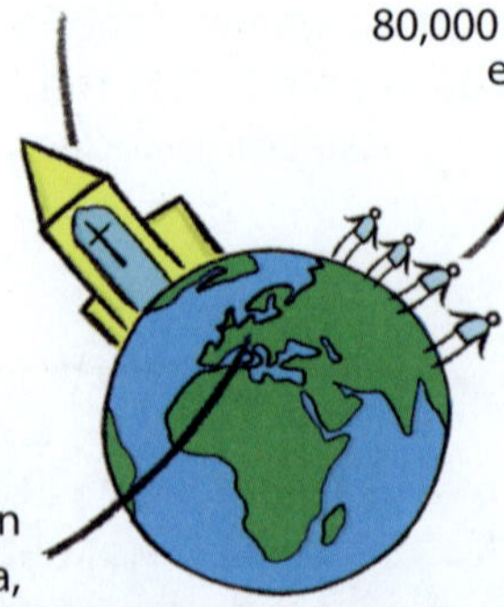

- The Church is growing rapidly in South America, Africa and Asia, but not in the USA, Europe and the Middle East (where Christians have been persecuted).
- Worldwide around 80,000 people become Christians each day, and over 500 new churches are formed.
- The Church's mission is to make disciples, not just new believers. This means **new Christians are also expected to help spread the faith**.
- Evangelism should therefore be followed up by training new **converts** (people who decide to change their religious faith) in the way of following Jesus.
- Every Christian has a role in **encouraging fellow believers**. They might do this in the following ways.

Ways Christians can spread the faith

- advertising and using media (such as Facebook, Twitter or Premier Christian Radio)
- praying for others to accept God
- sharing what God has done for them with others
- inviting people to Christian meetings, fellowship meals and social events

Christ for all Nations

- Christ for all Nations is an example of a **Christian organisation promoting evangelism**. They do this by holding evangelistic meetings throughout the world, but particularly in Africa.
- They are led by the evangelists Richard Bonnke and Daniel Kolenda.
- Some of their large open-air rallies held in Africa have drawn crowds of up to 1.6 million people.
- It is claimed that many miracles of healing take place at the meetings.
- Christ for all Nations claims that 74 million people have filled in decision cards to follow Christ at their meetings.

APPLY

A Give **one** way in which the Church gets its message to people.

B **Evaluate the following argument** in response to the statement, 'Christians should just rely on evangelists for Church growth.' Explain your reasoning and suggest how you would improve the argument.

"Christians should not just rely on evangelists for Church growth because there are not that many specially trained evangelists to promote Christianity. People are more likely to be drawn to Christianity by the inspiration of someone they know, like a neighbour who is kind and considerate and demonstrates the love that Jesus taught."

TIP

You will not be asked a specific question about Christ for all Nations in your exam, but being able to give examples of the work of Christian organisations or charities may be very helpful.

2.12 The importance of the worldwide Church

RECAP

Essential information:

- ☐ The worldwide Church has a mission to restore people's relationship with God and with one another.
- ☐ The Church therefore plays an important role in **reconciliation** (restoring harmony after relationships have broken down), through initiatives to develop peace and understanding.

Working for reconciliation

- Christians believe humans were **reconciled to God** through Jesus' death and resurrection. This means Jesus' death and resurrection helped to **restore the relationship between God and humanity**, which had been broken by sin (see page 22).
- For Catholics, the **sacrament of Reconciliation** also helps to restore people's relationship with God.
- Matthew 5:23–24 teaches that Christians should be **reconciled to each other**.
- Reconciliation is therefore an **important part of the Church's work**. This might involve anything from trying to restore relationships between individual people, to working for peace between different religious groups or nations at conflict.

> "For if, while we were God's enemies, we were reconciled to him through the death of his Son, how much more, having been reconciled, shall we be saved through his life!"
>
> *Romans 5:10* [NIV]

TIP

You could use this quote in your exam to show that humanity's relationship with God was restored (or reconciled) through the death of Jesus.

Examples of organisations working for reconciliation

- The **Irish Churches Peace Project** brings Catholics and Protestants together in Northern Ireland.
- The project aims to develop peace and understanding between these two denominations.

- The **World Council of Churches** works for reconciliation between different Christian denominations and members of other faiths.
- For example, the Pilgrimage of Justice and Peace initiative supports inter-religious dialogue and cooperation.

- After the bombing of Coventry Cathedral in World War II, local Christians showed forgiveness to those responsible, and the cathedral became a world centre for peace and reconciliation.
- The cathedral is home to the **Community of the Cross of Nails**, which works with partners in other countries to bring about peace and harmony.

- The **Corrymeela Community** brings together people from different backgrounds, including people of different faiths or political leanings.
- They meet at a residential centre in Northern Ireland to build trust and explore ways of moving away from violence so they can work together constructively.

APPLY

A Give **one** example of how the Church has helped to work towards reconciliation.

B 'Reconciliation to God is more important than reconciliation to other people.'

Develop the following argument to support the statement by explaining in more detail, adding an example, or referring to a relevant religious teaching or quotation.

"Reconciliation to God is more important because God is the Supreme Being. God will judge us when we die and if we are not sorry for our sins we will not receive eternal life with God in heaven."

2.13 Christian persecution

RECAP

Essential information:

- Christians have faced **persecution** (hostility and ill-treatment) from the beginning of the Church, and Christians are still persecuted worldwide today.
- For some Christians, persecution can have positive effects: it can strengthen their faith, allow them to share in Jesus' sufferings, and even inspire others to become Christian.
- The Church helps those who are persecuted through prayer, practical help and financial support, and by raising awareness of persecution and campaigning against it.

What is persecution?

- The International Society for Human Rights estimates 80% of all acts of religious discrimination today are aimed at Christians.
- This persecution happens around the world, but particularly in countries such as North Korea, Somalia, Iraq and Syria.
- It might involve:
  - being forced to pay extra tax
  - job discrimination
  - being forbidden to build churches
  - attacks on Christian homes, churches and families, including murder.

TIP
These examples of the kinds of persecution Christians face will be helpful if you need to give an explanation of persecution in your exam.

Some Christian responses to persecution

Response	Supporting quote from scripture
• For some Christians, persecution can have a **positive effect**, as it strengthens their faith and conviction. • It also allows them to share in the suffering of Jesus.	"I want to know Christ – yes, to know the power of his resurrection and participation in his sufferings" (*Philippians 3:10*) This quote shows that one way Christians can get to know Jesus is by sharing in his suffering.
• The Church believes it is important to **act against persecution**, by supporting persecuted Christians wherever possible and campaigning on their behalf.	"If one part suffers, every part suffers with it" (*1 Corinthians 12:26*) This quote refers to the Church. It shows that helping individual Christians also helps the whole Church.
• Christians are **encouraged to show love and forgiveness** towards their persecutors.	"Do not be overcome by evil, but overcome evil with good" (*Romans 12:21*) This quote shows that Christians should respond to evil with love.

Some ways the Church has helped persecuted Christians

- Christians smuggled Bibles into the USSR (Russia) to strengthen and give comfort to persecuted Christians.
- The Barnabas Fund sends money to support people persecuted for their faith.
- Christian Solidarity Worldwide campaigns for religious freedom for all.

APPLY

A Give **one** way in which Christians support people in countries where it is forbidden to follow Jesus.

B **Develop** one religious argument and one non-religious argument in response to the statement, 'It is not possible to "rejoice and be glad" if you are suffering persecution.'

TIP
'Develop' means you should write arguments that are supported by detail, for example by explaining them more fully and giving examples.

2.14 The Church's response to world poverty

RECAP

Essential information:

- [ ] Christian charities follow the example and teaching of Jesus in working to relieve poverty.
- [ ] Christians believe they should show Jesus to the world through helping the disadvantaged.
- [ ] Three Christian charities that help people living in poverty are Christian Aid, Tearfund and CAFOD.

Helping those in poverty

Christians try to help those living in poverty because Jesus taught that this was important. For example:

- Jesus once told a rich man to sell everything and give to people living in poverty (Mark 10:21).
- The parable of the Rich Man and Lazarus tells of a rich man who ends up in hell for ignoring a beggar.
- The parable of the Good Samaritan teaches the importance of helping all people.
- Jesus helped outcasts such as lepers, tax collectors and sinners.

> "If anyone has material possessions and sees a brother or sister in need but has no pity on them, how can the love of God be in that person? Dear children, let us not love with words or speech but with actions and in truth." *1 John 3:17–18* [NIV]

TIP
You only need to know about one of these organisations for your exam.

Three Christian charities that help those in poverty are Christian Aid, Tearfund and CAFOD (Catholic Agency for Overseas Development).

Charity	Examples of their work
Christian Aid	• Supports projects to encourage sustainable development. • Provides emergency relief, such as food, water, shelter and sanitation. • Campaigns to end poverty alongside organisations such as the Fairtrade Foundation, Trade Justice and Stop Climate Chaos.
Tearfund	• Works with over 90,000 churches worldwide to help lift people out of poverty. • Supplies emergency aid after natural disasters and conflict. • Provides long-term aid to help communities become more self-reliant, such as education or new farming equipment. • Supported by donations, fundraising events and prayer from churches in the UK.
CAFOD	• Works with local organisations to train, supply and support communities to work their own way out of poverty. • Gives short-term aid such as food, water and shelter during conflicts and disasters. • Lobbies UK government and global organisations for decisions that respect people living in poverty. • Encourages Catholic schools and parishes to pray, give money and campaign for justice.

APPLY

A Below are two ways in which a worldwide Christian relief organisation carries out its mission overseas. **Develop one of the points** by adding more detail and by referring to a relevant religious teaching or quotation. **Then apply the religious teaching or quotation** by explaining how it links to the point.

"One way that Christian Aid carries out its mission overseas is to provide emergency relief when there is a disaster."

"Another way they help is by setting up longer-term programmes that encourage sustainable development."

TIP
Emergency aid gives help such as food, water and temporary shelter to people immediately after a disaster. In contrast, long-term aid tries to help people to become more self-sufficient over a longer period of time.

B **Write a paragraph** either supporting or against the statement, 'Religious charities should just concentrate on emergency aid.' Include a Christian teaching in your answer.

REVIEW

2 Exam practice

Test the 1 mark multiple-choice question

1 Which **one** of the following is a type of worship that follows a set pattern?

A Informal worship

B Private worship

C Non-liturgical worship

D Liturgical worship **[1 mark]**

2 Which **one** of the following is the festival that celebrates the incarnation of Jesus?

A Easter B Good Friday C Christmas D Lent **[1 mark]**

Test the 1 mark question

3 Give **one** way in which the Church responds to world poverty. **[1 mark]**

____

4 Give **one** reason why prayer is important to Christians. **[1 mark]**

____

Test the 4 mark question

5 Explain **two** different ways in which Christians worship. **[4 marks]**

• **Explain one way.**	*Some Christians worship with other people in church on Sunday by going to a service called Holy Communion.*
• Develop your explanation with more detail/an example/ reference to a religious teaching or quotation.	*During the liturgy, they receive bread and wine that they believe is the body and blood of Jesus.*
• **Explain a second different way.**	*Other Christians prefer informal worship, sometimes meeting in someone's home.*
• Develop your explanation with more detail/an example/ reference to a religious teaching or quotation.	*These Christians share their faith by reading and discussing a passage from scripture and praying together in their own words.*

TIP

In this answer formal worship is contrasted with informal worship, but you could also contrast public worship with private worship or liturgical worship with charismatic worship.

6 Explain **two** different ways in which Christians practise baptism. **[4 marks]**

• **Explain one way.**	
• Develop your explanation with more detail/an example/ reference to a religious teaching or quotation.	
• **Explain a second way.**	
• Develop your explanation with more detail/an example/ reference to a religious teaching or quotation.	

TIP

The question asks for different 'ways' in which Christians practise baptism, not different beliefs about baptism. The clearest difference is between believers' baptism and infant baptism, but you should focus your answer on the way each of these is carried out, not what people believe about them.

7 Explain **two** different interpretations of the meaning of Holy Communion. **[4 marks]**

Test the 6 mark question

8 Explain **two** ways that Christian charities help people living in poverty in low-income countries.
Refer to sacred writings or another source of Christian belief and teaching in your answer. **[6 marks]**

• **Explain one way.**	*One way that Christian charities help people living in poverty in low-income countries is by providing emergency aid when there has been a natural disaster, like an earthquake or famine.*
• Develop your explanation with more detail/an example.	*For example, Tearfund, a Christian charity, was set up originally to provide emergency aid in response to the famine in Biafra, Nigeria, where it sent emergency food and clothing to refugees fleeing the famine-struck country.*
• **Explain a second way.**	*A second way that Christian charities help is by providing long-term aid that helps countries become self-sufficient or less dependent on aid.*
• Develop your explanation with more detail/an example.	*CAFOD, for example, works on development projects to give people access to education, healthcare and clean water.*
• **Add a reference to sacred writings or another source of Christian belief and teaching.** If you prefer, you can add the reference to your first way instead.	*These charities are inspired by Christian teachings such as the parable of the Rich Man and Lazarus, where Jesus taught that people who are rich and ignore the needs of people living in poverty will be punished by God.*
• Apply the reference by explaining how it links to the question.	*This can be interpreted to mean that helping people in poverty in low-income countries will be looked on favourably by God and may lead to going to heaven.*

TIP
Here the student has used a parable from the bible. Another 'source of Christian belief and teaching' could be official statements or documents by leaders of the Church.

9 Explain **two** reasons why Christians practise evangelism.
Refer to sacred writings or another source of Christian belief and teaching in your answer. **[6 marks]**

• **Explain one reason.**	
• Develop your explanation with more detail/an example.	
• **Explain a second reason.**	
• Develop your explanation with more detail/an example.	
• **Add a reference to sacred writings or another source of Christian belief and teaching.** If you prefer, you can add the reference to your first reason instead.	
• Apply the reference by explaining how it links to the question.	

TIP
It is helpful to start by explaining the meaning of 'evangelism' before explaining why Christians practise it.

10 Explain **two** ways that Christians may work for reconciliation.
Refer to sacred writings or another source of Christian belief and teaching in your answer. **[6 marks]**

Test the 12 mark question

11 'The most important duty of the Church is to help people in need.'

Evaluate this statement. In your answer you should:

- refer to Christian teaching
- give reasoned arguments to support this statement
- give reasoned arguments to support a different point of view
- reach a justified conclusion.

[12 marks]

REASONED ARGUMENTS IN SUPPORT OF THE STATEMENT • **Explain why some people would agree with the statement.** • Develop your explanation with more detail and examples. • Refer to religious teaching. Use a quote or paraphrase or refer to a religious authority. • **Evaluate the arguments.** Is this a good argument or not? Explain why you think this.	*'The Church' in this statement clearly stands for the Christian believers and not the actual building. So what does the Bible say about the duty of Christians? Jesus taught his followers that helping those in need is extremely important and he showed he believed that by the way he acted. If he saw a person suffering from an illness he healed them. He touched lepers in order that they might be cured, even though it was something other people would not do because it was against the law and they feared catching leprosy. He gave sight to the blind, healed the crippled and even cast out evil spirits that were tormenting a naked madman. Jesus did this because he had compassion and pity on those he saw were in need.* *Jesus also showed in his teaching that Christians should help people in need. In the parable of the Good Samaritan it is the traveller who showed pity on the wounded man and helped him that is the hero of the story. Furthermore Jesus warns that those who do not help will face the anger of God on judgement day in the parable of the Sheep and the Goats. The sheep represented the people who helped and were given the reward of eternal life, but the goats did not and were thrown out of God's presence. So you could argue that it is the most important duty of the Church to help people who are in need.*
REASONED ARGUMENTS SUPPORTING A DIFFERENT VIEW • **Explain why some people would support a different view.** • Develop your explanation with more detail and examples. • Refer to religious teaching. Use a quote or paraphrase or refer to a religious authority. • **Evaluate the arguments.** Is this a good argument or not? Explain why you think this.	*On the other hand, Jesus summed up the duty for Christians and the Church in two commandments. He said that the first, most important commandment is to love God. The second is to love our neighbour as ourselves. If that is the case, then the most important duty of the Church (Christians) is to love and worship God, and this is more important than helping those in need.*
CONCLUSION • **Give a justified conclusion.** • Include your own opinion together with your own reasoning. • **Include evaluation**. Explain why you think one viewpoint is stronger than the other or why they are equally strong. • Do not just repeat arguments you have already used without explaining how they apply to your reasoned opinion/conclusion.	*In conclusion I would say that the statement is wrong and I would argue that the most important duty is to love God. The only way the Church can show love of God is by loving human beings who need help. So that is also important, but not the most important duty. It merely follows on from the most important duty.*

TIP

The student has develo this argument by referr to the Bible. Although th are no direct quotation the answer shows excell knowledge of Jesus' acti and teaching and uses these to support the statement.

TIP

This argument could be developed further for more marks. For example, it could go into more detail about other important duties of the Church (such as preaching the gospel or administering the sacraments), and explain why these are equally or more important than helping people in need.

12 'The best way for Christians to grow closer to God is to go on a pilgrimage.'

Evaluate this statement. In your answer you should:

- refer to Christian teaching
- give reasoned arguments to support this statement
- give reasoned arguments to support a different point of view
- reach a justified conclusion.

[12 marks]

TIP
Look for the key words in questions. Here it is 'best'. The answer should focus on whether or not a pilgrimage is the best way for Christians to grow closer to God or whether there are other ways that might be better.

REASONED ARGUMENTS IN SUPPORT OF THE STATEMENT ● **Explain why some people would agree with the statement.** ● Develop your explanation with more detail and examples. ● Refer to religious teaching. Use a quote or paraphrase or refer to a religious authority. ● **Evaluate the arguments.** Is this a good argument or not? Explain why you think this.	
REASONED ARGUMENTS SUPPORTING A DIFFERENT VIEW ● **Explain why some people would support a different view.** ● Develop your explanation with more detail and examples. ● Refer to religious teaching. Use a quote or paraphrase or refer to a religious authority. ● **Evaluate the arguments.** Is this a good argument or not? Explain why you think this.	
CONCLUSION ● **Give a justified conclusion.** ● Include your own opinion together with your own reasoning. ● **Include evaluation**. Explain why you think one viewpoint is stronger than the other or why they are equally strong. ● Do not just repeat arguments you have already used without explaining how they apply to your reasoned opinion/conclusion.	

13 'A Christian's most important duty is to tell others about their faith.'

Evaluate this statement. In your answer you should:

- refer to Christian teaching
- give reasoned arguments to support this statement
- give reasoned arguments to support a different point of view
- reach a justified conclusion.

[12 marks]

TIP
'To tell others about their faith' is the meaning of evangelism, which is part of a Christian's mission. Try to use these terms in your answer to show the depth of your understanding about this topic.

Check your answers using the mark scheme on page 152. How did you do?
To feel more secure in the content you need to remember, re-read pages 28–41.
To remind yourself of what the examiner is looking for, go to pages 6–11.

3 Islam: beliefs and teachings

3.1 The Oneness of God and the supremacy of God's will

RECAP

Essential information:

- ☐ Islam is a **monotheistic** religion. This means that Muslims believe there is only one God (**Allah**).
- ☐ The belief in one, indivisible God is known as **Tawhid**.
- ☐ Muslims believe in the **supremacy** of God's will: the idea that God's will is above all things. This means that things only happen if God wants them to.

The Oneness of God

Tawhid is a fundamental belief in Islam. Surah 112 from the **Qur'an** (the main holy book in Islam) helps to explain this belief:

Verse in Surah 112	Meaning
'He is God the One'	• There is only one God • God is a unified, undivided being; God cannot be divided into different persons
'God the eternal'	• God has always existed
'He begot no one nor was He begotten'	• God was not born or came into being out of something else • God does not have any children
'No one is comparable to Him'	• God is unique • No other person or thing has God's qualities and attributes • No one can accurately picture or describe God because there is nothing to compare him to

The word 'Allah' in Arabic

Belief in Tawhid means that Muslims should:

- worship only one God
- never make anything in their lives more important than God, as God has no equal
- not use images or pictures of God, as it is impossible to portray God accurately.

TIP

Remember that Christianity and Islam are both monotheistic religions. This means they both believe in only one God. The difference is that Christians believe God is also three Persons.

The supremacy of God's will

- Muslims believe **God's will is supreme** (most powerful). This means God can make anything happen that he wants to happen (see page 50).
- It also means that **nothing happens unless God allows it to happen**.
- This helps to give Muslims confidence when something goes wrong, because they know it is part of God's plan for them.
- Muslims try to live according to God's will in their everyday lives, accepting that God knows best.

APPLY

A Identify **two** beliefs about God found in Surah 112 and explain what each teaches Muslims about God.

B 'Tawhid is the most important belief in Islam because it influences everything that Muslims do.'

Evaluate this statement.

TIP

To 'evaluate' this statement, explain the extent to which you think it is true or not and why. Consider how a belief in Tawhid affects the way a Muslim lives their life.

3.2 Key beliefs of Sunni Islam and Shi'a Islam

RECAP

Essential information:

- **Muhammad** was the last and most important of the prophets in Islam. After Muhammad died, there were disagreements about who should succeed him as the leader of Islam. The religion split into two branches: **Sunni** and **Shi'a**.
- The central beliefs of Sunni Muslims are given in the **six articles of faith**, while the central beliefs of Shi'a Muslims are shown in the **five roots of 'Usul ad-Din**.

Sunni and Shi'a Islam

Sunni Islam	Shi'a Islam
The Sunni leader (called the Caliph) should be elected	The Shi'a leader (called the Imam) should be a descendant of Muhammad and chosen by God
Only the Qur'an and the **Sunnah** (Muhammad's teachings and actions) have the authority to provide religious guidance	The Qur'an, Sunnah *and* the Shi'a leader have the authority to provide religious guidance
Abu Bakr, Muhammad's advisor, was the rightful leader after Muhammad died	Ali, Muhammad's cousin and son-in-law, was the rightful leader after Muhammad died
The six articles of faith give the main beliefs for Sunni Muslims	The five roots of 'Usul ad-Din give the main beliefs for Shi'a Muslims
There are many shared beliefs in Sunni and Shi'a Islam. For example, both Sunni and Shi'a Muslims: • believe in the same God • follow the teachings in the Qur'an	• follow the teachings in the Sunnah • acknowledge the importance of the prophets.

TIP

You will learn about further differences between Sunni and Shi'a Islam as you continue to read this chapter and Chapter 4.

The six articles of faith in Sunni Islam

1. **Tawhid** – belief that there is only one God.
2. **Angels** – belief in angels, who passed on God's message to the prophets.
3. **The holy books** – respect for the holy books and particularly the Qur'an, which is the highest authority in Islam.
4. **The prophets** – respect for the prophets and particularly Muhammad, who received the final revelation of Islam from God.
5. **The Day of Judgement** – belief that at the end of the world, every person will be judged by God and sent to paradise or hell.
6. **The supremacy of God's will** – belief that nothing happens unless God wants it to happen.

The five roots of 'Usul ad-Din in Shi'a Islam

1. **Tawhid** – belief that there is only one God.
2. **Prophethood** – respect for the prophets and particularly Muhammad, who received the final revelation of Islam from God.
3. **The justice of God (Adalat)** – belief that God will judge everyone on the Day of Judgement in a fair and just way, and hold them to account for their actions.
4. **The Imamate** – respect for the twelve Imams, who were chosen by God to lead Islam after Muhammad died.
5. **Resurrection** – belief that after death, Muslims will be resurrected and judged by God.

APPLY

A. Explain **two** different Muslim beliefs about God's nature.

B. 'The similarities between Sunni and Shi'a Islam are more important than the differences.'

Do you agree with this statement? Explain your reasoning. Make sure you refer to some of the key similarities and differences in your answer.

TIP

Being able to understand and use key terms such as 'Tawhid', 'Sunnah' and others will gain you marks in the exam.

3.3 The nature of God

RECAP

Essential information:

- ☐ There are 99 different names for God in the Qur'an and Hadith (Muhammad's sayings). These names describe God's characteristics, and help to give Muslims some idea of what God is like.
- ☐ Some of God's most important qualities are: **immanent**, **transcendent**, **omnipotent**, **beneficent**, **merciful**, **fair** and **just**.

The main qualities of God

Muslims believe God is so great he is beyond human understanding and imagination. But the 99 names for God can help them to understand what God is like. These names are given in the Qur'an and Hadith, and help to describe God's different qualities.

The qualities of God

Transcendent

- God created the universe, so is beyond and outside it. He is not limited by the physical world
- Muslims believe that God can be both transcendent and immanent because although he created the universe (so is outside it), he is also within all things and able to act within it

Immanent

- God is present everywhere in the world and the universe
- God is within all things and is involved with life on earth

Beneficent

- God is benevolent: all-loving and all-good
- God's generosity is seen in his gift to humans of everything they need to live on earth

Omnipotent

- God is all-powerful
- God has the power to create and sustain everything in the universe
- God is aware of everything, including human actions and thoughts

Merciful

- God shows compassion and mercy
- God cares for people and understands their suffering
- God forgives people who are truly sorry for the things they have done wrong

Fair and just

- God treats everyone fairly and justly
- God will judge all people equally on the Day of Judgement
- Shi'a Muslims in particular believe that people have full responsibility for their actions, and God will reward or punish people depending on the choices they make (see page 50)

TIP

Remember that Christians and Muslims share similar beliefs about how God is the all-powerful creator of everything.

APPLY

A Explain how God can be both transcendent and immanent.

B 'Of all God's qualities, his omnipotence is the most important one for Muslims to know about.'

Read the following response:

"I think it is more important for Muslims to know about God's mercy, because it's important to know that God will forgive them if they are sorry for what they have done wrong. People aren't perfect and always make mistakes, so knowing that God will forgive them helps people to keep trying to be better. Otherwise they might just give up, because it's impossible to be good all the time."

Write your own short paragraphs explaining why the most important quality of God for Muslims to understand is:

- fairness and justice
- immanence
- omnipotence.

Then write a short conclusion, in which you weigh up the arguments you have just written, to decide whether you consider the statement is true or not.

TIP

Remember, when you give your opinion in an answer, make sure you back it up by referring to religious beliefs and teachings.

3.4 Angels

RECAP

Essential information:

- ☐ **Angels** are spiritual beings who serve God and pass on his word to people through the prophets.
- ☐ **Jibril** is the angel of revelation, who revealed the Qur'an to Muhammad.
- ☐ **Mika'il** is the angel of mercy, who rewards good deeds and provides nourishment for the earth and human life.

The nature and role of angels

Muslims believe that angels have a number of different roles.

- Some act as **messengers of God**. They receive God's words directly from him and pass them on perfectly to the prophets.
- Some **take care of people** throughout their lives.
- Some **record everything a person does** in their own 'book of deeds'. This book is presented to God on the Day of Judgement, who will use it to judge the person and decide whether to send them to paradise or hell.
- Some **take people's souls to God** after they die, and escort them into paradise or hell.

Jibril and Mika'il

Jibril (Gabriel) and Mika'il (Michael) are two of the most important angels in Islam.

Jibril

The angel of revelation

Purified Muhammad's heart when he was a child, so he would later be able to receive God's revelation

Recited the Qur'an to Muhammad and continued to pass on God's messages to Muhammad to guide him through the rest of his life

Therefore played an important role in communicating the final version of Islam to humanity

Mika'il

The angel of mercy

Responsible for sending rain, thunder and lightning to earth

Brings nourishment to earth, and helps to provide food for humans, by sending rain to the ground

Believed to reward people who do good deeds

APPLY

A Give **one** role that angels have in Islam.

B 'Without angels, Islam would not exist.'

Do you think this statement is true or not? Explain your reasoning.

3.5 Predestination

RECAP

Essential information:

- ☐ **Predestination** is the idea that God knows or determines everything that will happen in the universe.
- ☐ Most Muslims believe that predestination means God knows everything that will happen, but people still have free will and can make their own choices.
- ☐ Most Muslims believe that they are responsible for their own actions, and will be rewarded or punished for them by God on the Day of Judgement.

What is predestination?

In Islam, ideas about predestination vary. Some Sunni Muslims believe that **God has already determined everything that will happen in the universe**. They believe that:

- God has written down everything that will happen in a 'book of decrees'
- because God created people, they must act according to his will
- God's will is so powerful that he is able to make anything happen that he wants to happen (see page 46)
- humans do not have the freedom to change their destiny, or the overall plan that God has set for them; but they do have some choice over how they behave.

Surah 9:51 from the Qur'an is sometimes used to support the view that God has already determined everything that will happen:

> "Only what God has decreed will happen to us."
>
> *Qur'an 9:51*

In contrast, many Shi'a Muslims believe that **God *knows* everything that is going to happen**, but this does not mean he *decides* what is going to happen. They believe that:

- as God is the creator of time, he is outside time and so not bound by it. This means that God can see everything that happens in the past, present and future
- God knows what choices people will make, but they still have the free will to make these choices for themselves.

Surah 13:11 from the Qur'an is sometimes used to support the view that people have the free will to change their own future:

> "God does not change the condition of a people [for the worse] unless they change what is in themselves"
>
> *Qur'an 13:11*

The Day of Judgement

- Muslims who believe they have the free will to make their own choices also believe they will be judged by God for these choices.
- They believe that on the Day of Judgement, God will judge them for everything they have done during their lives, and reward or punish them as a result.
- Even though God knows everything that will happen, people are still responsible for their actions, and will be rewarded or punished for them on the Day of Judgement.

APPLY

A Explain why Muslims believe it is important to take responsibility for their actions.

B 'Predestination means that Muslims have no free will to make their own choices.'

Evaluate this statement.

TIP

Sunni and Shi'a Muslims have slightly different ideas about whether or not predestination limits human freedom. Try to use their different understandings to support your evaluation of this issue.

3.6 Life after death

RECAP

Essential information:

- ☐ Muslims believe in **Akhirah** – everlasting life after death.
- ☐ They believe that after death, they enter a state of waiting until the Day of Judgement, when God judges them and sends them to **heaven** (**jannah**) or **hell** (**jahannam**).
- ☐ Belief in life after death encourages Muslims to take responsibility for their actions and to live in a way that pleases God.

Life after death

Muslims believe that after death the following three stages happen:

Barzakh

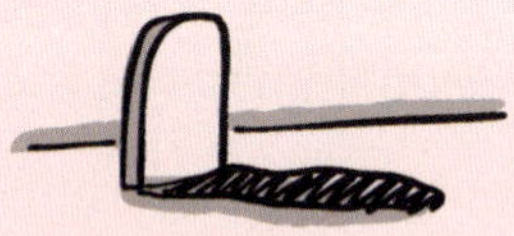

- After death, the state of waiting until the Day of Judgement is called **barzakh**, which means a 'barrier'. People are unable to come back across the barrier to right wrongs or to warn people
- While they are waiting, God sends two angels to question them about their faith
- Depending on how they answer, they will either see the rewards that will come or the punishments they will have to endure after the Day of Judgement

The Day of Judgement

- When God's purpose for the universe has been fulfilled, the world will be destroyed
- Everyone who has ever lived will be raised from the dead (**resurrected**)
- Everyone will be given their own 'book of deeds', which is a record of everything they did during their lives
- If they are given the book in their right hand, they will go to heaven; if they are given it in their left hand, they will go to hell

Heaven and hell

- People who have kept their faith in God and done good deeds will be rewarded with heaven (paradise)
- Heaven is described as a beautiful garden – it is a state of eternal happiness in the presence of God
- People who have rejected God and done bad things will be punished with hell
- Hell is described as a place of fire and torment, where people are separated from God

The importance of belief in Akhirah

- Belief in Akhirah encourages Muslims to **take responsibility for their actions**, because they know God will hold them accountable for their actions and reward or punish them accordingly.
- This motivates Muslims to follow the teachings in the Qur'an and to dedicate their lives to God.
- Belief in Akhirah helps to **give hope to Muslims who suffer**, as they know there is something better to look forward to. It also helps Muslims to **accept unjust situations**, because they know God will provide justice in the afterlife, and everyone will be fairly rewarded or punished for their actions on the Day of Judgement.

APPLY

A Which **one** of the following is the name given to the state of waiting that a Muslim enters after they die?

Akhirah/ Purgatory/ Paradise/ Barzakh

B 'A Muslim's approach to life should be based on their beliefs about the afterlife.'

Explain why some Muslims would agree with this statement. Why might some people disagree with this statement?

3.7 Prophethood and Adam

RECAP

Essential information:

- **Prophethood** refers to when someone is made a **prophet**: a messenger of God's word.
- **Risalah** is belief in the prophets and their importance as messengers of God.
- Muslims believe that Adam (the first human) was the first prophet.

What is prophethood?

Muslims believe that:

- prophethood is a gift from God to help humans to understand his message
- when people have forgotten, misunderstood or changed God's message, God has sent prophets to call people back to the right path
- there have been around 124,000 prophets, who have been sent to every nation on earth
- Muhammad was the last and most important of the prophets (see page 54).

Prophets are important in Islam because they are good role models and help Muslims to understand how to follow God. They do this both by conveying God's words and by setting a good example for how to live a life in obedience to God.

TIP

Jesus (Isa) is an important prophet in Islam. Muslims believe he was sent by God to help guide them in their faith. Muslims and Christians believe Jesus was fully human but only Christians believe that he was also fully God. Christians believe that Jesus had a unique relationship with God and they refer to him as the Son of God.

Adam

Adam is considered to be the father of the human race and the first prophet. The Qur'an teaches the following about Adam's beginnings:

1. God created Adam from the dust of the ground, and breathed his Spirit into him
2. God gave Adam knowledge and understanding and he taught Adam the names of all things
3. God told the angels to bow down to Adam out of respect for his knowledge
4. Iblis (Satan) refused to bow down to Adam, so God threw him out of paradise. Iblis vowed to always tempt humans to sin against God
5. God created Hawwa (Eve) to keep Adam company, and they lived together in the Garden of Bliss
6. God told Adam and Hawwa they could eat anything in the garden, except for the fruit from the forbidden tree
7. Iblis deceived Adam and Hawwa into eating fruit from the tree
8. God expelled Adam and Hawwa from the garden and their actions brought sin into the world
9. God forgave Adam after he accepted his mistake, and he became the first prophet

Adam is important to Muslims because God gave him knowledge and understanding. God taught Adam how to live a good life in obedience to God, and Adam passed on this knowledge to the rest of the human race through his descendants.

APPLY

A Give **one** reason why prophets are important in Islam.

B 'Adam is just as important a prophet as Muhammad.'

Explain why many Muslims would disagree with this statement.

What arguments could be given in support of this statement?

TIP

Some questions in the exam will require you to combine your knowledge from different parts of the course. Here, page 54 will help you to explain why Muslims disagree with this statement.

3.8 Ibrahim

RECAP

Essential information:

- Ibrahim (Abraham) is an important prophet in Islam.
- Ibrahim is a good role model for Muslims because he always had faith in God and showed obedience to God, at a time when many people worshipped a variety of gods and idols (statues).

Why is Ibrahim important?

Ibrahim is important because …

- he fulfilled all the tests and commands given to him by God
- he showed great faith in God
- he is a good role model for Muslims
- Muhammad was one of his descendants through his son, Ishmael
- he proclaimed belief in only one God at a time when people worshipped many different gods and idols

The Ka'aba in Makkah

How was Ibrahim a good role model?

How was Ibrahim a good role model?	Further explanation
He refused to worship idols and instead preached that there is only one God	• When Ibrahim was a young man, many people worshipped a number of different gods and idols • Ibrahim questioned their beliefs and decided there was only one God who had created everything in the universe • Ibrahim became determined to stop idol worship. One day, he took an axe and destroyed all the idols in the temple of his town • People were furious and demanded that Ibrahim be burned alive. He was thrown into a huge fire, but the fire only burned his chains and he walked out of it alive • This miracle prompted many people to start following Allah
He rebuilt the Ka'aba	• The **Ka'aba** is a small, cube-shaped building in the centre of the Grand Mosque in Makkah (Mecca). It is considered to be the house of God and the holiest place in Islam • The original Ka'aba was built by Adam but destroyed in the great flood • Following God's command, Ibrahim rebuilt the Ka'aba on the same site (see page 65) • When Muslims take part in Hajj (see pages 65–66), which starts at the Ka'aba, they remember Ibrahim and the steadfastness of his faith
He was willing to sacrifice his son to God	• Ibrahim had a dream in which God asked him to sacrifice his son to him • Ibrahim was willing to do this, but just before he carried out the sacrifice God stopped him, and told him he had passed the test • During the festival of Id-ul-Adha each year, Muslims kill an animal to remember Ibrahim's willingness to sacrifice his own son out of obedience to God

APPLY

A What is the Ka'aba, and why is it important to Muslims?

B 'Ibrahim is the perfect role model for Muslims.'

Evaluate this statement.

TIP

To 'evaluate' this statement, consider whether you think it is true or not and explain why. Are there any reasons why Ibrahim might not be a perfect role model (for example, regarding how he tried to stop idol worship)?

3.9 Muhammad and the Imamate

RECAP

Essential information:

- [ ] Muhammad is the last and most important prophet in Islam. He received the final revelation of Islam from God, which is recorded in the Qur'an.
- [ ] Shi'a Muslims believe in the importance of the **Imamate**: the leadership of the **Imams**. Shi'as believe that as the Imams have been appointed by God, they are able to maintain and interpret Islamic teachings without fault.

Why is Muhammad important?

Muhammad is the most important prophet in Islam because he is 'God's messenger' (Qur'an 33:40). He received the Qur'an from God, which all Muslims use as the basis of their faith. He is also remembered for helping to fully establish the religion by conquering Makkah, and for having travelled to heaven where he was in the presence of God.

Revelation of the Qur'an

- Muhammad grew up in Makkah (Mecca) and he would sometimes visit a cave in the mountains nearby to meditate and pray
- In 610 CE, Muhammad visited the cave and experienced a revelation from the angel Jibril
- Over the next 22 or so years, Muhammad continued to receive revelations from Jibril
- These were combined together to form the Qur'an

Conquering Makkah

- After the first revelation from Jibril, Muhammad started challenging people in Makkah to follow God's teachings
- Muhammad was persecuted for his preaching and fled with his followers to Madinah
- In Madinah he united the warring tribes, and with their help he conquered Makkah, converting the city to Islam
- This helped to bring harmony to the region, and firmly established Islam as a religion

The Night Journey

- Before Muhammad fled to Madinah, the angel Jibril took him on a miraculous journey to Jerusalem and then into heaven, where he spoke to prophets and saw great signs of God
- In heaven, Muhammad agreed with God that Muslims should pray five times a day
- Sunni Muslims still follow this practice (see page 61)

The Imamate

- The leader of Shi'a Muslims is called the Imam. The leadership of the Imams is known as the Imamate.
- Shi'as believe the Imam should be a **descendent of Muhammad and chosen by God**.
- The Twelver branch of Shi'a Islam teaches there have been **twelve Imams in total**. Each has been related to Muhammad in some way. The twelfth Imam has been kept alive by God and hidden somewhere on earth. He will return in the future to bring justice and equality to all.
- Because the Imams have been appointed by God, they are able to **interpret the Qur'an and Islamic law without fault**.
- Shi'as believe the Imams are necessary because people **need divine guidance on how to live correctly**. Although the final version of God's law was received by Muhammad, the Imams are important for helping to preserve and explain this law.

APPLY

A Give **one** reason why the Imamate is important to Shi'a Muslims.

B 'Muhammad has had more impact on Muslims' lives than any other prophet.'

List arguments to support this statement, and arguments to support a different point of view.

3.10 The holy books in Islam

RECAP

Essential information:

- ☐ The Qur'an is the most important holy book in Islam, and the highest source of authority for all matters relating to Islamic teaching, practice and law.
- ☐ The Qur'an was revealed to the prophet Muhammad by the angel Jibril.
- ☐ Other holy books in Islam are the Torah, Psalms, Gospel and Scrolls of Abraham.

The Qur'an

What is the Qur'an?

- includes a mixture of historical accounts and advice on how to follow God
- contains 114 surahs (chapters), roughly arranged in order of length
- nearly every chapter starts with the words 'In the name of God, the Lord of Mercy, the Giver of Mercy'
- written in Arabic
- the foundation of every believer's faith

- The Qur'an was revealed to Muhammad by the angel Jibril
- Jibril was directly passing on God's words, so the Qur'an is considered to be the word of God
- Jibril's revelations occurred over a period of about 22 years

→

- Muhammad learned by heart each revelation he received
- He recited these revelations to his followers
- Scribes later wrote them down

→

- As Islam spread, there was a danger that the original words would be distorted
- The third Caliph asked a team of Muslim scholars to compile an official version of the Qur'an that everyone could use
- This was completed around 650 CE

Other holy books

- Muslims believe there are other holy books that have been revealed by God.
- These holy books are mentioned in the Qur'an.
- Some Muslims think these books have been completely lost and no longer exist today.
- Others think they can still be found to some extent in the Bible. However, the original text has been corrupted or distorted, so it does not have the same authority as the Qur'an.

Name of the book	Who it was revealed to	Its authority in Islam
The Torah	Moses (Musa)	Some Muslims think the Torah is the first five books of the Bible, but altered from the original text
The Psalms	David	Many Muslims accept that the Psalms mentioned in the Qur'an are similar to the ones in the Bible
The Gospel	Jesus (Isa)	Muslims believe the Gospel has been lost but some of its message is still found in the Bible
The Scrolls of Abraham	Ibrahim	These are considered to be one of the earliest scriptures in Islam, and no longer exist

APPLY

A What is the name of the holy book that was revealed to David?

B 'The Qur'an is the highest authority in Islam.'

Why would many Muslims agree with this statement? List arguments to support it.

REVIEW

3 Exam practice

Test the 1 mark multiple-choice question

1 Which **one** of the following is the name of the holy book that was revealed to Moses?

A The Gospel
B The Psalms
C The Scrolls of Abraham
D The Torah
[1 mark]

2 Which **one** of the following revealed the Qur'an to Muhammad?

A Iblis
B Israfil
C Jibril
D Mika'il
[1 mark]

Test the 1 mark question

3 Give **one** difference between Sunni and Shi'a Islam. **[1 mark]**

____

4 Give a definition of 'Akhirah'. **[1 mark]**

____

Test the 4 mark question

5 Explain **two** ways in which a belief in prophethood influences Muslims today. **[4 marks]**

• **Explain one way.**	*A belief in prophethood influences Muslims to respect and follow the teachings in the Qur'an.*
• Develop your explanation with more detail/an example/ reference to a religious teaching or quotation.	*This is because the Qur'an was revealed to the prophet Muhammad. Believing in prophethood means believing that Muhammad passed on God's words in the Qur'an.*
• **Explain a second way.**	*A belief in prophethood also influences Muslims by encouraging them to show complete obedience to God.*
• Develop your explanation with more detail/an example/ reference to a religious teaching or quotation.	*This is because the prophets were always obedient to God. For example, Ibrahim was willing to sacrifice his son to God after God told him to.*

TIP

If you see a question asking you to explain how a belief in something influences people today, make sure your answer focuses on how people in the world today are affected by the belief. How does the belief change the way they practise their faith?

6 Explain **two** of God's qualities. **[4 marks]**

• **Explain one quality.**	
• Develop your explanation with more detail/an example/ reference to a religious teaching or quotation.	
• **Explain a second quality.**	
• Develop your explanation with more detail/an example/ reference to a religious teaching or quotation.	

7 Explain **two** ways in which a belief in the afterlife influences Muslims today. **[4 marks]**

3 Exam practice

Test the 6 mark question

8 Explain **two** Muslim teachings about predestination.

Refer to sacred writings or another source of Muslim belief and teaching in your answer. **[6 marks]**

• **Explain one teaching.**	*One teaching about predestination is that God has already determined everything that will happen in the universe.*
• Develop your explanation with more detail/an example.	*God has already written down everything that will happen in a 'book of decrees', and people have limited freedom to change their future.*
• **Explain a second teaching.**	*Another teaching about predestination is that God knows everything that will happen, but hasn't already decided what will happen.*
• Develop your explanation with more detail/an example.	*Because God is outside time, he already knows everything that will happen, but people can still make their own choices.*
• **Add a reference to sacred writings or another source of Muslim belief and teaching.** If you prefer, you can add the reference to your first teaching instead.	*This teaching is supported by Surah 13:11 in the Qur'an: 'God does not change the condition of a people ... unless they change what is in themselves.'*
• Apply the reference by explaining how it links to the question.	*This can be interpreted to mean that humans have some control over predestination because God responds to their efforts.*

TIP

To refer to Muslim belief and teaching in your answer, you could write out a short quote from the Qur'an or mention a specific passage from this text.

TIP

This answer is good because it explains a teaching about predestination and then supports it by referring to a specific passage from the Qur'an. If you cannot remember an exact quotation you can always paraphrase it.

9 Explain **two** reasons why Muhammad is considered to be the most important prophet in Islam.

Refer to sacred writings or another source of Muslim belief and teaching in your answer. **[6 marks]**

• **Explain one reason.**	
• Develop your explanation with more detail/an example.	
• **Explain a second reason.**	
• Develop your explanation with more detail/an example.	
• **Add a reference to sacred writings or another source of Muslim belief and teaching.** If you prefer, you can add the reference to your first reason instead.	
• Apply the reference by explaining how it links to the question.	

10 Explain **two** meanings of the concept of Tawhid.

Refer to sacred writings or another source of Muslim belief and teaching in your answer. **[6 marks]**

Test the 12 mark question

11 'The best way of understanding God is to describe God as transcendent.'

Evaluate this statement. In your answer you should:

- refer to Muslim teaching
- give reasoned arguments to support this statement
- give reasoned arguments to support a different point of view
- reach a justified conclusion.

[12 marks]
Plus SPaG 3 ma

> **TIP**
> 'Some [Muslims/Christians/Jews, etc.] might [agree/disagree] with this answer because...' can be a good way to introduce your arguments in the 12 mark answer.

REASONED ARGUMENTS IN SUPPORT OF THE STATEMENT ● **Explain why some people would agree with the statement.** ● Develop your explanation with more detail and examples. ● Refer to religious teaching. Use a quote or paraphrase or refer to a religious authority. ● **Evaluate the arguments.** Is this a good argument or not? Explain why you think this.	*Some Muslims might agree that the best way of understanding God's nature is to think of God as transcendent because this makes sense of God's ability to do things that humans can't. 'Transcendence' means that God is beyond and outside the universe. Because he is outside the universe, God is not limited by its rules. This is a good description of God because Muslims believe that God is above them and much greater than them. God created the universe, something humans cannot do. It also suggests that God can be omniscient and know everything that happens in the past, present and future because he is outside time. The Qur'an says, 'He is in charge of everything.'*
REASONED ARGUMENTS SUPPORTING A DIFFERENT VIEW ● **Explain why some people would support a different view.** ● Develop your explanation with more detail and examples. ● Refer to religious teaching. Use a quote or paraphrase or refer to a religious authority. ● **Evaluate the arguments.** Is this a good argument or not? Explain why you think this.	*Some Muslims might disagree with this statement because they think there are other qualities that describe God better. For example, God is also immanent. This means he is present in the world and involved with life on earth. Some Muslims might think this is the best way to understand God because it shows how people are able to have a relationship with God and be guided by him in their everyday lives.* *Another example of a way that God can be described is omnipotent. This means he is all-powerful. Some Muslims might think this is a good word for understanding God because it explains how he is able to create the whole universe, and make anything happen that he wants to happen.*
CONCLUSION ● **Give a justified conclusion.** ● Include your own opinion together with your own reasoning. ● **Include evaluation.** Explain why you think one viewpoint is stronger than the other or why you think they are equally strong. ● Do not just repeat arguments you have already used without explaining how they apply to your reasoned opinion/conclusion.	*In conclusion, I think all of the different qualities of God probably help Muslims to understand him in different ways. Knowing that God is transcendent helps to understand his greatness and special abilities, but knowing that God is immanent helps to understand how he can be close to humanity, and other qualities, for example that he is One, help to understand God in other ways too. All of these qualities teach Muslims something important about God.*

> **TIP**
> It is helpful to explain what transcendence means before evaluating whether it is a good description of God. Also, accurate use of key religious terms gains more marks for SPaG.

12 'The Qur'an contains all the guidance that Muslims need to live a perfect Muslim life.'

Evaluate this statement. In your answer you should:

- refer to Muslim teaching
- give reasoned arguments to support this statement
- give reasoned arguments to support a different point of view
- reach a justified conclusion.

[12 marks]
Plus SPaG 3 marks

REASONED ARGUMENTS IN SUPPORT OF THE STATEMENT ● **Explain why some people would agree with the statement.** ● Develop your explanation with more detail and examples. ● Refer to religious teaching. Use a quote or paraphrase or refer to a religious authority. ● **Evaluate the arguments.** Is this a good argument or not? Explain why you think this.	
REASONED ARGUMENTS SUPPORTING A DIFFERENT VIEW ● **Explain why some people would support a different view.** ● Develop your explanation with more detail and examples. ● Refer to religious teaching. Use a quote or paraphrase or refer to a religious authority. ● **Evaluate the arguments.** Is this a good argument or not? Explain why you think this.	
CONCLUSION ● **Give a justified conclusion.** ● Include your own opinion together with your own reasoning. ● **Include evaluation.** Explain why you think one viewpoint is stronger than the other or why you think they are equally strong. ● Do not just repeat arguments you have already used without explaining how they apply to your reasoned opinion/conclusion.	

13 'For Muslims, the prophets make better role models than the angels.'

Evaluate this statement. In your answer you should:

- refer to Muslim teaching
- give reasoned arguments to support this statement
- give reasoned arguments to support a different point of view
- reach a justified conclusion.

[12 marks]
Plus SPaG 3 marks

Check your answers using the mark scheme on page 153. How did you do?
To feel more secure in the content you need to remember, re-read pages 46–55.
To remind yourself of what the examiner is looking for in your answers, go to pages 6–11.

4 Islam: practices

4.1 The Five Pillars, the Ten Obligatory Acts and the Shahadah

RECAP

Essential information:

- ☐ The **Five Pillars** are the five most important duties for all Muslims. They are the fundamental practices of Islam on which everything else is built, and are seen as the key to living a perfect Muslim life.
- ☐ The **Ten Obligatory Acts** combine the Five Pillars with some additional duties. These are followed by Twelver Shi'a Muslims.
- ☐ The **Shahadah** is the Muslim declaration of faith. It expresses the basic beliefs of Islam.

The Five Pillars

1. **Shahadah** – the declaration of faith
2. **Salah** – prayer
3. **Zakah** – charitable giving
4. **Sawm** – fasting
5. **Hajj** – pilgrimage

The Ten Obligatory Acts

Salah – prayer
Sawm – fasting
Zakah – charitable giving
Khums – 20% tax (half goes to charity and half to religious leaders)
Hajj – pilgrimage
Jihad – the struggle to maintain the faith and defend Islam
Amr-bil-Maruf – encouraging people to do what is good
Nahi Anil Munkar – discouraging people from doing what is wrong
Tawallah – showing love for God and people who follow him
Tabarra – not associating with the enemies of God

Shahadah

> "There is no God but Allah and Muhammad is the Prophet of Allah."

- This phrase is called the Shahadah. It is important to Muslims because it **expresses the core beliefs of Islam**.
- The Shahadah is considered to provide the foundation for the other four pillars, which tell a Muslim how to live according to the beliefs expressed in the Shahadah.
- Shi'a Muslims add an extra phrase to the Shahadah: **'and Ali is the friend of God'**. This shows their belief that Ali, Muhammad's cousin and son-in-law, was the true successor to Muhammad (see page 47).
- To become a Muslim, a person only has to **sincerely recite the Shahadah in front of Muslim witnesses**.
- The Shahadah is recited many times during a Muslim's life. If they are born into a Muslim family, it is the first thing they hear. If possible, it is also the last thing they say before they die.

APPLY

A Name **two** of the Ten Obligatory Acts, and describe what they are.

B 'The Shahadah summarises the most important beliefs in Islam.'

Give arguments to support this statement. As part of your answer, explain how these beliefs influence Muslims in their practice of Islam.

TIP

To answer this question, think about why these beliefs are important and how they affect a Muslim's everyday life. For example, why is the belief that there is only one God central to Islam? And how does this belief affect the way a Muslim practises Islam?

4.2 Salah: the daily prayers (1)

RECAP

Essential information:

- [ ] To observe the duty of **salah** (prayer), Sunni Muslims pray five times a day and Shi'a Muslims three times a day.
- [ ] Muslims perform ritual washing (**wudu**) before they pray to make themselves spiritually clean. They always face the city of Makkah when they pray.
- [ ] When Muslims pray in a mosque, men and women are divided into separate groups. The prayers are led by an imam (religious leader).

The times of prayer

The times for each prayer are worked out from the times of sunrise and sunset, so they change slightly each day. Prayer timetables help Muslims to know when to pray. For Sunni Muslims, the five times for prayer are:

Fajr: just before sunrise

Zuhr: just after midday

Asr: afternoon

Maghrib: just after sunset

Isha: night

Differences between Shi'a and Sunni Muslims in prayer

Shi'a Muslims combine the midday and afternoon prayers, and sunset and night prayers, so they pray the same prayers but only pray three times a day. There are also a few differences in the movements Shi'a and Sunni Muslims make during salah. Another difference is that Shi'a Muslims believe in using only natural elements when prostrating themselves in prayer, so they place a clay tablet at the spot where their forehead will rest.

Preparing for prayer and the direction of prayer

	Preparing for prayer	The direction of prayer
What should Muslims do?	• Perform ritual washing (wudu) before they pray, to make themselves spiritually clean	• Face the city of Makkah
How is this achieved?	• Muslims wash their faces, hands and feet under running water • Mosques have two special rooms set aside for this, one for women and one for men • If water isn't available, Muslims can 'wash' themselves using sand or dust instead. This illustrates the fact that wudu is about becoming spiritually clean, not physically clean	• In a mosque, the **mihrab** indicates the direction of Makkah • This is a small niche in the **qiblah wall**, which is the wall that faces Makkah. Muslims use this to face the right direction when they pray • Muslims can also use a special compass to indicate the right direction
Why is it important?	• The purification of wudu helps Muslims to fully focus on God in their prayers	• Praying in the same direction means that all Muslims are focusing on one place associated with God

Prayer inside a mosque

- Many mosques have carpets that look like rows of prayer mats, giving each person their own space to pray.
- Prayers in the mosque are led by an imam, who is positioned at the front of the congregation, facing the mihrab.
- Men and women pray at the same time but in separate spaces.
- The imam will lead the prayers from the men's prayer room, but his voice is usually also broadcast in the women's prayer room, so he can lead everyone's prayers together.

APPLY

A Explain how Muslims prepare for prayer, and why this is important.

B 'Prayer is the most difficult of the Five Pillars for Muslims to follow.'

Give arguments for and against this statement.

Then write a short conclusion where you weigh up the arguments and decide whether you agree with the statement or not.

TIP

Some questions in the exam will require you to combine your knowledge from different sections of the course. This is one example.

4.3 Salah: the daily prayers (2)

RECAP

Essential information:

- ☐ Prayers are made up of a number of **rak'ah**: set sequences of actions and recitations.
- ☐ The **Jummah prayer** is a special prayer that is held at midday on Friday. Men are expected to attend a mosque for this prayer, but Muslims are otherwise allowed to pray at home if they want to.
- ☐ God commanded Muslims to pray, so it is important for Muslims to observe this pillar of Islam. Prayer is also important because it unites Muslims and brings them closer to God.

The rak'ah

Each prayer consists of a certain number of rak'ah. The rak'ah changes slightly depending on which prayer it is used in, and where it comes in the overall sequence, but it usually includes the following basic actions:

Stand and recite the first chapter from the Qur'an

Bow (showing respect to God) and recite in Arabic 'Glory be to my Lord who is the very greatest' three times

Stand and make a recitation praising God

Kneel with the forehead, nose, hands, knees and toes touching the floor (**prostration**) – this shows complete obedience to God. Recite 'How perfect is my Lord the most high'

Recite 'God is the greatest', first while sitting and then while prostrating

Jummah prayer and prayer at home

- The Jummah prayer is a special communal prayer held every Friday at midday.
- All men are expected to attend a mosque for this prayer, and women may do so if they wish.
- After the prayer, the imam will give a sermon that reminds Muslims about their duties to God.
- Muslims are otherwise allowed to pray at home, and women often do so if they have children to look after or find it hard to attend a mosque.
- Muslims must still perform wudu at home, although they do not need a special room to pray in.
- Many Muslims use a prayer mat at home, which is positioned facing Makkah.

The significance of prayer

Some Muslims may emphasise the ritualistic aspects of prayer, while others focus more on the spiritual quality of prayer. Either way, all Muslims agree that prayer is a very important part of worship in Islam.

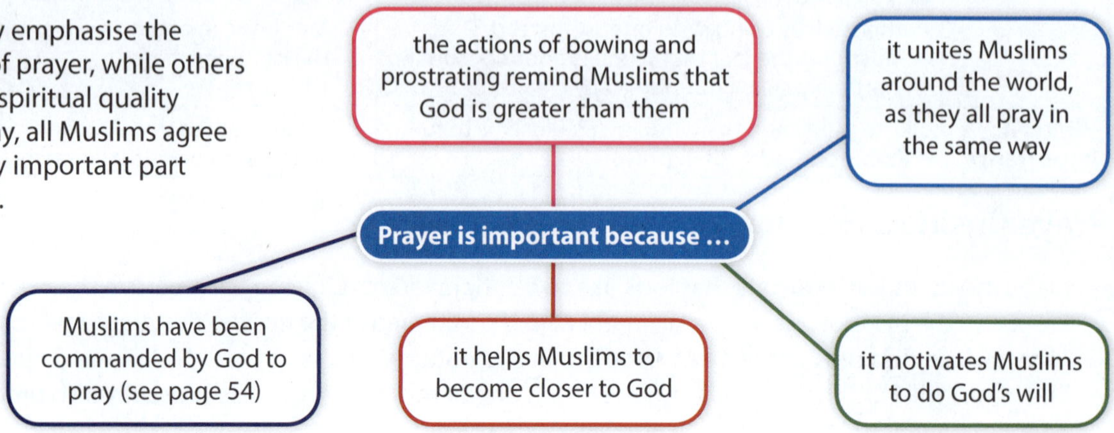

APPLY

A Explain **two** different ways in which prayer is practised in Islam.

B 'It is best that prayers are structured, with set actions and recitations.'

Give your opinion on this statement. Explain your reasoning, referring to Muslim practices in your answer.

TIP

Page 61 in this Revision Guide might help you to develop your opinion on this statement. But make sure your answer focuses on the religion in question, which in this case is Islam.

4.4 Sawm: fasting during Ramadan

RECAP

Essential information:

- ☐ **Ramadan** is the most important month in the Islamic calendar, as it is when the angel Jibril started to reveal the Qur'an to Muhammad (see page 54).
- ☐ Muslims focus on their faith during this month by **fasting** (not eating or drinking during daylight hours), studying the Qur'an, giving to charity, and trying to please God.
- ☐ The **Night of Power** is the night when Jibril first started to recite the Qur'an to Muhammad. Muslims celebrate this night during Ramadan.

Fasting during Ramadan

Origins of fasting	• The command to fast was revealed to Muhammad and can be found in the Qur'an: 'It was in the month of Ramadan that the Qur'an was revealed as guidance for mankind … So any one of you who sees in that month should fast' (Qur'an 2:185) • It has been obligatory for Muslims to fast during Ramadan since the seventh century
What it involves	• Muslims get up every day before sunrise to eat and drink enough to keep them going until sunset • Food, drink, smoking and sex are forbidden during daylight hours • The fast is broken at sunset. The evening meal is often shared with family and friends, and followed by extra prayers and readings from the Qur'an
The exceptions	• Children and people who are ill, pregnant or breastfeeding can be excused from fasting • People who can't fast are expected to make up for it later if they can
Its importance	• The self-discipline that is required to fast shows obedience and dedication to God • Fasting inspires Muslims to help those in poverty who can't afford enough to eat or drink

The Night of Power

- The Night of Power is when Jibril first appeared to Muhammad and started revealing the Qur'an.
- The words that Jibril spoke to Muhammad on this night can be found in Qur'an 96:1–5. They describe how Jibril instructed Muhammad to start reciting his words:

> "Read! In the name of your Lord who created: He created man from a clinging form [a blood clot]. Read! Your Lord is the Most Bountiful One who taught by [means of] the pen, who taught man what he did not know."
>
> *Qur'an 96:1–5*

- The exact date of the Night of Power is unclear, but it is believed to be one of the odd-numbered dates in the second half of Ramadan.
- Muslims try to stay awake throughout the night on each of these dates, praying and studying the Qur'an.
- Observing the Night of Power is thought to give Muslims the benefits of worshipping for a thousand months.

> "What will explain to you what that Night of Glory is? The Night of Glory is better than a thousand months"
>
> *Qur'an 97:2–3*

APPLY

A Explain **two** Muslim beliefs about the Night of Power.

Refer to scripture or another source of Muslim belief and teaching in your answer.

B 'It is more important to study the Qur'an during Ramadan than it is to fast.'

Evaluate this statement.

TIP

To 'evaluate' this statement, explain whether you think it is true or not and why. Consider arguments for and against the statement, then weigh them up to decide whether you agree or disagree with it.

4.5 Zakah: almsgiving

RECAP

Essential information:

- [ ] **Zakah** requires Muslims to give 2.5% of their savings to charity every year. Muslims believe that giving Zakah helps them to purify their souls, by removing selfishness and greed.
- [ ] In addition to giving Zakah, Shi'a Muslims also give **Khums**. This is 20% of their savings, half of which goes to Shi'a religious leaders and half to charity.

Zakah

Origins of Zakah	• Giving to charity is mentioned a number of times in the Qur'an; for example 'Whatever ... you give should be for parents, close relatives, orphans, the needy, and travellers. God is well aware of whatever good you do.' (Qur'an 2:215) • The exact amount that should be given was worked out at a later date by Muslim scholars
How much is given	• Only Muslims with savings greater than a certain amount (known as the nisab) are required to give Zakah • Muslims with savings greater than the nisab are expected to give 2.5% of their savings once a year
Who it is given to	• Zakah can be donated directly to a charity such as Islamic Relief or Muslim Aid • It can also be collected by a mosque, which will distribute the money among those in need
The importance of Zakah	• By giving Zakah, Muslims are fulfilling a duty to God • It helps to strengthen the Muslim community by supporting people living in poverty • It encourages Muslims to have a good attitude towards money, and to use their wealth in a way that would please God • It is a type of purification that helps Muslims to become closer to God

Khums

- Khums means 'fifth'. The giving of Khums started as a requirement for Muslim armies to donate one fifth (20%) of the spoils of war to their religious leader.
- Today, Shi'a Muslims give 20% of their savings.
- Half goes to Shi'a religious leaders, to be used for religious education or other religious matters, and the other half is given to charity or people living in poverty.

In addition to giving Zakah, Muslims are encouraged to voluntarily give their money and time to charity at any point of the year. This is called Sadaqah.

> "Alms are meant only for the poor, the needy, those who administer them, those whose hearts need winning over, to free slaves and help those in debt, for God's cause, and for travellers in need."
>
> *Qur'an 9:60*

APPLY

A Give **one** difference between Zakah and Khums.

B 'The most important reason to give Zakah or Khums is because it teaches Muslims to have a good attitude towards money.'

Do you agree with this statement? Explain your reasons.

Then explain why someone else might have a different point of view.

TIP

When you evaluate this question think about what 'a good attitude to money' would mean for a Muslim compared to a non-religious person.

4.6 Hajj: pilgrimage – origins and significance

RECAP

Essential information:

- **Hajj** is an annual pilgrimage that starts and ends in the city of Makkah (Mecca) in Saudi Arabia. Every Muslim is expected to take part in Hajj at least once during their life.
- Hajj remembers the actions of the prophet Ibrahim and his family, who rebuilt the **Ka'aba** (the cube-shaped building in the centre of the Grand Mosque, and the holiest place in Islam).
- Hajj strengthens a Muslim's faith and shows their commitment to God.

The origins of Hajj

Around 4000 years ago, God told the prophet Ibrahim to take his wife Hajira and son Ishmael to Arabia

→ God then told Ibrahim to leave Hajira and Ishmael on their own with some supplies of food and water

→ After a few days the supplies ran out, and Hajira and Ishmael were suffering from hunger and dehydration

→ Hajira ran up and down two hills called Safa and Marwah, looking for help or a source of water. After running between the hills seven times, she collapsed beside her son

→ Hajira prayed to God for help. Ishmael then struck his foot on the ground, and water began to gush up from the earth

→ Hajira and Ishmael survived by trading some of the water for food and supplies. This source of water became known as the well of Zamzam

→ When Ibrahim returned, God told him to build a shrine dedicated to him – the Ka'aba. Ibrahim was told to make the Ka'aba a pure place of worship and to call people to perform Hajj there

→ Over the years, as the city of Makkah grew, God's instructions to Ibrahim were forgotten. People worshipped idols and stored them in the Ka'aba

→ In 628 CE, Muhammad journeyed from Madinah to Makkah with a large group of Muslims to convert the city to Islam (see page 54). This is thought to have been the first pilgrimage in Islam

The significance of Hajj

Hajj is important because it …

- produces inner peace
- brings a person closer to God
- leads to a person's sins being forgiven
- fulfils a religious obligation
- emphasises equality and unity
- shows self-discipline and dedication to God
- reminds Muslims of the good examples set by the prophets

> "Pilgrimage to the House is a duty owed to God by people who are able to undertake it."
>
> *Qur'an 3:97*

APPLY

A Explain why the Ka'aba is important to Muslims.

B 'Going on Hajj is the best way for a Muslim to show their commitment to Islam.'

Give arguments for and against this statement.

Then write a short conclusion where you weigh up these arguments and decide whether you agree or disagree with the statement.

TIP

To answer this question, you need to explain why particular actions (such as going on Hajj, praying or fasting) show commitment to Islam. Then think about which of these actions is the 'best' way to show commitment to Islam, and why.

4.7 Hajj: pilgrimage – how Hajj is performed

RECAP

Essential information:

- ☐ Hajj takes place over five days, during which time pilgrims travel from Makkah to Mina, Arafat, Muzdalifah and back to Makkah.
- ☐ The actions that are performed on Hajj remember events in the lives of the prophet Ibrahim and his family, such as Hajira's search for water and Ibrahim's willingness to sacrifice his own son.

What happens on Hajj?

	What is involved	Its significance
Entering a state of Ihram 	• Before Hajj begins, pilgrims must enter a state of purity called **Ihram** • This involves performing ritual washing, praying, and putting on Ihram clothing • Men dress in two sheets of white cloth, and women wear a single colour (usually white) as well	• The colour white symbolises purity • The fact that everyone wears similar clothes emphasises unity and equality • It shows everyone is equal before God
Circling the Ka'aba 	• Hajj starts in Makkah at the Grand Mosque. Pilgrims walk in a circle seven times around the Ka'aba • As they circle the Ka'aba, they touch the black stone set into a corner of the building, or raise a hand towards it as they pass	• This stone is an ancient Islamic relic • It is believed to be the only surviving stone from the original Ka'aba • Some Muslims believe it comes from paradise, and was given by God to Adam
Walking between the two hills 	• After circling the Ka'aba, pilgrims walk seven times between the two hills of Safa and Marwah • They then collect water from the well of Zamzam	• This remembers Hajira's search for water (see page 65), and the miraculous appearance of the well of Zamzam
Standing at Arafat 	• Pilgrims travel to Arafat, where Muhammad preached his last sermon • They spend a whole afternoon praying under the hot summer sun (a reminder of what the Day of Judgement will be like) • Some Muslims stand while they pray to show the depth of their faith	• This afternoon is physically draining but allows Muslims to show their devotion to God • God is believed to forgive the sins of everyone at Arafat, providing they are sincerely sorry for what they have done wrong
Throwing pebbles at Mina 	• Pilgrims walk to Muzdalifah, where they spend the night. On their way they collect a handful of pebbles • The next day, at Mina, they throw these pebbles at three stone walls called the Jamarat	• The walls represent the devil and temptation • Pilgrims throw pebbles at the walls to show they reject evil and the temptation to sin
Sacrificing an animal 	• If they can, pilgrims then sacrifice an animal, as part of the celebration of Id-ul-Adha (see page 68) • The leftover meat is given to people living in poverty	• This sacrifice remembers Ibrahim's willingness to sacrifice his own son out of obedience to God (see page 53)

APPLY

A Describe what must happen before Hajj starts, and what this signifies.

B 'The most important reason for performing Hajj is to remember the actions of the prophets.' What is your opinion on this statement? **Explain your reasoning.**

4.8 Jihad

RECAP

Essential information:

- [ ] **Jihad** refers to the struggle against evil. It requires Muslims to strive to improve themselves and the societies they live in, in a way that would please God.
- [ ] **Greater jihad** is the inward, personal struggle to live according to the teachings of Islam.
- [ ] **Lesser jihad** is the outward, collective struggle to defend Islam from threat.

Greater jihad

Greater jihad refers to the constant struggle that Muslims undertake to improve themselves spiritually and to deepen their relationship with God, by living according to the teachings of Islam. It is considered to be more important than lesser jihad, and might involve some of the following actions.

Greater jihad involves ...

- observing the Five Pillars of Islam
- studying the Qur'an
- putting God above everything else
- avoiding temptations such as drugs and alcohol
- avoiding negative traits such as greed and jealousy
- helping and caring for those in need

> "... this is My path, leading straight, so follow it, and do not follow other ways"
>
> *Qur'an 6:153*

TIP

You can use this quote in your exam to show that greater jihad requires Muslims to follow God as best they can.

Lesser jihad

Lesser jihad refers to the outward struggle to defend Islam from threat. In the early days of Islam, this was important when Muslims were being persecuted and they needed to fight for their freedom to practise the faith.

Fighting for a religious cause is also sometimes called **holy war**. This refers to a war that must be:

- approved by a fair religious leader
- fought in self-defence in response to a threat
- not used to gain territory or wealth
- not used to convert people to Islam
- fought only after all peaceful methods to resolve the situation have been tried first.

This list shows that lesser jihad or holy war can only be used as a last resort, to defend the faith when it is under severe attack. Islam teaches that lesser jihad or holy war can never be used to justify terrorist attacks.

APPLY

A Explain **two** ways in which a belief in greater jihad influences Muslims today.

B 'Greater jihad is harder to follow than lesser jihad in today's world.'

Give arguments for and against this statement.

4.9 The festivals of Id-ul-Fitr and Id-ul-Adha

RECAP

Essential information:

- [ ] **Id-ul-Fitr** is a Muslim festival that celebrates the end of Ramadan.
- [ ] **Id-ul-Adha** is a Muslim festival that celebrates Ibrahim's willingness to sacrifice his son to God, and marks the end of Hajj.

Id-ul-Fitr

Origins	• The festival was started by Muhammad after he arrived in Madinah, having fled from persecution in Makkah (see page 54) • Muhammad told the people in Madinah that God had set aside two days for festivities: Id-ul-Fitr and Id-ul-Adha
Celebrations	• Muslims gather together in mosques or large outdoor areas to say special prayers. The imam's sermon usually reminds Muslims to forgive any disputes that have happened during the year, and focus instead on helping people living in poverty • Muslims decorate their homes, wear new clothes, eat special foods, and exchange cards and presents • Many Muslims visit their local cemetery to remember and pray for family members who have died • In the UK, Islamic businesses may give Muslims time off to celebrate
Importance	• The festival allows Muslims to celebrate the end of a month of fasting (see page 63) • It is a way for Muslims to give thanks to God for giving them the strength to complete the fast • It is also a way for Muslims to thank God for giving his wisdom and guidance in the Qur'an, which was first revealed to Muhammad during Ramadan

Id-ul-Adha

Origins	• Like Id-ul-Fitr, this festival was started by Muhammad (see above)
Celebrations	• Special prayers are held in the mosque, and the sermon will usually be on the theme of sacrifice • Muslims visit family and friends, and enjoy meals together. An effort is made to make sure everyone is included in the celebrations • Muslims who are able to, including those who are taking part in Hajj, will slaughter an animal (see page 66) • In Britain, some Muslims buy an animal from their local slaughterhouse, and share the meat with their family and friends. Traditionally some of the meat is given to people living in poverty, but today Muslims usually donate money to people in need instead
Importance	• The festival remembers and celebrates Ibrahim's willingness to sacrifice his son to God, as described in Surah 37 in the Qur'an. This reminds Muslims about the importance of showing complete obedience to God • The festival also celebrates the completion of Hajj, which is a demanding pilgrimage that helps strengthen a Muslim's faith • The festival allows Muslims around the world to connect with those on Hajj, even if they can't be there themselves

APPLY

A Describe the origins of Id-ul-Fitr and Id-ul-Adha.

B 'Muslim festivals are mainly about having fun.'

Read the following response:

"During Id-ul-Fitr and Id-ul-Adha, Muslims give each other presents, eat lots of nice food and have fun together. If they were really thinking about the religious meaning of the festival then they would be more solemn. Also, Id-ul-Adha remembers an event that happened years and years ago which isn't relevant to Muslims today, so I think the festival is mainly an opportunity to get together and share a meal with family and friends."

Write a paragraph in reply to this response, which argues against the statement above. Keep your answer focused on the festivals of Id-ul-Fitr and Id-ul-Adha.

4.10 The festival of Ashura

RECAP

Essential information:

- [ ] The **Day of Ashura** (Day of Remembrance) is an important Shi'a festival that remembers the death of Husayn at the battle of Karbala.
- [ ] Many Shi'a Muslims observe Ashura by taking part in mourning rituals or processions.
- [ ] Ashura is also observed by Sunni Muslims, for whom the festival is known as the Day of Atonement. However, for Sunni Muslims it is not as important or solemn an occasion as for Shi'a Muslims.

The origins and meaning of Ashura

- The Day of Ashura is important for Shi'a Muslims in particular, who view it as a day of great sorrow. This is because it remembers the death of Husayn, who was the son of Imam Ali and grandson of Muhammad.
- Husayn died in the battle of Karbala. This battle was held on 10 October 680 CE in Karbala, Iraq. It was fought between Husayn and his supporters (around 70 men, women and children) against the much larger army of Caliph Yazid I. Husayn and most of his supporters were killed in the battle.
- Husayn's death is seen by Shi'a Muslims as a symbol of the struggle against injustice, tyranny and oppression.

Sunni Muslims also observe Ashura, which they call the Day of Atonement. For some Sunni Muslims the festival celebrates the day the Jewish people were freed from slavery in Egypt, while for others it celebrates the day Noah left the ark after the flood.

How Ashura is commemorated

Shi'a Muslims commemorate Ashura in the following ways:

Action	Further explanation
Shi'a Muslims perform plays and re-enactments to tell the story of Husayn's death	• These help Muslims to remember the events at Karbala
Many Shi'a Muslims take part in public expressions of grief and mourning	• In London, thousands of Shi'a Muslims gather at Marble Arch to listen to speeches and take part in a procession of mourning • In some cities in Britain, some Shi'a men gather in the streets and slap themselves on their chests as part of a mourning ritual • Some Muslims believe they should shed blood to connect with Husayn's suffering and death • Some Shi'a religious leaders condemn this practice and encourage Muslims to donate blood to the blood transfusion service instead
In Iraq, many Shi'a Muslims visit Husayn's tomb	• Husayn's tomb is believed to be located in the Mashhad al-Husayn, which is a shrine in Karbala • Many Shi'a Muslims go on pilgrimage to the Mashhad al-Husayn each year for Ashura

Many Sunni Muslims observe Ashura by fasting for the day. They may also give to charity, show extra kindness to their family and people living in poverty, recite prayers, and learn from Islamic scholars.

APPLY

A Give **one** way in which Shi'a Muslims observe Ashura.

B On page 68, question B asked you to write a paragraph arguing against the statement 'Muslim festivals are mainly about having fun', focusing on the festivals of Id-ul-Fitr and Id-ul-Adha.

Now add another paragraph to your answer, arguing that the festival of Ashura is not 'mainly about having fun.'

TIP
When writing about Ashura, try to be specific about whether you are referring to Shi'a or Sunni Muslims. Remember that each group observes the festival in different ways, for different reasons.

REVIEW

4 Exam practice

Test the 1 mark multiple-choice question

1 Which **one** of the following is *not* one of the Ten Obligatory Acts?

A Hajj B Jihad C Shahadah D Zakah **[1 mark]**

2 Which **one** of the following people do Shi'a Muslims remember on the Day of Ashura?

A Hajira B Husayn C Muhammad D Ali **[1 mark]**

Test the 1 mark question

3 Give **one** object or feature that Muslims can use to know they are facing the right direction when they pray. **[1 mark]**

____

4 Give **one** way in which Muslims can give Zakah. **[1 mark]**

____

Test the 4 mark question

5 Explain **two** ways in which a belief in the importance of prayer influences Muslims today. **[4 marks]**

• **Explain one way.**	*A belief in the importance of prayer means that Muslims pray at least three times a day.*
• Develop your explanation with more detail/an example/ reference to a religious teaching or quotation.	*Muslims believe prayer is an important duty in their daily lives because it is one of the Five Pillars of Islam. One way that Muslims show it is important is by praying five times a day (Sunni Muslims) or three times a day (Shi'a Muslims). This helps Muslims remember God is with them throughout each day of their lives.*
• **Explain a second way.**	*A belief in the importance of prayer also means that Muslim men are expected to attend a mosque every Friday lunchtime.*
• Develop your explanation with more detail/an example/ reference to a religious teaching or quotation.	*Another way in which a belief in the importance of prayer is shown is by attending Friday prayers in the mosque to take part in the Jummah prayer, a special communal prayer that is said once a week. This is important to Muslims because it unites them with other members of the Muslim community and helps to strengthen their faith in God.*

TIP

Remember to be careful not to make generalisations in your answers. For example, here the student has correctly pointed out that Shi'a and Sunni Muslims pray a different number of times each day.

6 Explain **two** ways in which the actions of the prophet Ibrahim and his family are remembered on Hajj. **[4 marks]**

• **Explain one way.**	
• Develop your explanation with more detail/an example/ reference to a religious teaching or quotation.	
• **Explain a second way.**	
• Develop your explanation with more detail/an example/ reference to a religious teaching or quotation.	

7 Explain **two** different Muslim beliefs about why it is important to fast during Ramadan. **[4 marks]**

4 Exam practice

Test the 6 mark question

8 Explain **two** Muslim beliefs about the importance of festivals.

Refer to sacred writings or another source of Muslim belief and teaching in your answer. **[6 marks]**

• **Explain one belief.**	*Muslims believe festivals are important because they allow them to give thanks to God.*
• Develop your explanation with more detail/an example.	*For example, during the festival of Id-ul-Fitr Muslims give thanks to God for giving them the strength to complete a month of fasting.*
• **Explain a second belief.**	*Muslims also believe festivals are important because they help them to remember important events in the history of Islam.*
• Develop your explanation with more detail/an example.	*For example, Id-ul-Adha remembers Ibrahim's willingness to sacrifice his son to God.*
• **Add a reference to sacred writings or another source of Muslim belief and teaching.** If you prefer, you can add the reference to your first belief instead.	*In Surah 37, the Qur'an describes the dream Ibrahim had where God asked him to sacrifice his son, and tells how Ibrahim was willing to obey God's command.*
• Apply the reference by explaining how it links to the question.	*This suggests that festivals allow Muslims to celebrate things that are important in Islam, such as sacrifice and obedience to God. This then helps Muslims today follow Ibrahim's example.*

9 Explain **two** reasons why Muslims go on Hajj.

Refer to sacred writings or another source of Muslim belief and teaching in your answer. **[6 marks]**

• **Explain one reason.**	
• Develop your explanation with more detail/an example.	
• **Explain a second reason.**	
• Develop your explanation with more detail/an example.	
• **Add a reference to sacred writings or another source of Muslim belief and teaching.** If you prefer, you can add the reference to your first reason instead.	
• Apply the reference by explaining how it links to the question.	

10 Explain **two** Muslim beliefs about jihad.

Refer to sacred writings or another source of Muslim belief and teaching in your answer. **[6 marks]**

Test the 12 mark question

11 'The Shahadah is the most important pillar of Islam.'

Evaluate this statement. In your answer you should:

- refer to Muslim teaching
- give reasoned arguments to support this statement
- give reasoned arguments to support a different point of view
- reach a justified conclusion.

[12 marks]

TIP

Try to use religious terms in your answer, if it is appropriate, as this helps you to demonstrate your knowledge of the subject. For example, in this answer some of the names of the different pillars are given.

REASONED ARGUMENTS IN SUPPORT OF THE STATEMENT ● **Explain why some people would agree with the statement.** ● Develop your explanation with more detail and examples. ● Refer to religious teaching. Use a quote or paraphrase or refer to a religious authority. ● **Evaluate the arguments.** Is this a good argument or not? Explain why you think this.	*Many Muslims would agree with this statement because the Shahadah expresses the core belief of Islam. It provides the foundation for the other four pillars, which tell Muslims how to put into practice the belief expressed in the Shahadah. It is also the only pillar which people have to observe in order to become a Muslim, by reciting it sincerely in front of other Muslims.* *The Shahadah states that 'There is no God but Allah and Muhammad is the Prophet of Allah'. Muslims should carry out the other four pillars with this statement in mind. This means when they pray, they should pray only to God. When they go on Hajj, they should focus on God throughout the pilgrimage. If Muslims don't believe in the Shahadah, the other pillars become meaningless.*
REASONED ARGUMENTS SUPPORTING A DIFFERENT VIEW ● **Explain why some people would support a different view.** ● Develop your explanation with more detail and examples. ● Refer to religious teaching. Use a quote or paraphrase or refer to a religious authority. ● **Evaluate the arguments.** Is this a good argument or not? Explain why you think this.	*Some Muslims might disagree with this statement because the Shahadah doesn't tell Muslims how to live in a way that pleases God. It just tells Muslims what they should believe. But the other four pillars tell Muslims how to live a good life that gets them closer to God and helps them to get into heaven when they die.* *For example, the pillar of salah teaches Muslims they should pray three or five times a day. The pillar of sawm teaches Muslims they should fast during Ramadan. Observing these pillars helps Muslims to develop their relationship with God, so it could be argued they are more important than the Shahadah.*
CONCLUSION ● **Give a justified conclusion.** ● Include your own opinion together with your own reasoning. ● **Include evaluation.** Explain why you think one viewpoint is stronger than the other or why you think they are equally strong. ● Do not just repeat arguments you have already used without explaining how they apply to your reasoned opinion/conclusion.	*I think all of the pillars are important in Islam, because they all teach Muslims how to live in a way that would please God. This is important for becoming closer to God and getting into heaven in the afterlife. However, I also agree with the statement because Muslims have to believe in the Shahadah before they can observe the other four pillars. Also the Shahadah is a clear summary of the faith which Muslims share.* **TIP** This is a good answer that compares the Shahadah with the other pillars and comes to a justified conclusion about which is the most important.

12 'Giving to charity is the most important practice in Islam.'

Evaluate this statement. In your answer you should:

- refer to Muslim teaching
- give reasoned arguments to support this statement
- give reasoned arguments to support a different point of view
- reach a justified conclusion.

[12 marks]

REASONED ARGUMENTS IN SUPPORT OF THE STATEMENT ● **Explain why some people would agree with the statement.** ● Develop your explanation with more detail and examples. ● Refer to religious teaching. Use a quote or paraphrase or refer to a religious authority. ● **Evaluate the arguments.** Is this a good argument or not? Explain why you think this.	
REASONED ARGUMENTS SUPPORTING A DIFFERENT VIEW ● **Explain why some people would support a different view.** ● Develop your explanation with more detail and examples. ● Refer to religious teaching. Use a quote or paraphrase or refer to a religious authority. ● **Evaluate the arguments.** Is this a good argument or not? Explain why you think this.	
CONCLUSION ● **Give a justified conclusion.** ● Include your own opinion together with your own reasoning. ● **Include evaluation.** Explain why you think one viewpoint is stronger than the other or why you think they are equally strong. ● Do not just repeat arguments you have already used without explaining how they apply to your reasoned opinion/conclusion.	

13 'Id-ul-Fitr should be made an official public holiday in Britain.'

Evaluate this statement. In your answer you should:

- refer to Muslim teaching
- give reasoned arguments to support this statement
- give reasoned arguments to support a different point of view
- reach a justified conclusion.

[12 marks]

Check your answers using the mark scheme on page 154. How did you do?
To feel more secure in the content you need to remember, re-read pages 60–69.
To remind yourself of what the examiner is looking for in your answers, go to pages 6–11.

5 Relationships and families

5.1 Human sexuality

RECAP

Essential information:

- ☐ **Human sexuality** refers to how people express themselves as sexual beings. In Britain, sex before marriage, having children outside of marriage, and same-sex sexual relationships have become more common. The age of consent (when legally old enough to freely agree to have sex) is 16.
- ☐ Christianity and Islam regard sexual relationships between members of the opposite sex (**heterosexual relationships**) as natural, part of God's plan for humanity.
- ☐ Some Christians and most Muslims think same-sex sexual relationships are against God's will. In Britain, same-sex couples can now legally marry.

Opposite-sex sexual relationships

Christian views	Muslim views
• Marriage is the only valid place for opposite-sex sexual relationships because it is part of God's plan for humans. • Christian views about sex before marriage vary but all are against unfaithfulness. "That is why a man leaves his father and mother and is united to his wife, and they become one flesh." *Genesis 2:24* [NIV]	• Opposite-sex sexual relationships are the expected pattern of behaviour; Muslims are expected to marry and have a family. • The only permitted form of sexual relationship in Islam is that between husband and wife, considered a blessing from God. "Marry those who are single among you for [God] will develop their moral traits [through marriage]." *Hadith*

Same-sex sexual relationships

You might be asked to compare beliefs on same-sex sexual relationships between Christianity (the main religious tradition in Great Britain) and another religious tradition.

- Some Christians oppose same-sex sexual relationships because the Bible says sex between two men is forbidden (Leviticus 18:22) and Paul taught that the sexually immoral, including 'men who have sex with men', will not inherit the kingdom of God (1 Corinthians 6:9–10 [NIV]).
- Most Muslims believe the Qur'an and Hadith teach that same-sex sexual relationships are against God's will and forbidden.

> "Must you, unlike [other] people, lust after males and abandon the wives that God has created for you? You are exceeding all bounds." *Qur'an 26:165–166*

TIP: This is a good example of similarities between religious beliefs.

- Many Muslims agree with those Christians who believe that same-sex sexual relationships are against the natural law as they cannot produce children, therefore are not what God intended.
- The Catholic Church teaches that people who are attracted to people of the same sex are not sinful, but should remain chaste (not have sex) to avoid sinful acts. Many Muslims also believe that people who are attracted to people of the same sex should control their actions and not break God's law. Otherwise, Muslims believe, the person will have to answer to God on the Day of Judgement.
- Some Muslims agree with more liberal Christians who accept same-sex sexual relationships that are loving and committed. For example, the Church of England welcomes same-sex couples living in committed relationships, but does not allow marriage in church.

APPLY

A Explain **two** different religious beliefs about same-sex sexual relationships.

B 'Sex has been devalued in British society.'

Evaluate this statement, referring to **two** religious arguments, and **two** non-religious arguments.

TIP: Different religious beliefs may come from within religions as well as between religions. Make sure you write about religious beliefs and not just about commonly held opinions.

5.2 Sexual relationships before and outside marriage

RECAP

Essential information:

- [ ] The Anglican and Catholic Churches and Islam teach that **sex before marriage** (sex between two single unmarried people) is wrong.
- [ ] All religions teach that **sex outside marriage** or **adultery** (voluntary sexual intercourse between a married person and someone who is not their husband or wife) is wrong.
- [ ] In Britain, sex before marriage is widely accepted, but many people, religious and non-religious, think that adultery is wrong because it involves lies and secrecy, and betrays trust.

You might be asked to compare beliefs on sex before marriage between Christianity (the main religious tradition in Great Britain) and another religious tradition.

Sexual relationships before marriage

Christian views

- For many Christians, sex expresses a deep, lifelong union that requires the commitment of marriage.
- Paul warns against sexual immorality:

> "... whoever sins sexually, sins against their own body. Do you not know your bodies are temples of the Holy Spirit..."
>
> *1 Corinthians 6:18–19* [NIV]

- Some liberal Christians, however, think that sex before marriage can be a valid expression of love for each other, particularly if the couple are intending marriage.

Muslim views

- Muslims believe sex is a gift from God that must be managed responsibly within marriage.
- The Qur'an forbids sex before marriage; under Islamic law (Shari'ah), sex before marriage is considered a serious sin, like adultery and rape.

> "The only way to protect all within society is to maintain a society where only a man and his wife share the act of sex."
>
> Abdul Wahid Hamid, *Islam: The Natural Way*

Sexual relationships outside marriage

Christian views

- Adultery breaks vows Christian couples make before God and threatens the stable relationship needed for their children's security.
- It is against one of the Ten Commandments:

> "You shall not commit adultery."
>
> *Exodus 20:14* [NIV]

- It is against Jesus' teaching that lust, which could lead to adultery, is wrong:

> "Anyone who looks at a woman lustfully has already committed adultery with her in his heart."
>
> *Matthew 5:27–28* [NIV]

- Jesus forgave a woman caught in adultery but ordered her to leave her life of sin.

Muslim views

- Muslims should avoid situations that could lead to sexual sins.

> "A man should not stay with a woman in seclusion unless he is a Dhu-Mahram [relative]."
>
> *Hadith*

- The Qur'an forbids adultery:

> "And do not go anywhere near adultery: it is an outrage, and an evil path."
>
> *Qur'an 17:32*

- Married couples should not have to go outside of marriage for fulfilment.

APPLY

A Here are two religious beliefs about sexual relationships outside of marriage (adultery). Develop **one** of the points by referring to a relevant religious teaching or quotation. Then apply the religious teaching or quotation by explaining how it links to the point.

"Christians think sex outside marriage (adultery) is wrong because it breaks the vows couples make at their wedding."

"Muslims believe having an affair can affect children and cause pain to all concerned."

TIP

For an evaluation question it is important to develop the reasons that you give.

B Give **two** points in support and **two** points against the statement, 'It is not always wrong to have sex before marriage.'

Develop one of them by adding more detail or an example.

5.3 Contraception and family planning

RECAP

Essential information:

- [ ] There are three types of **contraception** (methods used to prevent pregnancy): artificial (e.g. condoms, the pill), natural (e.g. the rhythm method) and permanent (sterilisation).
- [ ] In Britain, there is widespread acceptance of contraception to help family planning, prevent unwanted pregnancies, reduce global overpopulation and prevent the spread of sexually transmitted infections.
- [ ] Most Christians and Muslims accept **family planning** (controlling how many children a couple has and when they have them) in certain circumstances, but not to prevent having children altogether.

Christian attitudes towards contraception and family planning

- All Christian Churches believe having children is God's greatest gift to married couples, but there are times when it may be acceptable to avoid bringing children into the world.

Religious group	Teaching	Methods
Catholic and Orthodox	• Artificial contraception goes against natural law/purpose of marriage and can encourage selfishness/infidelity. • The purposes of sex (having children and expressing love) should not be separated. • 'Every sexual act should have the possibility of creating new life.' (Humanae Vitae, 1968) • The Orthodox Church agrees with the Catholic position but recognises individuals' needs.	• Rhythm method/ avoiding sex at fertile times of month (Catholic) • Non-abortive forms of contraception only (Orthodox)
Anglican and non-conformist	• People should only have as many children as they can care for. • Allow contraception to enable couples to develop relationship first/space out pregnancies to avoid harming woman's health. • The Anglican Lambeth Conference approved artificial contraception used 'in the light of Christian principles' (1930).	• Preference for non-abortive forms of contraception

Muslim attitudes towards contraception and family planning

- Contraception is not for unmarried people, but may be used for family planning, e.g. if a wife's health is at risk, to space out pregnancies or to avoid serious financial difficulties.
- Some prefer natural methods, but artificial contraception is fine as long as it does not cause an abortion or prevent children altogether (permanent forms).

You might be asked to compare beliefs on contraception between Christianity (the main religious tradition in Great Britain) and another religious tradition.

For the use of contraception	Against the use of contraception
• No direct teaching in the Qur'an, but some scholars say this text shows that God does not want to make life difficult for people so would accept contraception: "God wishes to lighten your burden; man was created weak." *Qur'an 4:28* • Some hadith suggest Muhammad was aware of birth control and accepted it in appropriate circumstances.	• Some Muslims think contraception goes against God's will and God gives people strength to cope with any children. • These Muslims may quote this text, which is against killing infants once they are born, and argue it also applies to contraception: "Do not kill your children for fear of poverty – we shall provide for them and for you – killing them is a great sin." *Qur'an 17:31*

APPLY

A Give **one** religious belief about the use of contraception.

B 'Religious authorities should not preach about family planning.'

Evaluate this statement. Refer to religious arguments in your answer.

5.4 Marriage

RECAP

Essential information:

- ☐ **Marriage** is a legal union between a man and a woman (or in some countries, including the UK, two people of the same sex) as partners in a relationship.
- ☐ A **civil partnership** is a legal union of same-sex couples (2004).
- ☐ **Same-sex marriage** is marriage between partners of the same sex (2014).
- ☐ **Cohabitation** refers to a couple living together and having a sexual relationship without being married to one another.

The nature and purpose of marriage

Christian beliefs

- Marriage is a gift from God at creation/part of the natural law.
- It is a sacrament/a lifelong union blessed by God that reflects the sacrificial love of Jesus.
- It is a covenant (agreement) before God in which the couple promises to live faithfully till death.

> "That is why a man leaves his father and mother and is united to his wife, and they become one flesh." *Genesis 2:24* [NIV]

- It is a spiritual bond of trust that reflects the love of Christ for the Church.

Muslim beliefs

- Marriage is a faithful, lifelong commitment, intended by God for the sharing of love and companionship. It is an equal partnership under God.
- It is a social contract that brings two families together, impacting the whole community.
- It helps people develop spiritually by avoiding sexual sin and by adding value to worship.
- According to the Qur'an, husbands and wives are like garments for each other (Qur'an 2:187), meaning each should support and care for the other.

- The purpose of marriage is to provide a stable, secure environment for family life.
- Both Christians and Muslims believe marriage is the proper place to enjoy sex, raise children in a religious faith and provide lifelong support and companionship for a partner.
- In Islam, marriages can be arranged (where parents help to find a suitable partner) but young people have the right to refuse. Forced marriages are not allowed.

> "If a man gives his daughter in marriage while she is averse to it then such marriage is invalid." *Hadith*

- A Muslim woman must marry a Muslim; a Muslim man can marry a Muslim, Christian or Jew.

> "...to have and to hold from this day forward; for better, for worse, for richer, for poorer, in sickness and in health, to love and to cherish, till death us do part; according to God's holy law." *Anglican marriage service vows*

> "There is no institution in Islam more beloved and dearer [to God] than marriage." *Hadith*

Cohabitation and same-sex marriage

- Catholic and Orthodox Churches and Islam oppose cohabitation as they believe sex should only take place within marriage.
- Many Anglican and Protestant Christians accept that although marriage is best, people may cohabit in a faithful, loving and committed way without being married.
- Islam forbids same-sex sexual relationships. Many Muslims were opposed to the changes in law that made same-sex marriages legal.
- Many Christians were also opposed to legalising same-sex marriage, because it seemed to be changing the nature of marriage. The law protects Churches that oppose same-sex marriage and they are not forced to conduct same-sex marriages against their beliefs.

TIP
Show you understand that there are different perspectives on cohabitation within Christianity.

APPLY

A Give **one** religious belief about the nature of marriage.

B 'Marriage gives more stability to society than cohabitation.'
Develop an argument to support this statement.

TIP
Simply write down one belief. 'Give' indicates that there is no need to go into detail.

5.5 Divorce and remarriage

RECAP

Essential information:

- [ ] **Divorce** (legal ending of a marriage) is allowed after one year if a marriage cannot be saved. Reasons for divorce may include: adultery, domestic abuse, addiction, illness or disability, work or financial pressures, falling out of love, inability to have children, etc.
- [ ] **Remarriage** is when someone marries again while their former husband or wife is still alive.
- [ ] An **annulment** is a Catholic Church ruling that a marriage was never valid.
- [ ] Religions try to balance ethical arguments between the sanctity of marriage vows made before God and compassion for people whose marriage has broken down.

Christian teachings about divorce and remarriage

- In cases of marriage breakdown, Christian clergy offer counselling, prayer and sacraments, and may refer couples to outside agencies such as Relate and Accord.
- Jesus taught that anyone who divorced and remarried was committing adultery.

> "He answered, "Anyone who divorces his wife and marries another woman commits adultery against her. And if she divorces her husband and marries another man, she commits adultery."" *Mark 10:11–12* [NIV]

- Matthew 5:32 adds 'If a man divorces his wife for any cause other than unchastity (unfaithfulness) he involves her in adultery' [NIV].
- Vows made in God's presence must be kept.
- The Catholic Church teaches that marriage is a sacrament that is permanent and cannot be dissolved between two baptised people by civil divorce. Catholics can separate but not remarry while their partner is still alive, or they can obtain an annulment if there was never a true marriage.
- Other Christians believe marriage is for life, but sometimes divorce is the lesser of two evils. They think the Church should reflect God's forgiveness and allow couples a second chance for happiness.
- Most Anglican, Protestant and Orthodox churches allow divorce and remarriage in church as long as couples take the vows seriously.

TIP
This text shows why Christians have different attitudes towards divorce (because it seems to be allowing it for unfaithfulness).

Muslim teachings about divorce and remarriage

- The Qur'an encourages the couple to try to reconcile their differences by allowing a member of each partner's family to help bring them back together, if God wills (Qur'an 4:35).
- The Qur'an guarantees rights of both men and women to divorce, but divorce is 'hateful to Allah' (Hadith).
- For a religious divorce, the husband must declare it to his wife verbally or in writing, followed by a three month waiting period (iddah) to see whether his wife is pregnant. If so, they must wait until the baby is born.

> "...when any of you intend to divorce women, do so at a time when their prescribed waiting period can properly start... if you are in doubt, the period of waiting shall be three months." *Qur'an 65:1 and 4*

- A wife can apply for divorce, but if her husband is not at fault he does not have to support her and she must repay the marriage gift.
- The husband must support his children in all cases.
- Legally, Muslims in the UK require a British civil divorce. Religious divorces are granted through the Muslim Law (Shari'ah) Council in Wembley, Middlesex or through their local mosque.
- After divorce, Muslims can remarry, and it may be considered beneficial to do so particularly if there are children.

APPLY

A Explain **two** different religious views about remarriage.

B 'Divorce is never right.'

Evaluate this statement, supporting your answer with arguments from **two** different views, and evaluating them.

TIP
The difference can come from within the same religion or from between religions.

5.6 The nature of families

RECAP

Essential information:

- [ ] There are many types of **families** (people related by blood, marriage or adoption) in Britain: the **nuclear family** (a couple and their children), **stepfamily** (formed on the remarriage of a divorced or widowed person that includes a child/children) and **extended family** (includes grandparents/other relatives beyond just parents and children).
- [ ] **Same-sex parents** are people of the same sex who are raising children together.

The role of parents and children

- Christian parents raise their children in the Christian faith, teaching them to pray. Some parents send children to religious schools and teach them traditions of their faith. They teach them right from wrong and pass on values such as generosity, compassion and tolerance, enabling them to form loving relationships.
- Muslim parents bring children up in the faith of Islam: how to pray, keep halal food laws and live a good Muslim life. They support children in finding a suitable marriage partner. They also send children to a madrassah (mosque school) to learn how to read the Qur'an in Arabic.
- Both Christian and Muslim children are expected to respect and obey their parents, and care for them when they are old.

Religious beliefs about the nature of families

Christian beliefs	Muslim beliefs
• In Biblical times, people lived in extended families through which the religion, customs and traditions were passed to the next generation. • Christians must 'love one another' (John 13:34 [NIV]); it is in the family that a child learns to love. • The Commandment 'Honour your father and mother' (Exodus 20:12) is important, particularly when parents are elderly and need support.	• The extended family is the basis of Islamic society, part of God's plan for humanity. • The family shapes the moral values and character of children. • Muslims care for elderly parents with kindness and respect because they did the same for them when they were young (Qur'an 17:23).

Polygamy

- There are examples of **polygamy** (custom of having more than one wife at the same time) in the Bible, but Christians believe God's intention was for one man to marry one woman for life.
- Islam allows polygamy with the consent of the first wife but only if a husband is able to support, love and treat additional wives equally.
- Polygamous marriages cannot be performed in Britain because **bigamy** (the offence of marrying someone while already married to another person) is illegal.

Same-sex parents

- Some Christians believe that the ideal is for children to grow up with a male and female role model as parents.
- Other Christians think it is more important for children to be in a secure and loving family regardless of the gender of their parents.
- Muslims oppose same-sex parents because they believe same-sex sexual relationships are morally wrong so same-sex parents would not provide a good example for their children.

TIP
See page 77 for beliefs about same-sex marriage.

APPLY

A Give **one** religious belief about the nature of the family.

B 'Children should grow up in a loving, secure family whatever the gender of their parents.'

List arguments for and against the statement. **Include religious views.**

TIP
The 'nature' of families can mean the different types of families that exist nowadays, or it may also refer to what a family should ideally be like.

5.7 The purpose of families

RECAP

Essential information:

- The family is the main building block of society where **procreation** (bringing babies into the world) takes place. Happy, healthy families create **stability**, safety and security, for their members and society.
- An important purpose of the family is the **protection of children** (keeping children safe).
- For both Muslims and Christians, a purpose of the family is **educating children in their faith** (bringing up children according to the religious beliefs of the parents).

Christian beliefs about the purpose of families

- The family provides stability because it is where people learn to live as part of a community: parents teach children right from wrong and how to get along with others.
- Christians believe God reveals himself as Father, with Jesus his Son and humankind his children, so the idea of family is very important.
- The family reflects Christ's relationship with the Church.

> "Husbands, love your wives, just as Christ loved the Church and gave himself up for her."
> *Ephesians 5:25* [NIV]

Muslim beliefs about relationships in the family

- The Qur'an addresses married people as 'guarded' and 'protected', as if their relationship is like a fortress protecting them from sin, loneliness and danger. This protection is also offered to the extended family.
- Muslims have a responsibility to care for their elderly parents, so many have them living with them:

> "He who is good to his parents, blessings be upon him…" *Hadith*

- Most Muslims would not consider putting their elderly parents in a care home, but value their wisdom and experience and feel honoured to repay them for their love and support in life.

Christian beliefs about children in families

- Parents and children have responsibilities to each other. Children have duties to obey, love and respect their parents for their care.

> "Listen to your father, who gave you life, and do not despise your mother when she is old." *Proverbs 23:22* [NIV]

- Children are gifts from God so parents must respect their dignity.
- Christian parents are expected to be good role models, teach children their faith, pray with them, teach them moral values and nurture their spiritual lives.

> "Fathers do not embitter your children, or they will become discouraged." *Colossians 3:21* [NIV]

- Some Christians send children to faith schools or groups run by their church for religious education.

Muslim beliefs about children in families

- Children have a duty to respect their parents, even in adulthood. The Qur'an teaches that to be unkind or disrespectful to one's parents is a great sin.

> "Lower your wing in humility towards [your parents] in kindness and say, "Lord, have mercy on them, just as they cared for me when I was little."" *Qur'an 17:24*

- Children are a blessing from God.
- Parents have a duty to provide a stable environment and raise their children to be good Muslims:

> "Honour your children and perfect their manners." *Hadith*

- Some Muslims send children to faith schools or groups run by their mosque for religious education.

APPLY

A Develop **both** the points below by explaining in more detail, adding an example, and referring to and applying a relevant quotation from sacred writings.

"Christian parents teach their children moral values."
"Muslim parents bring their children up in their faith."

B 'Families should do more for their elderly relatives in Britain today.'

Evaluate this statement, giving **two** points of view.

TIP
The quotes from the Bible, the Qur'an and the Hadith would support an answer on the purpose of families and the role of parents.

5.8 Religious attitudes to gender equality

RECAP

Essential information:

- [ ] **Gender equality** means that people should be given the same rights and opportunities regardless of their gender identity.
- [ ] **Gender prejudice** means unfairly judging someone before the facts are known; holding biased opinions about people based on their gender.
- [ ] **Sexual stereotyping** means having a fixed idea of how men and women will behave.
- [ ] **Gender discrimination** means acting against someone on the basis of their gender; usually seen as wrong and may be against the law.

Gender equality in Britain

- In the past, men held more positions of power and had more rights than women.
- Traditional roles saw men working to support the family, while women cared for the home and raised any children.
- The Sex Discrimination Act (1975) made gender discrimination illegal, but examples still exist: on average women are paid less than men for the same jobs and men hold a higher proportion of senior positions.
- Roles are changing as more women work, and housework and childcare are shared.

Religious beliefs about gender equality

Christian beliefs	Muslim beliefs
• All people are created equal in the image of God (Genesis 1:27). • Jesus respected women, welcomed them as disciples, and showed that they were capable of more than domestic tasks (Luke 10:38–42). • The command to love one's neighbour means that discrimination is wrong. Paul taught that all people are equal (Galatians 3:28). • Some traditional Christians interpret Bible texts literally and think husbands should rule over their wives (Genesis 3:16) and that women should mainly stay at home and care for children, but most Christians today see marriage as an equal partnership.	• God created all people equal, from a single soul and with the same spiritual human nature (Qur'an 49:13). • Muhammad worked to unite the tribes in Madinah into one community (ummah) under God, with equality and justice for all. • Men and women have the same religious and moral responsibilities, and will be rewarded by God for their good deeds (Qur'an 16:97). • Islamic law recognises the full property rights of women before and after marriage. A wife can keep her maiden name and be financially supported.

Gender prejudice and discrimination

- Today Christians would oppose all forms of prejudice and discrimination, although some would argue it exists within the Christian Church (see page 138).
- Some Muslim women suffer prejudice and discrimination over issues such as wearing the veil, girls' education, employment or freedom to drive or vote in some countries. This may be due to different cultural practices rather than because of teachings in the Qur'an.
- In Britain, other reported examples of gender prejudice and discrimination include:
  - sexual harassment in the workplace
  - women being asked unfair questions in job interviews
  - top women earning less than top men in sport.

APPLY

A **Explain the difference** between prejudice and discrimination.

B **Develop an argument** in support of the statement, 'Men and women do not have equal rights' by explaining in more detail, adding an example and referring to a religious teaching or quotation.

TIP

You can also use information from the theme 'Human rights and social justice' in your answers.

5 Exam practice

Test the 1 mark multiple-choice question

1 Which **one** of the following is **not** a reason why some marriages fail?

A Domestic violence B Adultery C Addiction D Stability **[1 mark]**

2 Which **one** of the following describes a nuclear family?

A A couple, children and grandparents

B A couple and their children

C A couple, children, aunts and uncles

D A couple without children **[1 mark]**

Test the 1 mark question

3 Give **one** religious belief about gender equality. **[1 mark]**

____

4 Give **one** religious belief about cohabitation. **[1 mark]**

____

Test the 4 mark question

5 Explain **two** different beliefs in contemporary British society about sex before marriage.

In your answer you should refer to the main religious tradition of Great Britain and one or more other religious traditions. **[4 marks]**

• **Explain one belief.**	*Some Christians believe that sex before marriage is all right if the couple has a committed, loving relationship.*
• Develop your explanation with more detail/an example/ reference to a religious teaching or quotation.	*Although they think that it is better to get married, they accept that people can be faithful to each other and committed to the relationship even if they have not been officially married.*
• **Explain a second belief.**	*Muslims do not agree with sex before marriage because their holy book, the Qur'an, expressly forbids it.*
• Develop your explanation with more detail/an example/ reference to a religious teaching or quotation.	*They think that children have a right to be born into a secure family and that sex before marriage can lower the dignity of the people involved.*

TIP
It is important to say 'some' here, as many Christians, including the Orthodox and Catholic Churches, disapprove of sex before marriage.

6 Explain **two** different religious beliefs about divorce.

In your answer you must refer to one or more religious traditions. **[4 marks]**

• **Explain one belief.**	
• Develop your explanation with more detail/an example/ reference to a religious teaching or quotation.	
• **Explain a second belief.**	
• Develop your explanation with more detail/an example/ reference to a religious teaching or quotation.	

TIP
You can answer this question from the perspective of two denominations or from two religions.

7 Explain **two** different religious beliefs about human sexuality.

In your answer you must refer to one or more religious traditions. **[4 marks]**

Test the 6 mark question

8 Explain **two** religious beliefs about the nature of marriage.

Refer to sacred writings or another source of religious belief and teaching in your answer. **[6 marks]**

• **Explain one belief.**	*Muslims believe that marriage was intended by God for the sharing of love and companionship between a man and a woman.*
• Develop your explanation with more detail/an example.	*The Qur'an teaches that husband and wife should support and care for each other: they are like garments for each other (Qur'an 2:187).*
• **Explain a second belief.**	*A Christian belief about the nature of marriage is that marriage is a sacrament.*
• Develop your explanation with more detail/an example.	*This means that marriage is a lifelong union blessed by God, because the couple makes promises before God that they will be faithful to each other 'till death us do part'.*
• **Add a reference to sacred writings or another source of religious belief and teaching.** If you prefer, you can add the reference to your first belief instead.	*The Bible reflects this idea when it says, 'That is why a man leaves his father and mother and is united to his wife, and they become one flesh.' (Genesis 2:24)*
• Apply the reference by explaining how it links to the question.	*This can be interpreted to mean that the nature of marriage is a man and a women joining in union.*

TIP

There is no need to put the Qur'an or Bible reference in your answer as long as you quote or paraphrase the passage.

9 Explain **two** religious beliefs about the purpose of families.

Refer to sacred writings or another source of religious belief and teaching in your answer. **[6 marks]**

• **Explain one belief.**	
• Develop your explanation with more detail/an example.	
• **Explain a second belief.**	
• Develop your explanation with more detail/an example.	
• **Add a reference to sacred writings or another source of religious belief and teaching.** If you prefer, you can add the reference to your first belief instead.	
• Apply the reference by explaining how it links to the question.	

10 Explain **two** religious beliefs about the role of children in a religious family.

Refer to sacred writings or another source of religious belief and teaching in your answer. **[6 marks]**

Test the 12 mark question

11 'The love and care parents show in bringing up their children is all that matters; the sex of the parents is unimportant.'

Evaluate this statement. In your answer you:

- should give reasoned arguments in support of this statement
- should give reasoned arguments to support a different point of view
- should refer to religious arguments
- may refer to non-religious arguments
- should reach a justified conclusion.

[12 ma
Plus SPaG 3 r

REASONED ARGUMENTS SUPPORTING A DIFFERENT VIEW ● **Explain why some people would support a different view.** ● Develop your explanation with more detail and examples, which may include non-religious ideas. ● Refer to religious teaching. Use a quote or paraphrase or refer to a religious authority. ● **Evaluate the arguments.** Is this a good argument or not? Explain why you think this.	*It is true that the love and care parents show in bringing up their children is the most important thing for a good family life. Without love and care, children would grow up deprived of stability and security. But the statement says 'the sex of the parents is unimportant' and that is where people may have different views.* *Some Christians disapprove of same-sex parents because they think God made people male and female so that they would 'be fruitful and increase in number' (Genesis 1:28). Same-sex couples cannot do this naturally. Some also think the ideal for children is to grow up with a male and female role model as parents. Muslims believe that same-sex sexual relationships are morally wrong so do not approve of such couples raising children. An important role of religious parents is to bring up their children in their faith. If their religion disagrees with same-sex sexual relationships, then it is difficult for same-sex parents to bring their children up within the religion that disapproves of their behaviour.*
REASONED ARGUMENTS IN SUPPORT OF THE STATEMENT ● **Explain why some people would agree with the statement.** ● Develop your explanation with more detail and examples, which may include non-religious ideas. ● Refer to religious teaching. Use a quote or paraphrase or refer to a religious authority. ● **Evaluate the arguments.** Is this a good argument or not? Explain why you think this.	*On the other hand, many liberal Christians think that it is more important that children are raised in a secure and loving family regardless of the gender of their parents. There is nothing to say same-sex parents are not religious even if particular faiths disapprove of their relationships. Many can still bring their children up to love God or live spiritual and morally good lives.*
CONCLUSION ● **Give a justified conclusion.** ● Include your own opinion together with your own reasoning. ● **Include evaluation**. Explain why you think one viewpoint is stronger than the other or why they are equally strong. ● Do not just repeat arguments you have already used without explaining how they apply to your reasoned opinion/ conclusion.	*In conclusion, I think that whether parents are good at bringing up children depends on the individuals and not on their gender. Some opposite-sex couples spoil their children or even abuse them, which does not show good parenting. Many children live in single-parent families so do not have the benefit of a male and female role model anyway. The most important thing any family should have is love, and this is at the heart of all religions.*

TIP
In this answer the student begins presenting a different point of vie followed by arguments supportin the statement. It doesn't matte which order the arguments appear in, as long as you remember to include both sides.

TIP
Religious attitudes to some issues vary within religions as well as betwe religions, so it helps to s 'some Christians' or 'libe Christians' to show you understand that not al Christians share the same views.

TIP
This is a top level answer which uses logical chains of reasoning and well supported arguments with reference to religion. The justified conclusion does r merely repeat what w said but offers a perso viewpoint supported examples.

12 'Marriage is the proper place to enjoy a sexual relationship.'

Evaluate this statement. In your answer you:

- should give reasoned arguments in support of this statement
- should give reasoned arguments to support a different point of view
- should refer to religious arguments
- may refer to non-religious arguments
- should reach a justified conclusion.

[12 marks]
Plus SPaG 3 marks

REASONED ARGUMENTS IN SUPPORT OF THE STATEMENT	
• **Explain why some people would agree with the statement.** • Develop your explanation with more detail and examples, which may include non-religious ideas. • Refer to religious teaching. Use a quote or paraphrase or refer to a religious authority. • **Evaluate the arguments.** Is this a good argument or not? Explain why you think this.	
REASONED ARGUMENTS SUPPORTING A DIFFERENT VIEW	
• **Explain why some people would support a different view.** • Develop your explanation with more detail and examples, which may include non-religious ideas. • Refer to religious teaching. Use a quote or paraphrase or refer to a religious authority. • **Evaluate the arguments.** Is this a good argument or not? Explain why you think this.	
CONCLUSION	
• **Give a justified conclusion.** • Include your own opinion together with your own reasoning. • **Include evaluation**. Explain why you think one viewpoint is stronger than the other or why they are equally strong. • Do not just repeat arguments you have already used without explaining how they apply to your reasoned opinion/conclusion.	

TIP

When evaluating a statement like this one, do not simply list what different people think about the issue, for example 'Christians would agree that the best place to enjoy sex is in marriage. Muslims also think...' Remember to explain the reasons why they hold these opinions and to add an evaluation of how convincing you find these views to be.

13 'It is wrong for religious couples to use artificial contraception within marriage.'

Evaluate this statement. In your answer you:

- should give reasoned arguments in support of this statement
- should give reasoned arguments to support a different point of view
- should refer to religious arguments
- may refer to non-religious arguments
- should reach a justified conclusion.

[12 marks]
Plus SPaG 3 marks

Check your answers using the mark scheme on page 154. How did you do?
To feel more secure in the content you need to remember, re-read pages 74–81.
To remind yourself of what the examiner is looking for, go to pages 6–11.

6 Religion and life

6.1 The origins of the universe

RECAP

Essential information:

- ☐ Teachings in the Qur'an and the story in Genesis 1:1–2:3 describe the creation of the **universe** (the planets, galaxies and everything in them).
- ☐ The scientific explanation for the origins of the universe is the Big Bang theory.

Christian beliefs about the creation of the universe

Christians believe the universe was designed and made by God out of nothing. The creation story in Genesis says that God made the world in six days and rested on the seventh.

- **Fundamentalist Christians** believe that the statements in the Bible are literally true. Some believe the creation stories describe exactly how the universe was created. Others believe that the seven days describe seven long periods of time.
- **Liberal Christians** believe that the creation stories are symbolic, where the main message is that God created the universe. They might look to science to understand *how* God did this.

Muslim beliefs about the creation of the universe

- Muslims believe the universe was designed and made by God out of nothing.
- Most Muslims believe that 'six days' refers to six periods of time. There is no indication of what was created in each day or period and no mention of a day of rest as in the Bible.

> "Your Lord is God who created the heavens and earth in six days … He created the sun, moon and stars … All creation and all command belongs to Him." *Qur'an 7:54*

- God organised the universe to be under his watchful command. The work of creation continues with every new life that is born or seed that grows.

The Big Bang theory

Started with a tiny dense hot 'something'. → Over 13.8 billion years it expanded to become the cosmos as we know it. → It continued to expand and cool. → Matter that had been flung everywhere became stars grouped into galaxies.

Both the creation stories and the Big Bang theory leave many questions unanswered and neither can be proved.

- Many Muslims and Christians believe in the Big Bang theory and also that God created the universe.
- Islam encourages scientific investigation which may provide greater understanding of God. Some would argue that what is written about creation in the Qur'an closely resembles theories like the Big Bang. For example, the Qur'an describes how when God created the universe, the heavens and the earth were one and God split them into two smoke-like forms (Qur'an 21:30).

APPLY

A Give **one** reason why Muslims encourage scientific discovery.

B Can the Big Bang theory be a way of explaining how God created the earth? Give at least **one** reason for agreeing and **one** for disagreeing.

TIP

Importantly, the Qur'an and Bible try to focus on why the earth came into being and science on how.

6.2 The value of the world

RECAP

Essential information:

- [ ] Muslims and Christians believe the earth to be valuable because God created it.
- [ ] Both Muslims and Christians believe that people have a duty to protect and care for the earth and its environment; this is known as **stewardship** (khalifah).

How valuable is the world?

- For Christians and Muslims the beauty of the world can give a sense of **awe** (devout respect for God's power of creation) and **wonder** (marvelling at the complexity of the universe).
- They believe the earth and nature are so amazing because they provide everything humans and other living things need to survive.
- Muslims see the world in the same way as a place of worship; damaging the earth is a serious sin similar to harming a mosque.
- It is a Muslim's duty to respect, nurture and care for the environment.

> "When I consider your heavens … what is mankind that you are mindful of them, human beings that you care for them?" *Psalm 8:3–4* [NIV]

> "Every single Muslim that cultivates or plants anything of which humans, animals or birds may eat is counted as charity towards them on his behalf." *Hadith*

Stewardship (khalifah) and dominion

- The Qur'an and the Bible make it clear that humans were given responsibility to look after the earth for God.

Christian beliefs	Muslim beliefs
• Genesis 2 says that Adam, the first man on earth, was given the role of stewardship over the earth, looking after it for God. "The Lord God took the man (Adam) and put him in the Garden of Eden to work it and take care of it." *Genesis 2:15* [NIV] • This responsibility has been passed down to humankind which means it is the role of all humans to look after the earth for God. If they use it wrongly, they are destroying what belongs to God. • In return for looking after the earth, humans are allowed to use it to sustain life.	• Both Sunni and Shi'a Muslims believe that humans have the role of stewards (khalifah) and so should protect the environment – the natural world around us – for future generations. "It is He who has made you successors on the earth." *Qur'an 6:165* • There is only one creator and people are responsible to him for their actions. On the Day of Judgement, humans will be answerable to God for how they have fulfilled this role. • The Qur'an states that the laws of God's creation should not be changed.

- Christians teach that God gave humans power and authority to take charge of the earth. This is called **dominion**.
- A minority interpret this as meaning that humans can do whatever they want because they are in charge.

> "Rule over the fish in the sea and the birds in the sky and over every living creature that moves on the ground." *Genesis 1:28* [NIV]

Use of natural resources

Population growth is having a great impact on the environment and natural world.

- Forests are being destroyed (**deforestation**). **Non-renewable resources** such as oil, coal and gas are being used up and will eventually run out.
- It is increasingly important to encourage **sustainable development** (progress that tries to reduce the impact on the natural world for future generations). Scientists are developing **renewable energies** from sources that won't run out, such as wind or solar energy.
- Christians and Muslims believe they should avoid waste and conserve energy, for example by turning off unused electrical appliances, reusing bags when shopping and recycling waste, e.g. glass and paper.

APPLY

A What does stewardship (khalifah) mean?

B 'God's earth is a wonderful and valuable place.'

Give **two** reasons to agree with this and develop each one.

TIP

Stewardship (khalifah) has a specific religious meaning. Use terms like this accurately to show your knowledge.

6.3 The use and abuse of the environment, and pollution

RECAP

Essential information:

☐ Muslims and Christians show their concern by taking action to help to protect the earth against **abuse** – misuse of the world and the environment.

☐ Air, land and water **pollution** (making something dirty and contaminated, especially the environment) are a major threat to life on earth.

Pollution

Pollution has increased with the growing population.

Pollution type	Cause	Possible problems caused
Air	Fumes from factories and transport	Global warming, climate change, acid rain, diseases such as asthma and lung cancer
Land	Poor disposal of waste	Chemicals pollute the earth causing wildlife to be poisoned, inefficient farming and poisoned food
Water	Dumping waste into rivers and seas	Oil spills and plastic waste kill birds and marine life including whales

Christian and Muslim beliefs

- In order to emphasise the need to help the environment, Muslims follow the hadith:

> "Do not seek from it more than what you need." *Hadith*

- The Qur'an reinforces the need for stewardship and living sustainably:

> "Eat and drink [as we have permitted] but do not be extravagant." *Qur'an 7:31*

- Christians believe the world is on loan to humans, who have been given the responsibility by God to look after it (Genesis 1:28).
- The parable of the Talents/Bags of Gold (Matthew 25:14–30) warns that God will be the final judge about how responsible humans have been in looking after the earth.

> "The earth is the Lord's and everything in it." *Psalm 24:1* [NIV]

TIP
If writing about what Christians or Muslims believe, it is good to include and explain a quote or paraphrase rather than just providing a vague idea.

What do Christians and Muslims do about the environment?

- In **1986**, religious leaders met at **Assisi** in Italy to discuss how religious people everywhere could help to care for the environment.
- As part of their statement in The Assisi Declarations on Nature, Christians wrote: 'Every human act of irresponsibility towards creatures is an abomination [disgrace]' (*Alliance of Religions and Conservation (ARC)*).
- They met again in **Ohito** in Japan in **1995** where they stressed that being in charge of creation does not give people the right to abuse, spoil, waste or destroy the earth.
- Christians and Muslims join groups such as The Islamic Foundation for Ecology and Environmental Sciences (IFEES, which has developed a specifically Islamic approach to environmental protection by emphasising stewardship/khalifah) or Greenpeace and Friends of the Earth.
- Christians and Muslims encourage people to reduce waste, recycle and reuse materials.

APPLY

A Explain **two** types of pollution and give a cause of each one.

B 'Religious believers are not doing enough to help the environment'. **Evaluate this statement.**

TIP
Questions like this one do not need any religious beliefs and teachings.

6.4 The use and abuse of animals

RECAP

Essential information:

- [ ] Christians and Muslims believe that God made all living creatures and they should be treated well.
- [ ] There are different Christian and Muslim views about animal experimentation and using animals for food.

You might be asked to compare beliefs on animal experimentation between Christianity (the main religious tradition in Great Britain) and another religious tradition.

The use of animals for food

- People who don't eat meat or fish are called **vegetarians**.
- **Vegans** will not use anything from an animal including leather, milk and eggs.

Christian teachings	Muslim teachings
• Christianity has no rules about whether Christians can eat meat or not. • Some believe God gave humans animals for food and are happy to eat meat (Genesis 9:3). • Non-meat eaters, including some Christians, say there is no need to eat animals because a non-meat diet provides all the nutrition humans need. • Some point out that if crops were grown on land currently used to raise animals for meat, there would be much more food to go round and this would please God.	• To provide food is a just cause for killing animals but hunting for entertainment or pleasure is not. • Muslims have strict laws about how and which animals must be killed for food. No animal should be killed for food in front of other animals. • To be permissible (halal), the animal is killed 'in the name of God' and its throat is cut with a very sharp knife to prevent it from suffering. The blood is drained out. • Pigs must not be eaten, nor should any animal that is not halal, including those that have died in the wild.

> "The one who eats everything (including meat) must not treat with contempt the one who does not, and the one who does not eat everything must not judge the one who does, for God has accepted them."
>
> *Romans 14:3* [NIV]

> "It is God who provides livestock for you, some for riding and some for your food." *Qur'an 40:79*

Christian and Muslim beliefs about animal experimentation

- Scientists use animals such as rats, chimpanzees and rabbits to test new products such as medicines and food, to make sure they are safe for humans to use.
- Causing animals unnecessary harm and stress is against Muslim principles.
- Most Christians and Muslims believe testing should be allowed for essential human needs (e.g. to test new medicines) but that animals should be treated with compassion.
- Islam teaches that animal experimentation that is not essential for human needs (e.g. to test the effects of drugs) is not allowed.
- Many Christians believe that stewardship involves treating all life with care as it was given by God. So saving human life is important. Some Christians would use the principle of dominion to support their use of animals to benefit humans.

APPLY

A Explain **two** different beliefs in contemporary British society about animal experimentation. You should refer to the main religious tradition in Great Britain and one or more other religious traditions.

B 'Experimenting on animals is wrong because it is cruel.'

Develop this statement and elaborate it with religious teachings, explaining how the teachings are relevant to the argument.

TIP

You should use the Christian idea of dominion and one other in order to have different beliefs.

6.5 The origins of human life

RECAP

Essential information:

- [ ] Religion and science both attempt to explain the origins of human life.
- [ ] Many Christians and Muslims believe it is possible to believe both the creation story and the theory of **evolution** (how organisms are thought to have developed from earlier forms of life).

Christian beliefs

- In the story in Genesis 1, God created all life with human life being created last.
- Genesis 2 describes how God created the first man, Adam, from the soil and breathed life into him. Adam was given responsibility to look after his environment – the Garden of Eden.
- Some time later, while Adam was asleep, God took one of his ribs and used it to create a woman, Eve. God intended for Eve to help Adam, and that they would live in a close relationship with each other and with him.
- The story shows that humans are very special to God because they were created in his image.

Muslim beliefs

- After God made the universe and everything that lives in it, he created humans.
- God created Adam as the first man by moulding him from clay and breathing life into him.
- God created Eve (Hawwa) from the same soul as Adam and she became his wife.
- They were allowed to live in paradise and given free will, but forbidden to eat from one tree.
- The evil Iblis convinced them to eat fruit from the forbidden tree. Adam and Eve regretted their disobedience.
- Being aware of the regret shown by Adam and Eve is an essential part of following and serving God.
- God created everything necessary for Adam and Eve to live on the earth and to be the start of the human race.

> "You humans were lifeless and He gave you life."
> *Qur'an 2:28*

Evolution

In 1859, in a book called *The Origin of Species by Means of Natural Selection*, Charles Darwin put forward the theory of evolution. He suggested that as the earth cooled, conditions became right to support life:

Life started with single-celled creatures in the sea. → Over a long period of time they evolved (changed) into creatures capable of living on land. → Next came creatures with the ability to fly, such as insects and birds. → Around 2.5 million years ago creatures resembling humans formed. → They gradually changed into humans about 200,000 years ago.

- Genes passed on from their parents have resulted in different individuals from the same species, some of which found it easier to survive and breed successfully.
- They were able to change or **adapt** to their surroundings and thrived. This is called survival of the fittest.

Religious debate on evolution

- Some Christians and Muslims are creationists who believe that the origin of human life is exactly as recorded in scripture and who reject the theory of evolution.
- Many Christians and a minority of Muslims accept the mainstream scientific view of evolution and do not believe it should cause conflict with their faith. God created the beginnings of life and set everything in motion to develop over the course of history.
- Some Muslims argue that the theory of evolution is correct for all living beings except humans. God inserted Adam into the natural order and evolution has progressed from God's first moment of creation.

APPLY

A Explain **two** religious responses to the theory of evolution.

B 'The story of Adam and Eve (Hawwa) is more important than whether or not life evolved on earth.'

Write one chain of reasoning for each of **two points of view**. A chain of reasoning includes an opinion, a reason, development of your reasoning and religious beliefs and teaching.

TIP
Chains of reasoning are important in 12 mark questions.

6.6 Abortion

RECAP

Essential information:

- [ ] **Abortion** (the removal of a foetus from the womb to end a pregnancy) is legal in the UK.
- [ ] Christians and Muslims believe in the **sanctity of life**, that life is holy and given by God, therefore only God can take it away.
- [ ] However when considering the issue of abortion, many people will also consider **quality of life** (the general well-being of a person, in relation to their health and happiness).

You might be asked to compare beliefs on abortion between Christianity (the main religious tradition in Great Britain) and another religious tradition.

The legal position on abortion in the UK

- In 1990, the Human Fertilisation and Embryology Act set various conditions to govern abortion.
- An abortion must take place in a licensed clinic and only during the first 24 weeks of pregnancy.
- The 24-week limit does not apply if the woman's life is in danger or if the child will be born with a severe disability.
- Two doctors must agree to it taking place but only if it meets at least one of the following conditions:

1. Pregnancy endangers the woman's life.
2. The woman's physical or mental health is endangered.
3. There is a strong risk that the baby will be born with a severe disability.
4. An additional child may endanger the physical or mental health of other children in the family.

Christian and Muslim beliefs about abortion

Christian beliefs	Muslim beliefs
• Christians believe in the sanctity of life. • Jeremiah 1:5 shows that God has a plan for everyone – abortion takes this away, so is considered wrong. • Psalm 139:13 suggests to Christians that abortion is taking away what God has created. "For you created my inmost being; you knit me together in my mother's womb." *Psalm 139:13* [NIV] • Some Christians may agree with abortion if the baby will have a very poor quality of life. • Other Christians believe that if abortion is the kindest option, for example in instances of rape, they may support it. • The Catholic Church, along with many evangelical Christians, believes that abortion is wrong because life begins at conception so abortion is taking away life.	• Most Muslims believe that abortion is haram (forbidden) but there are some circumstances when it may be allowed. • The woman's life should be saved if the pregnancy is putting her in danger. Her life takes priority if the pregnancy will cause her physical or mental harm. • Some Muslims believe abortion is justified if the child will be born with a disability. • Some may believe it is justified if the pregnancy is the result of a rape. • Under no circumstances should financial situations be considered to be an acceptable reason for abortion: "Do not kill your children for fear of poverty – We shall provide for them and you" *Qur'an 17:31* • Abortion must happen before **ensoulment** – when Muslims believe the foetus is given a soul. Some believe this is after 40 days, others after 120 days. Abortion after ensoulment is considered to be taking life and therefore forbidden.

APPLY

A **Explain two legal points** that are used to decide whether an abortion should be allowed.

B 'If the quality of life is not going to be good, abortion is the best option.'

Write and fully develop an argument to support each of two different points of view about this statement. Include religious arguments in your answer.

TIP
It may be a good idea to define terms such as quality of life in your answer.

6.7 Euthanasia

RECAP

Essential information:

- [ ] **Euthanasia** means 'a good or gentle death', painlessly ending the life of someone who is dying.

You might be asked to compare beliefs on euthanasia between Christianity (the main religious tradition in Great Britain) and another religious tradition.

What is euthanasia?

Active euthanasia involves taking deliberate steps to end a person's life, for example by giving a lethal injection. This is illegal in the UK. There are three main types of euthanasia:

Voluntary: the ill person asks for their life to be ended because they don't want to live any more.

Involuntary: the person is capable of expressing a choice but is not given the opportunity to do so.

Non-voluntary: the person is unable to express a choice, for example a baby or a person in a coma.

- Doctors can decide to withhold treatment if it is in the patient's best interests, for example by not resuscitating a person after a heart attack or withdrawing food. This would not be considered euthanasia as it is allowing death to take place rather than actively ending a life.
- Some countries in Europe allow euthanasia under certain strict criteria and in 2025, a new bill supporting assisted dying was debated in the UK parliament.

Christian beliefs

Some Christians believe that euthanasia may be acceptable in some cases to end a person's suffering, but many believe it is never right to take a life.

Arguments in favour	Arguments against
• God gives people free will to end their own life. • Euthanasia may be the most loving and compassionate thing to do, following Jesus' teaching to 'love your neighbour' (Luke 10:27). • Euthanasia allows a good and gentle death which may not be the case if natural death occurs. • Euthanasia allows a dignified death. • Drugs to end life are God-given so can be used.	• Euthanasia is deliberate killing – murder. • It is open to abuse and may be against the will of the ill person. • Only God should take life at the time of his choosing. • Inheritance issues may encourage relatives to pressurise a member of their family to agree to euthanasia. • Once certain types are allowed it may encourage compulsory euthanasia at a certain age at some time in the future.

Muslim beliefs

- Euthanasia is haram (forbidden) in Islam. It goes against the sanctity of life.
- No one knows God's plans – the person may be suffering for a purpose known only to God, for example their illness may enable others to do good by looking after them, thereby gaining a place in paradise.
- Euthanasia is a sin against God, the individual and the community.
- Al-Qadr – predestination – means that God has planned a person's life and ending it early goes against his plan. Only God decides when it will be ended.

> " No soul may die except with God's permission at a predestined time. "
>
> *Quran 3:145*

APPLY

A **Explain** an argument in favour of euthanasia and show how religious beliefs may disagree with this.

B 'Active euthanasia should never be allowed.'

Explain why and develop your reasoning. Add and explain some religious teaching to elaborate your answer.

TIP

If you include love and compassion in your answer, make sure you explain who it is loving and compassionate towards.

6.8 Death and the afterlife

RECAP

Essential information:

- [ ] Both Christians and Muslims believe that death is not the end but the beginning of an afterlife.
- [ ] Both believe that God will judge everyone (both believers and non-believers) on how they have lived their lives on earth.
- [ ] God's judgement will determine what happens to people after death.

Is death the end?

- **Christians** believe that death is the beginning of an eternal life that depends on faith in God.
- It begins at death or on the Day of Judgement when God judges people's behaviour as well as their faith in following Jesus.
- God's judgement results in the person spending **eternity** (a state that comes after death and never ends) either with God in heaven or without God in hell.
- **Muslims** believe in an afterlife known as **Akhirah**.
- Life on earth is a test or trial which will determine what happens in the afterlife.
- On the Day of Judgement, each person will be brought before God and the book of their life will be opened. Their good and bad deeds are weighed. God uses this to decide their fate.
- Those who rejected God, Muhammad and the teachings of the Qur'an, together with those who did not do enough good deeds, are sent to hell.
- Muslims who did more good than bad deeds are rewarded with eternity in paradise with God.
- For both Christians and Muslims, belief in an afterlife and God's judgement has an effect on how they live their lives.

TIP

See pages 18–21 and 51 for more about Christian and Muslim beliefs about life after death and God's judgement.

The value of human life

Everybody can choose how to live their one life. → Being given free will shows that God considers human life to be of great value. → Human life should be respected in the way people behave towards each other. → How people decide to act has eternal consequences. → This encourages believers to follow God and obey his instructions.

- All religions emphasise that everyone is accountable for their actions on earth and all actions have consequences, good or bad. Both Christians and Muslims believe that God gives guidance about how to live their lives, but God also gives humans free will to choose between doing right and doing wrong.
- Doing the right thing involves resisting temptation to stray from God's path.
- These decisions have important consequences for eternal life after death. Making the right choices, resisting temptation and following their faith in the way God requires (e.g. worship, prayer, obeying the teachings and example of their faith leaders) will ensure an eternal afterlife with God.

APPLY

A **Explain** what Muslims believe will happen on the Day of Judgement.

B 'The fear of eternal punishment is the only thing that makes religious people value human life.'

Develop an idea that agrees with this statement and one that does not. Include religious teaching.

REVIEW

6 Exam practice

Test the 1 mark multiple-choice question

1 Which **one** of the following gives the meaning of the term euthanasia?

A A type of abortion
B A method of animal testing
C A good or gentle death
D A scientific view about the origin of the earth **[1 mark]**

2 Which **one** of the following gives the meaning of the term sanctity of life?

A Life never ends
B Life is sacred
C Life is of high quality
D Life has an end **[1 mark]**

Test the 1 mark question

3 Give **one** legal criterion that would allow an abortion in the UK. **[1 mark]**

4 Give **one** belief about heaven. **[1 mark]**

Test the 4 mark question

5 Explain **two** different beliefs in contemporary British society about abortion.
In your answer you should refer to the main religious tradition of Great Britain and one or more other religious traditions. **[4 marks]**

• **Explain one belief.**	*Muslims believe that life is God-given and part of his plan.*
• Develop your explanation with more detail/an example/ reference to a religious teaching or quotation.	*Ending life prematurely is not allowed because it is against God's plan for that person, even if they haven't yet been born.*
• **Explain a second belief.**	*Some Christians believe that in certain circumstances abortion is the best option.*
• Develop your explanation with more detail/an example/ reference to a religious teaching or quotation.	*If the child is unlikely to survive or if the woman's life is in danger then abortion is the loving thing to do.*

TIP
This question says that 'you should refer to the main religious tradition of Great Britain' so you need to make at least one reference to Christianity.

6 Explain **two** similar religious beliefs about animal experimentation.
In your answer, you must refer to one or more religious traditions. **[4 marks]**

• **Explain one belief.**	
• Develop your explanation with more detail/an example/ reference to a religious teaching or quotation.	
• **Explain a second belief.**	
• Develop your explanation with more detail/an example/ reference to a religious teaching or quotation.	

TIP
This question asks for 'two similar religious beliefs', so make sure both beliefs from different traditions are similar.

7 Explain **two** different religious beliefs about the use of natural resources.
In your answer, you must refer to one or more religious traditions. **[4 marks]**

6 Exam practice

Test the 6 mark question

8 Explain **two** religious beliefs about what happens when a person dies.

Refer to sacred writings or another source of religious belief and teaching in your answer. **[6 marks]**

• **Explain one belief.**	*Muslims believe in the resurrection of the dead.*
• Develop your explanation with more detail/an example.	*On the Day of Judgement Muslims will be resurrected and face judgement when Allah decides who goes to heaven and who goes to hell.*
• **Add a reference to sacred writings or another source of religious belief and teaching.** If you prefer, you can add the reference to your second belief instead.	*The Qur'an says that those whose good deeds weigh heavily will go to heaven.*
• Apply the reference by explaining how it links to the question.	*This suggests that, when a person dies, they will be judged by God and, if they have more good deeds, they will go to heaven.*
• **Explain a second belief.**	*After judgement, Muslims believe everybody crosses the Sirat bridge over hell.*
• Develop your explanation with more detail/an example.	*Those who carry the book of their life in their right hand cross to paradise, the others fall into hell.*

TIP
In this answer, the reference to sacred writing has been added here to the first belief.

TIP
The question asks for two religious beliefs. Even though these are from the same religion, they are separate beliefs so can be used.

9 Explain **two** religious beliefs about the duty of human beings to protect the earth.

Refer to sacred writings or another source of religious belief and teaching in your answer. **[6 marks]**

• **Explain one belief.**	
• Develop your explanation with more detail/an example.	
• **Explain a second belief.**	
• Develop your explanation with more detail/an example.	
• **Add a reference to sacred writings or another source of religious belief and teaching.** If you prefer, you can add the reference to your first belief instead.	
• Apply the reference by explaining how it links to the question.	

10 Explain **two** religious beliefs about the origins of the universe.

Refer to sacred writings or another source of religious belief and teaching in your answer. **[6 marks]**

Test the 12 mark question

11 'Religious believers should not eat meat.'

Evaluate this statement. In your answer you:

- should give reasoned arguments in support of this statement
- should give reasoned arguments to support a different point of view
- should refer to religious arguments
- may refer to non-religious arguments
- should reach a justified conclusion.

[12 marks
Plus SPaG 3 m

REASONED ARGUMENTS IN SUPPORT OF THE STATEMENT • **Explain why some people would agree with the statement.** • Develop your explanation with more detail and examples, which may include non-religious ideas. • Refer to religious teaching. Use a quote or paraphrase or refer to a religious authority. • **Evaluate the arguments.** Is this a good argument or not? Explain why you think this.	*Eating meat involves the killing of animals to provide the meat. This is seen by many religious believers as cruel and unnecessary and they are quite happy to be vegetarians. For others, it is not just the killing of the animals that is the problem – the way they are treated throughout their short lives is much worse. Their death, so they can be used as meat, is often merciful because it ends their inhumane treatment. Some of the worst abuse happens to chickens who live their lives in cages in barns and never see daylight or breathe fresh air because they never leave their cage. This completely ignores the stewardship role humans have which means they should care for all living creatures. All living beings are valuable to God: 'not one of them is forgotten by God'.*
REASONED ARGUMENTS SUPPORTING A DIFFERENT VIEW • **Explain why some people would support a different view.** • Develop your explanation with more detail and examples, which may include non-religious ideas. • Refer to religious teaching. Use a quote or paraphrase or refer to a religious authority. • **Evaluate the arguments.** Is this a good argument or not? Explain why you think this.	*Most Christians and Muslims do eat meat because they believe that it is a good source of protein. Although they believe that animals should not be treated cruelly, they believe that they were created by God for human use which includes killing them for food. As far as we know Jesus and Muhammad ate meat, and the fact that food laws are part of Islam and they make it clear how animals should be killed for meat means that Islam is in favour of meat eating.*
CONCLUSION • **Give a justified conclusion.** • Include your own opinion together with your own reasoning. • **Include evaluation.** Explain why you think one viewpoint is stronger than the other or why they are equally strong. • Do not just repeat arguments you have already used without explaining how they apply to your reasoned opinion/conclusion.	*So there is a difference of opinion concerning whether it is right to eat meat. Although I can see why some people prefer not to kill animals, I believe that meat is important for a balanced diet. Also many farmers would lose their livelihoods if people stopped eating meat. In my opinion it would be unfair on religious believers if they were prevented from enjoying meat. I can see that if your religion opposes meat eating then you would need to keep the rules of your faith. However, within Islam this does not apply, especially as sacrificing an animal is part of a Muslim festival.*

TIP
This section about the treatment of animals shows an excellent chain of reasoning. It starts with an introductory statement, followed by developmen opinion and including religion which is further elaborated.

TIP
Although there is good content in here, greater development about food law in Islam would improve it, e further explanation about h animals are killed humanely

TIP
This is a good conclusion because it includes reference to the arguments already made and supports them with more reasoning, not just the same as before.

12 'The law on abortion should be changed.'

Evaluate this statement. In your answer you:

- should give reasoned arguments in support of this statement
- should give reasoned arguments to support a different point of view
- should refer to religious arguments
- may refer to non-religious arguments
- should reach a justified conclusion.

[12 marks]
Plus SPaG 3 marks

REASONED ARGUMENTS IN SUPPORT OF THE STATEMENT • **Explain why some people would agree with the statement.** • Develop your explanation with more detail and examples, which may include non-religious ideas. • Refer to religious teaching. Use a quote or paraphrase or refer to a religious authority. • **Evaluate the arguments.** Is this a good argument or not? Explain why you think this.	
REASONED ARGUMENTS SUPPORTING A DIFFERENT VIEW • **Explain why some people would support a different view.** • Develop your explanation with more detail and examples, which may include non-religious ideas. • Refer to religious teaching. Use a quote or paraphrase or refer to a religious authority. • **Evaluate the arguments.** Is this a good argument or not? Explain why you think this.	
CONCLUSION • **Give a justified conclusion.** • Include your own opinion together with your own reasoning. • **Include evaluation**. Explain why you think one viewpoint is stronger than the other or why they are equally strong. • Do not just repeat arguments you have already used without explaining how they apply to your reasoned opinion/conclusion.	

13 'Humans should use the earth's resources however they wish.'

Evaluate this statement. In your answer you:

- should give reasoned arguments in support of this statement
- should give reasoned arguments to support a different point of view
- should refer to religious arguments
- may refer to non-religious arguments
- should reach a justified conclusion.

[12 marks]
Plus SPaG 3 marks

Check your answers using the mark scheme on page 155. How did you do?
To feel more secure in the content you need to remember, re-read pages 86–93.
To remind yourself of what the examiner is looking for, go to pages 6–11.

7 The existence of God and revelation

7.1 The Design argument

RECAP

Essential information:

- The **Design argument** says that because everything is so intricately made it must have been created by God.
- Christians and Muslims are **theists** (people who believe in God). They believe that God planned and created the earth. **Atheists**, who don't believe in God, believe the universe was not created, but evolved naturally. **Agnostics** believe there is not enough evidence that God exists or that God created the universe.

Some different Design arguments

Muslim argument	God created humans to serve him. He created order in the world and put humans in charge of creation. The world is so well ordered and balanced to sustain life. It is beautiful and has complex, independent parts that make up a whole. It must have been designed and only God is able to do this.
William Paley	Paley (1743–1805) argued that the workings of a watch are so intricate that they must have been designed and made by a watchmaker. It cannot be accidental. Similarly, the universe is so complex and intricate that it must have been designed and made, and the only possibility is that it was the work of God.
Isaac Newton	Newton (1642–1726) used the existence of the human thumb as evidence that God designed the universe. The 'opposable thumb' that humans and some primates have allows precise and delicate movement and allows humans to do such things as tying a shoelace or writing with a pen. This is sufficient evidence of design which can only have been achieved by God.
Thomas Aquinas	In the thirteenth century, Aquinas stated that only an intelligent being could keep everything in the universe in regular order. The fact the planets rotate in the solar system without colliding is because of God.
F. R. Tennant	In the 1930s, Tennant said that since everything was just right for humans to develop, the world must have been designed by God. He referred to the strength of gravity being absolutely right and said that if the force and speed of the explosion caused by the Big Bang was slightly different, life could not have developed on earth.

Objections to the Design arguments

- Natural selection happens by chance. The fact that the fittest survive and the rest die out is pure chance. Species design themselves through the process of evolution not through a designer God.
- The amount of suffering in the world proves there is no designer God, because a good God would not have designed and allowed bad things, such as natural disasters and evil.
- The order in the universe, necessary to support life, makes it look as though it is designed when in fact the order and structure in nature is imposed by humans.

TIP

You should learn strengths and weaknesses of the Design argument and be prepared to argue the case for each, regardless of what you believe.

APPLY

A Write the main points of **two** Design arguments.

B 'The Design argument proves that God exists.'

Write **two** developed arguments, one in agreement and one against.

7.2 The First Cause argument

RECAP

Essential information:

- [ ] The **First Cause argument** (or cosmological argument) states that there has to be an uncaused cause that made everything else happen.

The First Cause argument

The logical chain of reasoning for the First Cause argument runs like this:

1. Everything that exists or begins to exist has a cause to explain its existence. →
2. As the universe exists and had a beginning, it too must have a cause. →
3. There must be something existing with no cause, that is **eternal** (has no beginning or end) to cause everything else to exist. →
4. This eternal first cause can only be God. →
5. This means God must exist.

The key point in the First Cause argument is that the universe had a starting point or cause like all other things that exist. Muslims and Christians say the starting point was God, who set a chain of events into motion that created the universe. As God is eternal, he has no starting point.

Many scientists believe the universe started with the Big Bang. Theists ask what existed before the Big Bang. They believe the answer is God and that he was the cause of it.

Thomas Aquinas' First Cause argument

In the thirteenth century, Thomas Aquinas argued that everything in the universe is caused to exist. Nothing can become something by itself. According to Thomas Aquinas, as everything we see is caused to exist, including the universe, it must have a creator. This uncaused cause of creation can only be God, who is eternal.

The Kalam cosmological (First Cause) argument

In the eleventh century, Muslim philosophers argued:

- The difference between the universe and God is that the universe has a starting point; God does not.
- Everything that has a starting point has a cause of its existence.
- The cause of the universe is God, who is eternal and therefore does not need a cause to exist.

Objections to the First Cause argument

- Atheists argue that if everything that exists has a cause, who or what caused God?
- Surely if God is eternal the universe can be eternal as well.
- The idea that everything has a cause does not necessarily mean the universe has to have a cause as well.
- The Big Bang was a random event and had nothing to do with God.
- Religious **creation** stories, about how God brought the universe into being, are myths. The truth they tell is spiritual, not actual.

APPLY

A Explain carefully **two** of the objections to the First Cause argument.

B 'The First Cause argument proves that God exists.'

Write **two** developed arguments, one in agreement and one against.

TIP

The five-point logical chain of reasoning gives a simple overview of the First Cause argument.

7.3 The argument from miracles

RECAP

Essential information:

The argument from **miracles** – seemingly impossible events that cannot be explained by natural or scientific laws – tries to prove that God exists.

You might be asked to compare beliefs on miracles between Christianity (the main religious tradition in Great Britain) and another religious tradition.

What is a miracle?

Christians and Muslims believe that a true miracle is an event performed by God which appears to break the laws of nature. An example would be someone recovering from an illness when doctors had given up hope. Through miracles, God shows his love and a believer's faith is strengthened.

The argument from miracles and objections to it

Theists argue that:

- There is no scientific reason for an event happening so it must be caused by something outside nature.
- God is the only thing that exists outside nature.
- These events must be the result of God's intervention in the world.
- **Therefore God must exist.**

Atheists and agnostics may argue that:

- Miracles are no more than happy coincidences.
- They may be explained by scientific explanations we don't yet realise.
- Healings could be the result of mind over matter or wrongly diagnosed illnesses.
- Some miracles are deliberately made up for fame or money.
- **Therefore what appear to be miracles have nothing to do with God, so they cannot prove God exists.**

David Hume, a philosopher in the eighteenth century, argued against miracles:

- Miracles deny the laws of nature but **there can never be enough evidence** to prove this can happen.
- **Witnesses to miracles are unreliable**, as most of them are uneducated, primitive people.
- Religions depend on miracles to prove they are true but **all religions cannot be right**.

Even some theists object to miracles because they make God seem unfair. They ask why God chooses someone to benefit from a miracle over millions who are not so fortunate. An all-just and all-loving God wouldn't do that.

Christian and Muslim responses to miracles

Christian responses	Muslim responses
• Christians view miracles as evidence of God's existence and work in the world. The fact that some people convert to Christianity after experiencing a miracle is seen as proof of God's existence. • Jesus worked many miracles, e.g. healings, bringing the dead back to life. • Jesus' incarnation and resurrection are considered the most important miracles in Christian teaching. • Lourdes is recognised by the Church as a place where miracles have occurred – the Catholic Church has recorded 69 miracles there.	• For Muslims, belief in miracles is not a strong argument for God and there are few modern examples of miracles. • The supreme miracle in Islam is the revelation of the Qur'an to Muhammad. No human could write such a book without God's intervention. • Muslims do not see most miracles as important – some religious experiences can be seen as miracles but they are individual cases. Muhammad's ascent into heaven (al Mi'raj) can be seen as a miraculous religious experience.

APPLY

A Explain carefully **one** example of a miracle.

B Finish the sentence below with a **detailed explanation**, then write a detailed explanation of a different point of view.

"When David Hume argued against miracles I believe he was right because…"

7.4 Further arguments against the existence of God

RECAP

Essential information:

- Some people use science and the existence of **suffering** (living with unpleasant conditions) and **evil** (a force of negative power) to challenge the existence of God.
- None of the arguments for God's existence provide **proof** (evidence that supports the truth of something) that God exists. Theists have **faith** (a commitment that goes beyond proof) in God and these arguments make their faith stronger.

How science is used to challenge belief in God

- Atheists believe that religious beliefs, especially about God, were invented by people to answer questions about the origins of the universe and matters of life that they could not answer in any other way.
- Science can now answer the questions that in the past couldn't be answered without inventing the idea of God.
- In the future, science will be able to answer all currently unanswered questions.
- The fact that science is getting closer to creating human life provides further evidence that God does not exist.

Christian and Muslim responses to arguments based on science

- Scientific accounts of the origins of the universe and life do not have to conflict with what the Bible or Qur'an says.
- As God gave humans intelligence to learn more about God's creation, it is important to do so because it gives a clearer understanding of God.
- Science reveals the laws by which God created the universe.
- Some Christians reject evolution because they take the Genesis account literally and some Muslims reject it because they believe humans are a special creation of God.
- Science and faith are partners in understanding the meaning of life.
- Although science answers many questions, it cannot disprove God.
- God created science along with everything else.

> "The big bang … does not contradict the divine act of creation; rather, it requires it."
> *Pope Francis*

Evil and suffering as an argument against the existence of God

Atheists use the existence of evil and suffering as another reason why they do not believe there is a God.

1. Christians believe God to be all-knowing, all-powerful and all-loving. → 2. If this is true, God should be aware of evil and use his powers to prevent it because he loves his creation. → 3. God doesn't do this, so he doesn't exist.

Christian and Muslim responses to arguments based on evil and suffering

Christian responses	Muslim responses
• Adam was given free will to make choices by God. • If God constantly intervened against evil, humans would have less freedom. • If there was no good and evil, people would not be able to show their human qualities, e.g. compassion. • Allowing suffering means people can make mistakes and learn from them.	• Adam was given free will to make choices by God. • If God constantly intervened against evil, humans would have less freedom. • Shaytan (the source of evil) was given the job of testing people's faith and character through suffering. God does not allow more suffering than a person can bear. • God allows evil but he doesn't will it. He has reasons for allowing it that humans cannot know.

> "The work of Satan … cannot harm [believers] in the least, unless God permits it. Let the believers put their trust in God" *Qur'an 58:10*

APPLY

A Explain **two** reasons why atheists may believe evil and suffering prove God doesn't exist.

B Write **two** logical chains of reasoning, one to agree that science is correct in challenging the existence of God and the other to disagree.

TIP
Remember that a logical chain of reasoning can express an opinion, give a reason to support the opinion and further develop the reason, possibly using religious arguments to elaborate it.

7.5 Special revelation and enlightenment

RECAP

Essential information:

- [ ] All religions believe that there is supreme, final, fundamental power in all reality, an **ultimate reality**. This ultimate reality could be a God or gods which are referred to as being **divine**.
- [ ] **Special revelation** is God making himself known through direct personal experience.
- [ ] Special revelation and enlightenment are both sources of knowledge about the divine.

How may God be known?

- Some say that God cannot be known because he is pure mystery and beyond human understanding.
- Human language limits God and so he cannot be adequately described.
- Others believe that two ways that God can be known is if he chooses to reveal himself through either special or general **revelation** – an enlightening, divine or supernatural experience in which God shows himself.

Special revelation

- Special revelation is a person experiencing God directly in an event. It usually has a profound effect on those involved and can be life changing.
- In the Bible, Mary received a special revelation from the angel Gabriel that she would become the mother of Jesus (Luke 1:26-38).
- Christians consider special revelations to be rare and many believe in God all their lives without experiencing such events.
- An example in Islam is the revelation of the Qur'an to Muhammad.
- Some Muslims would say there is no special revelation and that the revelation of the Qur'an to Muhammad was a divine revelation. Divine revelations are only given to prophets and messengers, of which Muhammad was the last.
- Muslims can gain nearness to God and experience dreams, visions or miracles but these are not divine revelation.
- God may send angels as a spiritual experience. However they are neither prophets nor messengers.

Visions

- **Visions** involve seeing a picture or image that shows something about the nature of God.
- In Christianity and Islam, this is interpreted as being a spiritual experience and holds great meaning for the person receiving it.
- However, both religions study reports of visions carefully and reject them if they are against the Bible or Qur'an.
- Christians believe there are several examples of visions in the Bible, including Saul's vision on the Damascus Road in Acts 9:1–19. He experienced a blinding light and was spoken to by Jesus. Afterwards he changed his name to Paul, was baptised as a Christian and committed himself to the Christian faith – a faith whose followers he had previously persecuted.
- Some atheists believe visions can be explained by sleep deprivation or drug use.

> You might be asked to compare beliefs on visions between Christianity (the main religious tradition in Great Britain) and another religious tradition.

Enlightenment

Buddhists do not believe in God or gods. However, they use meditation and self-discipline to discover the meaning of ultimate reality by gaining true knowledge (**enlightenment**). They hope to discover how to end suffering and achieve happiness.

APPLY

A Using **one** detailed example, explain the meaning of special revelation.

B 'Those who see visions are only hallucinating.'

Write a detailed argument to explain what you think about this statement.

7.6 General revelation

RECAP

Essential information:

- Some seek to understand the divine by using **general revelation** – God making himself known through ordinary experiences. These ordinary experiences could be through **nature** (the physical world or environment) or **scripture** (the sacred writings of a religion).

What is general revelation?

Below are some forms of general revelation – such experiences do not convince everyone that God is real but help others to strengthen their faith.

- God's presence in nature
- The lives of religious leaders close to God
- A person's reason, conscience or morality
- Worship and reading scriptures

Nature as a way of understanding the divine

Many Christians and Muslims believe that God is revealed to them through the beauty of the world he created (e.g. through the power of storms and the sea, the wonder of a newborn baby, the order of the natural world). This may lead to awe and wonder at his power to create and destroy.

You might be asked to compare beliefs on nature as a general revelation between Christianity (the main religious tradition in Great Britain) and another religious tradition.

> "The heavens declare the glory of God; the skies proclaim the work of his hands … night after night they reveal knowledge." *Psalm 19:1–2* [NIV]

> "It is He who spread out the earth, placed firm mountains and rivers on it and made two of every kind of fruit; He draws the veil of night over the day. There truly are signs in this for people who reflect." *Qur'an 13:3*

Scripture as a way of understanding the divine

- Some Christians believe that the Bible contains God's actual words and must not be changed or questioned.
- More liberal Christians believe that the Bible was inspired by God and can be interpreted in different ways by looking at the words in their original context and applying them to today's world.
- When Christians read or listen to the words of the Bible, they hope to get a better understanding of the teachings of Christianity and to receive spiritual strength from God's words.
- Muslims believe the writings in the Qur'an are the actual words of God revealed directly to Muhammad.
- Readers of scripture can feel God's presence in the words they are reading because the words have hidden depths.
- The power of the words is so strong that people come to believe in the faith just by reading or hearing them.

The atheist and humanist view

- **Nature:** Atheists and humanists may argue that observing nature does not provide a greater understanding of God but can lead to greater scientific truth.
- **Scripture:** For atheists the writings in scripture are merely the authors' opinions. The words reveal nothing about God.

APPLY

A Explain **two** forms of general revelation.

B **Develop the following point** about whether scripture can help people to believe in God.

"It is easy to believe that an ancient book can help people to believe in God even though it was written so long ago."

TIP

Including your personal view may improve your answer, but don't forget to develop your point with reasons to support it.

7.7 Different ideas about the divine

RECAP

Essential information:

- Religions have different ideas about the divine.
- Christianity and Islam see God as omnipotent, omniscient, benevolent, personal, impersonal, immanent and transcendent.

Descriptions of God's nature

The limitations of language make describing a God without limits very difficult. However all of the major religions, apart from Buddhism, believe in one God who is creator, controller and maintainer of the universe. The table explains the main words used to describe God and his nature.

Description	Explanation
omnipotent	Almighty and all-powerful; capable of doing anything including creation.
omniscient	All-knowing and aware of everything that has happened in the past, present or future.
benevolent	All-loving and all-good – provider of everything humans need to survive.
personal	The idea that God has human characteristics, such as being merciful and compassionate. Humans can have a relationship with God through prayer.
impersonal	The idea that God has no human characteristics, is unknowable and mysterious and more like an idea or a force.
immanent	A belief that God is present in, and involved with, life in the universe. People can experience God in their lives as he influences events.
transcendent	A belief that God is beyond and outside life on earth. He is not limited by the world, time or space. As God existed before the universe was made, he is separate from it so does not act in the world or interfere in people's lives.

TIP
As all of these terms are listed in the specification, you may need to know about any or all of them.

Can God be immanent and transcendent, personal and impersonal?

For Christians and Muslims, God can be immanent and transcendent; personal and impersonal.

- Even though God is the eternal, unlimited creator of the universe (transcendent and impersonal), theists can have a personal relationship with him (immanent and personal).
- Christians believe God is personal because he allows followers to join in a relationship with him, described as a Father who loves and cares for his children. This relationship is enabled by prayer.
- For Christians, God's immanence is revealed both in Jesus, who they believe is God made man, and also in the work of the Holy Spirit.
- God is omnipotent, omniscient and beyond human understanding, but as the Qur'an says, he is also close to people.

> "You have searched me, LORD, and you know me. You know when I sit and when I rise; you perceive my thoughts from afar." *Psalm 139:1–2* [NIV]

> "For God so loved the world that he gave his one and only Son, that whoever believes in him shall not perish but have eternal life." *John 3:16* [NIV]

> "He is with you wherever you are" *Qur'an 7:180*

- Muslims have 99 Beautiful Names of God which all describe qualities God has revealed about himself.
- Despite all this, God remains a mystery beyond human understanding.
- Muslims stress the one-ness of God (Tawhid) and that he has no equal. Images of him are forbidden.

APPLY

A For each of the seven ideas about the divine, **design and draw a simple symbol** to help you remember them.

B 'It is not possible to fully express God's nature in words.'

Write **two** developed points of view about this statement, one in favour and one that expresses a different opinion.

TIP
Even though a quote such as this has a specific religious theme, don't forget to include specific religious content in your answer.

7.8 The value of revelation and enlightenment

RECAP

Essential information:

- Theists believe that revelation and enlightenment are sources of knowledge about the divine.
- Some people find it difficult to accept the reality in some examples of revelation.

The value of revelation

For theists revelation can:

- provide proof of God's existence
- help to start a religion
- enable believers to have a relationship with the divine
- help people know how God wants them to live.

Individual revelations have a great impact on the lives of those who receive them, even to the extent that they change their religious thinking completely.

Revelation: reality or illusion?

Revelation cannot be proved, so how do believers know it is real? They may ask themselves these questions.

Question	Religious responses
Does their revelation match the real world?	It is probably unlikely if it claims that people can fly. If it claims that water in a holy place can cure, and it does, then it is more likely to be a real revelation.
Does it fit with other revelations acknowledged to be correct in a religion?	If it contradicts the long-held belief of a religion, it is less likely to be a true revelation. However, beliefs may change over time (e.g. about slavery) so this is not always the case.
Does it change a non-believer into a believer, or convert someone from one religion to another?	Cat Stevens was raised in a Christian family and found fame as a singer and songwriter in the 1960s and 70s. He used drugs and alcohol and while he was in hospital his brother gave him a copy of the Qur'an, which he studied carefully. As a result of his revelation he became a Muslim, changed his name to Yusuf Islam, gave up his music career and became strongly involved in the Muslim community. Nicky Cruz was the leader of a gang in New York in the 1950s. He led a life of brutal violence until he met a street preacher who converted him to Christianity. He eventually became a minister in his old neighbourhood.
How is it that different religions have different revelations? They can't all be correct.	Different religions are different paths to the divine chosen by different people. Within a faith there are different interpretations of sacred texts and how these apply to moral issues. If a particular interpretation disagrees with another verse in the Bible/Qur'an it is likely that the interpretation is questionable.

Alternative explanations for the experiences

Atheists and others who do not believe in revelation put forward alternative explanations for what believers call their revelation experience:

- drugs or alcohol
- wishful thinking
- genuine error
- physical illness or a mental health problem
- deliberate lying for fame/money

APPLY

A Develop **three** of the alternative explanations for revelations.

B 'Revelation proves that God exists.'

Write a reasoned answer to express the atheist point of view on this statement.

TIP

You can develop each of these alternative explanations by providing an example. For instance, there have been cases in the news of people who have claimed to have had revelations from God and later their claims were found to be fraudulent.

REVIEW

7 Exam practice

Test the 1 mark multiple-choice question

1 Which **one** of the following describes a person who believes in God?

A Atheist B Agnostic C Theist D Humanist **[1 mark]**

2 Which **one** of the following is not an attribute of God?

A Compassionate B Mortal C Transcendent D Eternal **[1 mark]**

Test the 1 mark question

3 Give **one** weakness of the First Cause argument. **[1 mark]**

____

4 Give **one** possible cause of suffering. **[1 mark]**

____

Test the 4 mark question

5 Explain **two** different beliefs in contemporary British society about the Design argument for God's existence.

In your answer you must refer to one or more religious traditions. You may refer to a non-religious belief. **[4 marks]**

• **Explain one belief.**	*Muslims believe that the beauty and intricacy of nature proves that God created the world.*
• Develop your explanation with more detail/an example/ reference to a religious teaching or quotation.	*He created order in the world and put humans in charge of creation in order to make it easier for them to serve him by following his words and showing stewardship.*
• **Explain a second belief.**	*Atheists disagree with the Design argument because they do not believe there is a God.*
• Develop your explanation with more detail/an example/ reference to a religious teaching or quotation.	*They think that the natural world evolved after the Big Bang, a random event, and through natural selection creatures designed themselves without a need for God.*

TIP

The question asks for different beliefs, and the answer refers to Islam and contrasts it with an atheist view.

6 Explain **two** different beliefs about miracles.

In your answer you must refer to one or more religious traditions. You may refer to a non-religious belief. **[4 marks]**

• **Explain one belief.**	
• Develop your explanation with more detail/an example/ reference to a religious teaching or quotation.	
• **Explain a second belief.**	
• Develop your explanation with more detail/an example/ reference to a religious teaching or quotation.	

7 Explain **two** similar beliefs about general revelation.

In your answer you must refer to one or more religious traditions. You may refer to a non-religious belief. **[4 marks]**

7 Exam practice

Test the 6 mark question

8 Explain **two** religious beliefs about visions.

Refer to sacred writings or another source of religious belief and teaching in your answer. **[6 marks]**

● **Explain one belief.**	*Muslims believe that God can be revealed to people in a special, direct way through visions.*
● Develop your explanation with more detail/an example.	*Some people who have had visions may become aware of reality in a new way that follows teachings in the Qur'an.*
● **Explain a second belief.**	*A Christian belief about visions is that they reveal a message to a person which makes them want to spread the word of God to other people.*
● Develop your explanation with more detail/an example.	*Since they believe the vision was given for a specific purpose, they often begin a life of preaching or sharing their experiences with others.*
● **Add a reference to sacred writings or another source of religious belief and teaching.** If you prefer, you can add the reference to your first belief instead.	*An example of a vision in the Bible is in Acts 9:1–19, where it says Saul (who later became Paul) received a vision of Jesus on the Damascus Road. Saul was temporarily blinded and when he regained his sight he changed from persecuting Christians to preaching the gospel of Jesus to everyone.*
● Apply the reference by explaining how it links to the question.	*This demonstrates the belief that visions can include a revelation that changes a person to make them evangelise.*

TIP

When questions ask for two religious beliefs, it is fine to answer from different religions, as here. Visions is one of the three topics in this chapter about which you may be asked (in a differently worded question) to give a view from Christianity (the main religious tradition of Great Britain) and one or more other religious traditions.

9 Explain **two** religious beliefs about special revelation.

Refer to sacred writings or another source of religious belief and teaching in your answer. **[6 marks]**

● **Explain one belief.**	
● Develop your explanation with more detail/an example.	
● **Explain a second belief.**	
● Develop your explanation with more detail/an example.	
● **Add a reference to sacred writings or another source of religious belief and teaching.** If you prefer, you can add the reference to your first belief instead.	
● Apply the reference by explaining how it links to the question.	

TIP

Make sure you write about special revelation, <u>not</u> general revelation.

TIP

This question is not an evaluation, so do <u>not</u> give your opinion or write arguments against revelation. Don't forget to refer to a source of religious teaching in the answer <u>and</u> to link it to the question.

10 Explain **two** religious ideas about God.

Refer to sacred writings or another source of religious belief and teaching in your answer. **[6 marks]**

Test the 12 mark question

11 'The First Cause argument proves that God exists.'

Evaluate this statement. In your answer you:

- should give reasoned arguments in support of this statement
- should give reasoned arguments to support a different point of view
- should refer to religious arguments
- may refer to non-religious arguments
- should reach a justified conclusion.

[12 marks]

Plus SPaG 3 ma

REASONED ARGUMENTS IN SUPPORT OF THE STATEMENT ● **Explain why some people would agree with the statement.** ● Develop your explanation with more detail and examples, which may include non-religious ideas. ● Refer to religious teaching. Use a quote or paraphrase or refer to a religious authority. ● **Evaluate the arguments.** Is this a good argument or not? Explain why you think this.	*The First Cause argument says that everything that exists has a cause. It is obvious to everyone that the universe exists because we live in it! Therefore the universe too must have a cause – something must have started it. But that something had to be eternal and not caused by something else, otherwise that other thing would be the cause, and so on. Christians and Muslims believe that God is the eternal, almighty cause that began the process of creation of everything we know. Everything except God has a beginning in time. God was the eternal being that set off the Big Bang in time, which led to evolution and the world as we know it today.*
REASONED ARGUMENTS SUPPORTING A DIFFERENT VIEW ● **Explain why some people would support a different view.** ● Develop your explanation with more detail and examples, which may include non-religious ideas. ● Refer to religious teaching. Use a quote or paraphrase or refer to a religious authority. ● **Evaluate the arguments.** Is this a good argument or not? Explain why you think this.	*Atheists are people who do not believe there is a God. They would argue that the First Cause argument does not prove there is a God because there are flaws in the logic – the argument contradicts itself. For example, if everything has a cause, what caused God?* *They also point out that saying God is eternal so nobody made him is just a convenient excuse. If God is eternal, why cannot the universe be eternal? Of course, if the universe is eternal, it doesn't need a first cause and was never created. This then removes the need for a God to cause the universe to exist. They also point out that the Big Bang just happened and there was no cause for it.*
CONCLUSION ● **Give a justified conclusion.** ● Include your own opinion together with your own reasoning. ● **Include evaluation.** Explain why you think one viewpoint is stronger than the other or why they are equally strong. ● Do not just repeat arguments you have already used without explaining how they apply to your reasoned opinion/conclusion.	*In conclusion, I think that although the First Cause argument may seem convincing because it depends on something everyone can observe, that everything that happens has a cause, in the end it fails to convince me that a God is the First Cause of the universe. The argument relies on the universe having a beginning and a cause, but just because things in our world have causes does not necessarily mean the universe itself had one. Christians may use the Bible's creation stories to support their arguments in favour of the statement, but as I am an atheist, I am not persuaded by myths.*

TIP

It is good to mention the Big Bang here, and it links well to the previous argument. This point could be developed further, perhaps with a brief explanation of the Big Bang theory, and some evaluation as to how convincing it is.

TIP

This conclusion is good because it doesn't just repeat points already made to justify the opinion. It is also clearly linked to the quote in the question.

12 'Miracles prove that God exists.'

Evaluate this statement. In your answer you:

- should give reasoned arguments in support of this statement
- should give reasoned arguments to support a different point of view
- should refer to religious arguments
- may refer to non-religious arguments
- should reach a justified conclusion.

[12 marks]
Plus SPaG 3 marks

REASONED ARGUMENTS IN SUPPORT OF THE STATEMENT ● **Explain why some people would agree with the statement.** ● Develop your explanation with more detail and examples, which may include non-religious ideas. ● Refer to religious teaching. Use a quote or paraphrase or refer to a religious authority. ● **Evaluate the arguments.** Is this a good argument or not? Explain why you think this.	
REASONED ARGUMENTS SUPPORTING A DIFFERENT VIEW ● **Explain why some people would support a different view.** ● Develop your explanation with more detail and examples, which may include non-religious ideas. ● Refer to religious teaching. Use a quote or paraphrase or refer to a religious authority. ● **Evaluate the arguments.** Is this a good argument or not? Explain why you think this.	
CONCLUSION ● **Give a justified conclusion.** ● Include your own opinion together with your own reasoning. ● **Include evaluation.** Explain why you think one viewpoint is stronger than the other or why they are equally strong. ● Do not just repeat arguments you have already used without explaining how they apply to your reasoned opinion/conclusion.	

TIP
Make sure your focus is on both miracles and the existence of God.

13 'The existence of evil and suffering proves that God does not exist.'

Evaluate this statement. In your answer you:

- should give reasoned arguments in support of this statement
- should give reasoned arguments to support a different point of view
- should refer to religious arguments
- may refer to non-religious arguments
- should reach a justified conclusion.

[12 marks]
Plus SPaG 3 marks

Check your answers using the mark scheme on page 156. How did you do?
To feel more secure in the content you need to remember, re-read pages 98–105.
To remind yourself of what the examiner is looking for, go to pages 6–11.

8 Religion, peace and conflict

8.1 Introduction to religion, peace and conflict

RECAP

Essential information:

- [ ] Throughout history people have gone to **war** (fighting between nations to resolve issues between them). Often the intention of those fighting a war is to create **peace** – an absence of conflict, which leads to happiness and harmony.
- [ ] Many wars are fought to achieve **justice** – what is right and fair, according to the law, or making up for a wrong that has been committed. Christians and Muslims believe that **forgiveness** (pardoning someone for what they have done wrong) and **reconciliation** (restoring friendly relationships after conflict) should follow after a war.

Christian and Muslim beliefs about war

- Although the Church teaches that killing is wrong, many Christians have been prepared to fight for their faith or their country.
- Other Christians, e.g. Quakers (who are pacifists), believe war is always wrong and they work to prevent it.
- The main message of Islam is peace (salam means 'peace' or 'safety').
- Fighting in self-defence or in defence of faith can be justified, but fighting without just cause is against the will of God and Muslim teachings.
- For Muslims and Christians the concepts of peace, justice, forgiveness and reconciliation are important both in the aftermath of conflict and as tools to prevent war happening in the first place.

Peace

- Peace may be hard to achieve through war because its aftermath is often instability and resentment.
- Christians and Muslims seek inner peace and tranquillity through prayer and meditation.
- The prophet Isaiah spoke of a time when God will bring peace, and the Qur'an also emphasises peace.

> "He will judge between the nations and will settle disputes for many peoples ... Nation will not take up sword against nation, nor will they train for war any more."
>
> *Isaiah 2:4* [NIV]

> "The servants of the Lord of Mercy are those who walk humbly on the earth, and who, when aggressive people address them, reply with words of peace."
>
> *Qur'an 25:63*

Justice

- Isaiah says God, the ultimate judge, will establish justice. Justice is linked to equality of opportunity.
- If more privileged parts of the world are seen to be the cause of injustice, conflict may result.
- In Islam 'the Just' is one of the 99 names for God who gives humans laws to follow.

Forgiveness

- Christians are taught to forgive others if they wish to be forgiven (the Lord's Prayer).
- Forgiveness does not mean no action should be taken to right a wrong, but when conflict is over forgiveness should follow. Actions to establish peace and justice need to be taken to avoid future conflict.
- Both Muslims and Christians believe God offers forgiveness to all who ask in faith.

Reconciliation

- Reconciliation means a conscious effort to rebuild a relationship which has been damaged by conflict.
- It is also important in the prevention of conflict.

APPLY

A Explain **two** religious beliefs about forgiveness.

B Make a list of **three** arguments for and **three** arguments against the statement, 'Religious believers should not take part in wars.'

8.2 Violence, violent protest and terrorism

RECAP

Essential information:

- The right to **protest** (express disapproval, often in a public group) is a fundamental democratic freedom.
- UK law allows peaceful public protest marches if police are told six days before so that **violence** (actions that threaten or harm others) can be avoided.
- **Terrorism** (the unlawful use of violence, usually against innocent civilians, to achieve a political goal) is a more serious form of violent protest.

You might be asked to compare beliefs on violence between Christianity (the main religious tradition in Great Britain) and another religious tradition.

Violence and protest

- Christians believe that protest to achieve what is right is acceptable as long as violence is not used.
- The Christian pastor Dr Martin Luther King Jr organised peaceful protests against unjust racist laws, which succeeded in bringing civil rights to African-American citizens.
- No religion's teachings promote violence, but they have different views about when violence may be justified.
- In Islam, fighting is only allowed in self-defence or defence of the faith and only against those who actively fight against you.

"Do not kill each other, for God is merciful to you. If any of you does these things, out of hostility and injustice, We shall make him suffer Fire."

Qur'an 4:29–30

"Do not repay anyone evil for evil ... If it is possible, as far as it depends on you, live at peace with everyone."

Romans 12:17–19

Terrorism

- Some individuals or groups use terrorism to further their cause by killing innocent people.
- Suicide bombers, car bombs, gunmen shooting into crowds and using vehicles to injure pedestrians are all tactics of terrorism.
- The aim of terrorism is to make society aware of their cause, make people frightened and push the authorities into giving way to their demands.
- Terrorists may link their cause with a religion, but no religion promotes terrorism.
- Most Christians and Muslims believe terrorism is wrong as it targets innocent people.

"The purpose of terrorism lies not just in the violent act itself. It is in producing terror. It sets out to inflame, to divide, to produce consequences which [terrorists] then use to justify terror."

Former UK Prime Minister, Tony Blair

APPLY

A Give **one** reason why some religious people may wish to protest.

B **Develop the following argument** to support the statement, 'Terrorism is never justified' by explaining in more detail, adding an example, or referring to a relevant religious teaching or quotation.

"Terrorism kills innocent people. It uses violence to frighten and intimidate ordinary citizens who are just going about their daily lives. It can never be justified no matter what the cause."

8.3 Reasons for war

RECAP

Essential information:

Some reasons for war include:

- **greed** (selfish desire for something)
- **self-defence** (acting to prevent harm to yourself or others)
- **retaliation** (deliberately harming someone as a response to them harming you).

TIP

Other reasons for war such as political disputes, regime change, clash of cultures or disputes between ethnic groups within a nation can be included in your answers on this topic.

Reasons for war

Greed:
- To gain more land/regain land previously lost
- To control important resources, e.g. oil
- To deprive the enemy of main source of income

Self-defence:
- To defend one's country against invasion or attack/to defend allies who are under threat
- To defend one's values, beliefs and ways of life
- To defeat evil, e.g. genocide (deliberate killing of a whole nation or ethnic group)

Retaliation:
- To fight against a country that has done something very wrong
- To fight against a country which has attacked or damaged your country

Christian and Muslim beliefs

- The Bible and the Qur'an warn against greed.

> "For the love of money is the root of all kinds of evil." *1 Timothy 6:10* [NIV]

> "God does not like arrogant, boastful people, who are miserly ... hiding the bounty God has given them." *Qur'an 4:36–37*

- Many Christians and Muslims think that fighting in self-defence is justified if all other ways of resolving conflict have been tried and failed. Their views can be supported by sacred writings:

> "Do not repay anyone evil for evil … If it is possible, as far as it depends on you, live at peace with everyone." *Romans 12:17–19* [NIV]

> "Those who have been attacked are permitted to take up arms because they have been wronged – God has the power to help them." *Qur'an 22:39*

- Jesus taught that retaliation is wrong.

> "But I tell you, do not resist an evil person. If anyone slaps you on the right cheek, turn to them the other cheek also." *Matthew 5:39* [NIV]

- Many Christians follow this teaching in their own lives but find it more difficult in situations of war.
- Islam teaches that God knows the need for justice so permits 'fair retribution' (Qur'an 2:179), but retaliation must be measured: torture and mutilation are strictly forbidden under Islamic law. Forgiveness is a better response to avoid bloodshed and be rewarded by God.

APPLY

A Which **one** of the following is **not** a reason for war?

a) Self-defence b) Greed c) Retaliation d) Forgiveness

B 'Retaliation is a justifiable reason for war.'

Write a paragraph to **explain whether you agree or disagree** with the statement. Include religious teachings and explain how the teachings are relevant to the argument.

8.4 Nuclear war and weapons of mass destruction

RECAP

Essential information:

- [ ] **Nuclear weapons** are weapons that work by a nuclear reaction; they devastate huge areas and kill large numbers of people.
- [ ] Other types of **weapons of mass destruction** (that kill large numbers of people/cause great damage) include:
  - **chemical weapons** (that use chemicals to poison, burn or paralyse humans and destroy the natural environment)
  - **biological weapons** (that have living organisms or infective material that can lead to disease or death).
- [ ] No religion supports the use of these weapons.

The use of nuclear weapons

- US forces used atom bombs on Hiroshima and Nagasaki during the Second World War, causing 140,000 people to die in Hiroshima alone.
- Japan surrendered, ending the war, so some people say their use was justified.
- Since then many countries have developed powerful nuclear weapons as a deterrent (to prevent an enemy attack).

Weapons of mass destruction

- The Chemical Weapons Convention (1993) made the production, stockpiling and use of these weapons illegal worldwide. Chemical weapons are thought to have been used in Iraq and Syria.
- Biological weapons introduce harmful bacteria and viruses into the atmosphere, food or water supplies that can kill large numbers of people. Biological weapons are illegal but many countries have them.

You might be asked to compare beliefs on weapons of mass destruction between Christianity (the main religious tradition in Great Britain) and another religious tradition.

Christian and Muslim beliefs

Christian beliefs	Muslim beliefs
• Only God has the right to end life. • Nuclear, chemical and biological weapons kill huge numbers of innocent civilians so their use can never be justified. "You shall not murder." *Exodus 20:13* [NIV] • The quote 'eye for eye' (Exodus 21:24 [NIV]) is sometimes used to justify war but this cannot justify the use of weapons of mass destruction. • Some Christians see the possession of nuclear weapons as a deterrent to maintain peace and prevent attack.	• God created all life on earth and Muslims have a duty to care for and preserve it. • The use of nuclear weapons would destroy God's creation, killing millions of innocent people. • The Qur'an gives advice that seems to rule out using all weapons of mass destruction: "Do not contribute to your destruction with your own hands, but do good, for God loves those who do good." *Qur'an 2:195* • Some Muslims see the possession of nuclear weapons as a deterrent to maintain peace and prevent attack.

APPLY

A Explain **two** different beliefs in contemporary British society about weapons of mass destruction. In your answer you should refer to the main religious tradition of Great Britain and one or more other religious traditions.

B **Develop the following argument** to support the statement, 'There are no good reasons for countries to possess nuclear weapons' by referring to a relevant religious teaching or quotation.

"Nuclear weapons could kill huge numbers of people and destroy much of the earth. They have a long lasting impact on the earth because of radiation that will poison the ground."

TIP
Make sure you choose different viewpoints.

8.5 The just war

RECAP

Essential information:

- A **just war** is a war which meets internationally accepted criteria for fairness, following traditional Christian rules for a just war that are now accepted by other religions.
- Christian writers Augustine (fourth century) and Thomas Aquinas (thirteenth century) developed the concept of a 'just war'.
- The just war theory gives the conditions that must apply if a war is justifiable and rules on how the war must be fought to make sure it is ethical.
- **Lesser jihad** (the outward struggle to defend one's faith, family and country from threat) obliges Muslims to fight under certain conditions.

TIP Muslims have the same conditions for lesser jihad.

Conditions of a just war

For a war to be just it must:

- be fought for a **just cause** (e.g. in self-defence or to defend others, not to gain territory or resources or in retaliation)
- be declared by a **proper legal authority**
- have a **just intention** (fought to promote good or defeat wrongdoing; justice and peace must be restored afterwards)
- be a **last resort** (other ways of solving the problem tried first)
- have a reasonable **chance of success** (the good gained by winning should outweigh the evil which led to the war)
- be **proportional** (excessive force should not be used and innocent civilians must not be killed)

TIP The mnemonic 'CLIPS' will help you remember some conditions for a just war:

C – just CAUSE
L – LAST resort
I – Right INTENTION
P – PROPORTIONALITY
S – reasonable chance of SUCCESS

But don't forget proper legal authority!

Rules about how a war must be fought

- The war should be fought by **just means** (innocent civilians should not be targeted or harmed).
- Only **appropriate force should be** used (including type of force and how much force).
- **Internationally agreed conventions** must be obeyed (Geneva Convention rules).

TIP It will be helpful if you know some examples of wars so that you can support your opinion about whether war can be justified according to the just war theory.

Muslim attitudes to conduct in a war

- The first Caliph, Abu Bakr, devised rules for Muslims:
  - Muslim armies must not harm innocent civilians, animals, fruit-bearing trees or people who are devout in their faith, such as monks.
  - Dead bodies must not be mutilated and prisoners must be treated in a civilised way.
- Muslims generally believe:
  - wars should be proportional and fought without anger, but it is better to avoid war if possible
  - soldiers must be of sound mind and body and prisoners should be treated in a civilised way.

> “Know that the evil of war is swift, and its taste bitter.”
> *Hadith*

APPLY

A Give **one** reason why some religious people believe it is right to fight in a war.

B **Develop the following argument** against the statement, 'The just war theory is the best religious response to whether it is right to fight' by explaining in more detail, adding an example, or referring to a relevant religious teaching or quotation.

"The just war theory is not the best religious response because it accepts that sometimes war is right, when in fact it is never right."

8.6 Holy war and religion as a cause of violence

RECAP

Essential information:

- [ ] A **holy war** is fighting for a religious cause or God, probably controlled by a religious leader.
- [ ] Religion is sometimes seen as a cause of violence in the contemporary world.

Holy war

- A holy war seems to be a contradiction – how can killing large numbers of people be holy?
- The Old Testament refers to God helping the Jewish people win battles to settle in the Promised Land.
- In the Crusades (11–14th century battles between Christians and Muslims) both sides believed God was on their side.
- For both Muslims and Christians a holy war must:
  - be authorised by a religious leader with great authority
  - only be fought to defend the faith from attack (e.g. the right to worship and practise the religion is being denied).
- Those who take part gain spiritual rewards (e.g. if they die in battle they will go straight to heaven/paradise).
- In Islam, holy war must meet the criteria for a just war.

Religion as a cause of violence

- In the UK today most Christians and Muslims do not respond violently to an attack on their faith.
- During 'the Troubles' in Northern Ireland (1968–98) conflict between Catholics and Protestants led to violence against each community.
- Some groups such as al-Qaeda and ISIS (IS) use the Muslim idea of holy war to wage civil war and commit acts of terrorism.

TIP

Although some conflicts may seem to be about two religious groups fighting each other, the reasons for conflict may be more political or economic than religious.

Religious attitudes to the use of violence

Christian beliefs	Muslim beliefs
• The words 'eye for eye, tooth for tooth' (Exodus 21:24) are sometimes used to justify retaliation, but this teaching was intended to reduce violence by limiting retaliation to the individual offenders rather than their whole tribe, many of whom were innocent. • Most Christians accept Jesus' teaching that not only violence, but the anger that leads to violence, is wrong. • Some Christians cite Jesus' advice to his disciples to buy a sword (Luke 22:36) as justification for violence, but most believe Jesus was warning his disciples of dangerous times ahead, not suggesting violence. • Jesus' example at his arrest showed his non-violent stance: "'Put your sword back in its place,' Jesus said, 'for all who draw the sword die by the sword.'" *Matthew 26:52* [NIV]	• Holy war must follow just war criteria (e.g. not for gaining territories/financial gain/for a leader's own power/must be a last resort/in self-defence/not to force conversion to Islam, etc.) • Holy war can only be declared by a proper religious leader. • It cannot be declared to force people to convert to Islam. • It must be fought for God and not to allow a leader to show power. "Fight in God's cause against those who fight you, but do not overstep the limits: God does not love those who overstep the limits." *Qur'an 2:190*

APPLY

A Give **one** feature of holy wars.

B **Evaluate the following argument** to support the statement, 'There is no place for a holy war in contemporary Britain.'

"People have religious freedom. No one has to fight for the right to worship God in the way they wish."

8.7 Pacifism and peacemaking

RECAP

Essential information:

- **Pacifism** is the belief of people (**pacifists**) who refuse to take part in war and any other form of violence.
- **Peacemaking** is the action of trying to establish peace.

You might be asked to compare beliefs on pacifism between Christianity (the main religious tradition in Great Britain) and another religious tradition.

What is pacifism?

- Pacifists believe that **war and violence can rarely be justified** – conflicts can be settled in a peaceful way.
- They think that it is better to prevent war by promoting justice and peace.
- They believe prayer and meditation can help people be at peace with themselves and others.
- Some Christians are pacifists and follow Jesus' example and teaching:

> "Blessed are the peacemakers..." *Matthew 5:9* [NIV]

- The Religious Society of Friends (Quakers) are a Christian denomination that strongly supports pacifism.
- During the First and Second World Wars some people called conscientious objectors refused to fight and faced punishment. Many conscientious objectors took non-fighting roles as cooks, doctors, nurses or mechanics instead, e.g. volunteering for the Friends' Ambulance Unit.
- Islam is a religion of peace, but not a pacifist religion because of the duty of jihad and the instruction in the Qur'an:

> "Fighting has been ordained for you, though it is hard for you." *Qur'an 49:9*

- Muslims must not refuse peace if it is offered, as the Qur'an teaches:

> "But if they [non-believers] incline towards peace, you [Prophet] must also incline towards it, and put your trust in God..." *Qur'an 8:61*

- Muslims seek inner peace through submission to God's will and being part of the ummah (Brotherhood of Muslims).

Examples of peacemaking in contemporary Britain

The Anglican Pacifist Fellowship

- Works to overcome the inequality and injustice that lead to war within and between nations.
- Sponsors the Week of Prayer for World Peace, contributes to peace-related events and religious services and raises awareness of the issue of pacifism.

> "We believe that as Christians we are called to follow the way of Jesus in loving our enemies and becoming peacemakers." *The Anglican Pacifist Fellowship*

The Muslim Peace Fellowship

- Works against injustice and for peace in local communities and globally.
- Affirms commitment to peace on behalf of all Muslims.
- Tries to deepen people's understanding of Muslim teachings about peace through publications and conferences and works to develop non-violent strategies for issues in society.

APPLY

A Describe **two** examples of peacemaking in contemporary Britain.

B Write down **two** reasons in support of the statement, 'Promoting justice and human rights is the best way of preventing conflict.'

Now **develop each reason** by explaining in more detail or by giving examples.

8.8 Religious responses to victims of war

RECAP

Essential information:

- [ ] Victims of war include injured members of the armed forces, the families of those who died or were injured in war, civilians left in a war zone where everything has been destroyed and refugees from war-torn countries.
- [ ] Christians believe they should show love of neighbour by helping victims through Christian charities such as Caritas and Christian Aid.
- [ ] Muslims injured in war receive help from their local community and mosques and through Muslim charities such as Islamic Relief and Muslim Aid.

Providing help to victims of war

Victims of war may need:

- psychological support
- money to live on if the main wage earner dies
- a safe place to live
- medical help for injuries
- access to food and clean water
- a means of earning a living

Christian reasons for helping	Muslim reasons for helping
• Jesus taught 'Love your neighbour as yourself' (Mark 12:31) • Jesus' parable of the Good Samaritan (Luke 10:25–37) taught that everyone is everybody else's neighbour, regardless of race, age, gender, religion or political beliefs.	• The Qur'an teaches 'Whoever saved a life, it would be as if they saved the life of all mankind.' (Qur'an 5:32) • Principles such as compassion, empathy, generosity and helping those in need motivate Muslims to help.

Christian organisations that help	Muslim organisations that help
• **Caritas**, a Catholic charity that serves people living in poverty and promotes charity and justice worldwide. They provided food, shelter, translators and legal services to Syrian refugees who escaped to Greece in 2015. • **Christian Aid** works to end poverty and promotes peace, justice and human rights so that war is prevented. It raises money to support local organisations that help refugees from places such as Gaza, Afghanistan and Syria.	• **Muslim Aid** provides short- and long-term aid to victims of war and other disasters. In 2014 they helped set up the Beity orphanage in Turkey to give health care, education and spiritual support to children whose parents were killed in Syria. • **Islamic Relief** provides short-term aid to victims of war during disasters and emergencies. They also work alongside communities to help prepare and strengthen them in the long term.

> "The need to address the root causes of refugee flows and the migration of the desperate – conflict, inequality, and the impacts of climate change, to name but three – has never been greater."
>
> *Christian Aid*

TIP

Be careful to choose a religious organisation that helps victims of war, rather than secular charities like Help for Heroes or the Red Cross which do good work but which are not required for your examination. You will only need to know about one organisation.

APPLY

A Give **one** way in which religious believers help victims of war.

B 'The point of war is to kill the enemy, not help them to survive.'

Give **two** reasons to agree with this statement and **two** reasons to oppose it. Develop one of them by adding religious teaching to your answer.

8 Exam practice

Test the 1 mark multiple-choice question

1 Which **one** of the following best expresses the religious ideal of bringing about what is right and fair?

A Peace B Forgiveness C Justice D Defence **[1 mark]**

2 Which **one** of the following are **not** weapons of mass destruction?

A Chemical weapons B Nuclear weapons C Biological weapons D Conventional weapons **[1 mark]**

Test the 1 mark question

3 Give **one** condition of a just war according to some religious believers. **[1 mark]**

____

4 Give **one** reason why many religious people do **not** support violent protest. **[1 mark]**

____

Test the 4 mark question

5 Explain **two** different beliefs in contemporary British society about whether countries should possess weapons of mass destruction.

In your answer you should refer to the main religious tradition of Great Britain and one or more other religious traditions. **[4 marks]**

• **Explain one belief.**	*Some Christians, while following Jesus' teaching to 'turn the other cheek' and not to use violence, might approve of countries possessing some weapons of mass destruction in order to stop people being tempted to use them.*
• Develop your explanation with more detail/an example/ reference to a religious teaching or quotation.	*They would believe that possessing them is necessary in order to prevent war and help to keep the peace.*
• **Explain a second belief.**	*Many Muslims believe that no country should possess weapons of mass destruction because they are dangerous and overstep the limits of how humans should behave towards each other. They do not believe God would approve.*
• Develop your explanation with more detail/an example/ reference to a religious teaching or quotation.	*Muslims would support this belief from the words of the Qur'an, 'Fight in God's cause against those who fight you, but do not overstep the limits: God does not love those who overstep the limits.'*

TIP

It is good practice to include a religious teaching to support your explanation of religious beliefs.

6 Explain **two** different beliefs in contemporary British society about pacifism.

In your answer you should refer to the main religious tradition of Great Britain and one or more other religious traditions. **[4 marks]**

• **Explain one belief.**	
• Develop your explanation with more detail/an example/ reference to a religious teaching or quotation.	
• **Explain a second belief.**	
• Develop your explanation with more detail/an example/ reference to a religious teaching or quotation.	

8 Exam practice

7	Explain **two** similar religious beliefs about forgiveness. In your answer you must refer to one or more religious traditions. **[4 marks]**

Test the 6 mark question

8	Explain **two** religious beliefs about helping victims of war. Refer to sacred writings or another source of religious belief and teaching in your answer. **[6 marks]**

• **Explain one belief.**	*One Christian belief about helping victims of war is that Christians should treat everyone as if they were a neighbour to them, as Jesus commanded.*
• Develop your explanation with more detail/an example.	*Victims of war may be suffering because they have lost everything including people they love, so even if Christians do not know them, they should not ignore their suffering but offer to help them in whatever way they can.*
• **Explain a second belief.**	*Muslims believe that they should help those in need, particularly those injured in war, out of compassion for others.*
• Develop your explanation with more detail/an example.	*Giving to those in need is one of the five pillars of Islam.*
• **Add a reference to sacred writings or another source of religious belief and teaching.** If you prefer, you can add the reference to your first belief instead.	*They follow the teaching in the Qur'an that says, 'Whoever saved a life, it would be as if they saved the life of all mankind.'*
• Apply the reference by explaining how it links to the question.	*This can be interpreted to mean that helping victims of war, by saving their lives in some way, is a significant deed, equal to saving all of humanity.*

TIP

If you cannot remember an exact quotation from sacred writings, you may express it in your own words.

9	Explain **two** reasons why some religious people believe it is right to fight in a war. Refer to sacred writings or another source of religious belief and teaching in your answer. **[6 marks]**

• **Explain one reason.**	
• Develop your explanation with more detail/an example.	
• **Explain a second reason.**	
• Develop your explanation with more detail/an example.	
• **Add a reference to sacred writings or another source of religious belief and teaching.** If you prefer, you can add the reference to your first reason instead.	
• Apply the reference by explaining how it links to the question.	

10 Explain **two** religious beliefs about reconciliation.
Refer to sacred writings or another source of religious belief and teaching in your answer. **[6 marks]**

Test the 12 mark question

11 'The just war theory is the best religious response to whether it is right to fight.'
Evaluate this statement. In your answer you:

- should give reasoned arguments in support of this statement
- should give reasoned arguments to support a different point of view
- should refer to religious arguments
- may refer to non-religious arguments
- should reach a justified conclusion.

[12 marks]
Plus SPaG 3 m

REASONED ARGUMENTS IN SUPPORT OF THE STATEMENT ● **Explain why some people would agree with the statement.** ● Develop your explanation with more detail and examples, which may include non-religious ideas. ● Refer to religious teaching. Use a quote or paraphrase or refer to a religious authority. ● **Evaluate the arguments.** Is this a good argument or not? Explain why you think this.	*Although religious people think it is better to avoid war and violence, if faced with a decision about whether or not it is right to fight, the just war theory gives them some guidance. The theory has several criteria including that the war must be declared by a leader of a state, it should be proportional in the amount of force that is used and that civilians should be protected. Although the theory was originally developed by Christians (Augustine and Aquinas), its principles are accepted by Muslims too.* *The theory is a good response because it makes sure wars are not fought about something unimportant or in a way which breaks internationally agreed rules. This is important because God wants people to protect innocent civilians rather than killing them. The first Caliph, Abu Bakr, added that children, women and old men should not be killed and that the environment should also be protected in a war. Muslims believe they are stewards of the earth and should not destroy it.*
REASONED ARGUMENTS SUPPORTING A DIFFERENT VIEW ● **Explain why some people would support a different view.** ● Develop your explanation with more detail and examples, which may include non-religious ideas. ● Refer to religious teaching. Use a quote or paraphrase or refer to a religious authority. ● **Evaluate the arguments.** Is this a good argument or not? Explain why you think this.	*Some Christians do not agree with the just war theory. These Christians may be pacifists like the Quakers who think that all war is wrong whether it is considered 'just' or not. The best religious response to whether it is right to fight is to follow the teaching of Jesus who said 'Blessed are the peacemakers'. Jesus taught people to 'turn the other cheek' and he forgave his persecutors on the cross.*
CONCLUSION ● **Give a justified conclusion.** ● Include your own opinion together with your own reasoning. ● **Include evaluation.** Explain why you think one viewpoint is stronger than the other or why they are equally strong. ● Do not just repeat arguments you have already used without explaining how they apply to your reasoned opinion/conclusion.	*In conclusion, I would agree with the statement that the just war theory is the right religious response. I have sympathy with the views of pacifists, and ideally war should be avoided, but in the real world there are always countries that will bully other countries or try to take their land or resources, so war is sometimes necessary. It is better to have rules that limit the damage war can do, and the just war theory helps in that way.*

TIP
It is good practice t show that you know what the just war theory is before sayir whether it is a gooc response to whether is right to fight in a war.

TIP
The conclusion does not always have to come down on one side of the argument or the other. In this example the student shows they understand the complexity of the moral issue of whether it is right to fight.

12 'Religion is the main cause of wars.'

Evaluate this statement. In your answer you:

- should give reasoned arguments in support of this statement
- should give reasoned arguments to support a different point of view
- should refer to religious arguments
- may refer to non-religious arguments
- should reach a justified conclusion.

[12 marks]
Plus SPaG 3 marks

REASONED ARGUMENTS IN SUPPORT OF THE STATEMENT ● **Explain why some people would agree with the statement.** ● Develop your explanation with more detail and examples, which may include non-religious ideas. ● Refer to religious teaching. Use a quote or paraphrase or refer to a religious authority. ● **Evaluate the arguments.** Is this a good argument or not? Explain why you think this.	
REASONED ARGUMENTS SUPPORTING A DIFFERENT VIEW ● **Explain why some people would support a different view.** ● Develop your explanation with more detail and examples, which may include non-religious ideas. ● Refer to religious teaching. Use a quote or paraphrase or refer to a religious authority. ● **Evaluate the arguments.** Is this a good argument or not? Explain why you think this.	
CONCLUSION ● **Give a justified conclusion.** ● Include your own opinion together with your own reasoning. ● **Include evaluation.** Explain why you think one viewpoint is stronger than the other or why they are equally strong. ● Do not just repeat arguments you have already used without explaining how they apply to your reasoned opinion/conclusion.	

TIP

When evaluation questions ask whether something is the 'main' cause or 'best' response or whether a religious belief is the 'most important' belief, they are asking you to think about whether other causes/responses/beliefs are more significant or whether there can be many of equal merit.

13 'Religious people should be the main peacemakers in the world today.'

Evaluate this statement. In your answer you:

- should give reasoned arguments in support of this statement
- should give reasoned arguments to support a different point of view
- should refer to religious arguments
- may refer to non-religious arguments
- should reach a justified conclusion.

[12 marks]
Plus SPaG 3 marks

Check your answers using the mark scheme on page 156. How did you do?
To feel more secure in the content you need to remember, re-read pages 110–117.
To remind yourself of what the examiner is looking for, go to pages 6–11.

9 Religion, crime and punishment

9.1 Crime and punishment

RECAP

Essential information:

☐ **Crime** (an offence which is punishable by law) and **punishment** (something legally done to somebody after being found guilty of breaking the law) are both governed by the law.

What are crime and punishment?

- In the UK, magistrates and, for more serious cases, crown courts are involved in hearing cases against someone charged with committing a crime.
- The courts decide whether the accused is *guilty or not guilty* and if guilty, impose a *sentence* as punishment.
- In the UK, the most severe sentence is life in prison. This is reserved for the most serious crimes such as murder, rape and terrorist activity.
- Many Muslim countries follow **Shari'ah law**, which is derived from the teachings of the Qur'an, Hadith and Sunnah.
- In some Muslim countries, such as Egypt and Saudi Arabia, the death penalty is the most severe sentence.
- The death penalty does *not* exist in UK, and no legal punishment can deliberately cause any physical harm to the offender, whereas Shari'ah law allows corporal punishment such as caning.

TIP

It is unlikely that you will need to answer a question directly about the legal process but you may find it useful to have some knowledge and understanding of it, especially in the 12 mark question.

Good and evil intentions and actions

Some people assume a **good action** is an action that does not break a law. However, there are many good actions that people perform that exist outside the law.

- There is no law telling people that they have to give to charity or to help people in need.
- Being kind and compassionate is a natural human reaction and has nothing to do with the law.
- People who do such good things intend to do them; it is not accidental.
- However, some Christians and Muslims believe that adultery and abortion are wrong despite them not being illegal.
- Actions encouraged by genuine religious faith are good.

There are many evil actions that are against the law. **Evil** can be described as the opposite of good; a force of negative power which is seen in many traditions as destructive and against God.

- Evil actions may cause suffering, injury or death.
- Not all evil actions come from evil **intentions** (the plan that someone has before they act); sometimes a person may be influenced by the situation in which they find themselves.
- In the UK, the intentions of the criminal will often be taken into account when setting a punishment. Under Shari'ah law, the severity of the punishment depends on the seriousness of the religious value breached.
- Many Muslims would claim that human beings are not perfect and make mistakes – evil actions may be blamed on not resisting temptation rather than the offender being wicked or evil.
- Christians believe no one is evil and everybody makes mistakes. Because people are created good, there is usually a reason why they do wicked things (e.g. a mental health problem that should be treated in addition to the person being punished).

APPLY

A **Explain the difference** between evil actions and evil intentions.

B 'Intentions are more important than actions.'

Write a developed argument on **each** side of this statement. Elaborate your arguments with religious teaching.

TIP

When faced with a statement that you strongly agree or disagree with, you must also focus on an alternative opinion and explain why a person might hold it.

9.2 Reasons for crime

RECAP

Essential information:

- Religious believers think crime is hardly ever justified, no matter the reason.
- Some reasons why people commit crimes include **poverty** (being without money, food or other basic needs), a **mental health problem** (a medical condition that affects a person's emotions or moods), **addiction** (a physical or mental dependency on a substance or activity) and **greed** (a selfish desire for something).

Reasons why some people commit crimes

Reason	Development	Christian view	Muslim view
Poverty	There are millions of people in the UK who cannot always afford to buy food. Some believe the only way out of this is to steal food for their family.	Society should ensure that nobody has to steal food. Christians support foodbanks and may campaign for the living wage and to improve public services.	Zakah exists to ensure that no one lives in poverty. However, it cannot help everybody who needs help so the community should become involved as well.
Upbringing	Some people grow up in a household where crime is a way of life and they may be encouraged to commit crime.	Parents should teach their children the right way to behave through their own words and actions.	The strong extended family should ensure Muslims are guided to respect the law.
Mental health problem	There is a link between some mental health problems and crime. For example, antisocial personality disorder affects how a person thinks and relates to others, and can lead to lawbreaking.	Christians believe that treating the causes of the illness is the most loving and compassionate thing to do.	Mental health problems should be treated, although punishment is still justified.
Addiction	Taking illegal drugs is a crime, even though the person is addicted. They may commit further crimes to be able to buy drugs. Legal drugs, e.g. alcohol, can also play a part in crimes such as violence, rape and drunk driving.	Christians are against taking illegal drugs and support rehabilitation as a way of defeating the addiction. Christians permit alcohol but not to excess.	Illegal drugs and alcohol are not allowed in Islam so addiction is no excuse for criminal behaviour.
Greed	Some people want personal possessions that they do not need and cannot afford. Their greed for them may lead them to steal.	The Ten Commandments forbid envy and it is envy that often causes greed. "You shall not covet... anything that belongs to your neighbour." *Exodus 20:17*	Greed is a temptation that should be avoided. "Competing for more distracts you until you go in your grave." *Qur'an 102:1–2*
Hate	Hate, the opposite of love, can lead to violence or aggression.	Jesus taught to love everybody, even enemies.	Hatred is against Muslim morality.
Opposition to an unjust law	Some people break laws that they believe to be unjust in order to protest against them. These could be laws based on inequality or that deny basic human rights.	Some Christians may agree with this but only if no violence is involved and nobody is harmed.	Shari'ah law is believed to be God's law so it cannot be unjust. Therefore this is not a good reason.

Even though some people believe they have a justified reason for committing crimes, everybody must obey the law. This helps society to live in peace without fear of danger. Christians believe God put the system of government in place to rule every citizen.

Regardless of the reasons why crimes are committed, most crimes are selfish because they harm innocent people in order that the criminal can get what they want or need.

> "Let everyone be subject to the governing authorities, for there is no authority except that which God has established."
> *Romans 13:1* [NIV]

APPLY

A Explain **two** reasons why people commit crimes.

B 'Addiction is the only good reason for committing crimes.'
Write down your own thoughts about this and **develop them by adding religious views**.

RECAP

9.3 Attitudes to lawbreakers and different types of crime

Essential information:

☐ Many Christians and Muslims condemn the crimes people commit but do not hate the people who commit them.

Attitudes to lawbreakers

Christian views

- Christians believe the law should be respected.
- Offenders must be punished by the law according to the seriousness of the crime.
- Offenders have basic rights and so should not be given a punishment that is inhumane or harmful. Through their punishment they should be helped to become a useful member of society so they do not re-offend.
- The parable of the Sheep and Goats makes it clear that helping prisoners is helping Jesus:

> “I was in prison and you came to visit me.” *Matthew 25:34–36* [NIV]

- Some Christians think the punishment should be as severe as the crime committed.

Muslim views

> “God commands justice … and prohibits wrongdoing, and injustice.” *Qur'an 16:90*

- Muslims believe that the law must be obeyed, especially by those living in countries governed by Shari'ah law.
- In Britain, Muslims support the UK legal system, despite it not being Shari'ah, even though there may be some laws they do not agree with.
- Shari'ah punishments fit the seriousness of the crime. Severe punishments are given for crimes prohibited in the Qur'an (such as murder, adultery, theft and drinking alcohol), but the most severe are not used in Britain.
- Shari'ah punishments are intended to be severe enough to make sure the offender does not re-offend.

Different types of crime – hate crime, theft and murder

- **Hate crimes** often involve violence and are usually targeted at a person because of their race, religion, sexuality, disability or gender.
- **Theft** is less serious than some other crimes but it still results in a victim suffering loss.
- **Murder** is one of the worst crimes. Some murders involve the victim being put in great pain before they die. Some murders are classed as hate crimes.

Religious attitudes to different types of crime

- Hate crimes are widely condemned by both Christians and Muslims. When Jesus taught that people should love their neighbour, he was referring to showing compassion, care and respect to everybody. This means that Jesus himself would condemn criminal actions because no crime shows love towards the victim.
- Murder is wrong because both Christians and Muslims believe only God has the right and authority to take life.

> “You shall not murder.” *Exodus 20:13* [NIV]

> “Do not take life which God has made sacred, except by right.” *Qur'an 17:33*

- Similarly, theft is not permitted in the Ten Commandments. Neither Christians nor Muslims justify theft caused by the need to supply food for a family.

TIP
See page 123 for Christian and Muslim beliefs about poverty as a reason for crime.

APPLY

A Explain the similarities and differences between a hate crime and murder.

B Should religious believers hate the crime but not the criminal who has committed it? **Explain your opinion** and elaborate it with religious teachings.

TIP
When elaborating a developed idea with religious teachings, you should show how the teachings are relevant.

9.4 Three aims of punishment

RECAP

Essential information:

☐ Three aims of punishment are retribution, deterrence and reformation.

> **TIP** To protect other people in the community is another aim of punishment that you can use if you wish.

Aim	Explanation	Christian attitude	Muslim attitude
Retribution – to get your own back 	• Society is getting its own back on the offender. • It is supported by the Old Testament idea of 'life for life, eye for eye, tooth for tooth' (Exodus 21:23–25 [NIV]), which is interpreted as meaning that criminals should receive back the same (not greater) injuries and harm that their criminal actions caused. • In the case of murder, the murderer should be killed as a punishment.	• Christians believe the 'eye for eye' teaching should not be taken literally but that punishment should be severe enough (but not more severe) to match the seriousness of the crime. • This means murderers should not necessarily be killed as punishment. • Most Christians prefer other aims which they believe are less harmful and more positive. "Do not take revenge... but leave room for God's wrath for it is written: "It is mine to avenge; I will repay," says the Lord." *Romans 12:19* [NIV]	• The Qur'an says 'We prescribed for them a life for a life, an eye for an eye' (Qur'an 5:45), which is interpreted as meaning that criminals should receive back the same (not greater) injuries than their criminal actions caused. • Murderers should not always be killed as punishment. The victim's family can accept compensation for showing mercy to the murderer and prevent him from being executed. • Retribution is favoured because actions against Shari'ah law are actions against God.
Deterrence – to put people off committing crimes 	• The idea of deterrence is to use the punishment an offender receives as an example and warning to others. • If the punishment is harsh, it is less likely that others will copy the crime. • In addition, harsh punishment may deter the offender from repeating their crime.	• Although most Christians agree with deterring people from committing crimes, they do not support punishments that cause physical or mental harm to the offender or infringe their rights. • They oppose public punishments because they think offenders should be treated with respect, despite what they have done.	• Some Shari'ah punishments are carried out in public to deter people watching from committing similar crimes. Punishments might include the amputation of the hand of a thief or the execution of a murderer. "Cut off the hands of thieves, whether they are man or woman, as punishment for what they have done – a deterrent from God." *Qur'an 5:38*
Reformation – to change someone's behaviour for the better 	• Offenders may be given treatment such as counselling and made to carry out community service to help them to understand that their behaviour was wrong because it harmed society. • It is hoped that offenders will change their attitude so that they can return to the community as a responsible law-abiding citizen.	• Most Christians favour reformation over other aims of punishment. • It is positive rather than negative and works with individuals to improve their life chances. • It is not a replacement for punishments but happens alongside punishment even for the worst offenders.	• It is necessary for offenders to seek forgiveness from God and become purified. This becomes more likely if the offender is reformed. Education and financial advice may be used to assist reform. • It is not a replacement for punishment but happens alongside punishment even for the worst offenders.

APPLY

A Write **two** sentences to explain what each of the three aims of punishment are.

B **Write a detailed argument** to support your own opinion about whether offenders should be punished severely. Try to include some religious teaching.

> **TIP** The three aims of punishment may be useful to develop your ideas if writing about other aspects of punishment.

RECAP

9.5 Religious attitudes to suffering and causing suffering to others

Essential information:

- ☐ Suffering can be caused by natural events (e.g. illness, an earthquake) or by human behaviour (e.g. assault, a car crash etc.).
- ☐ Both Christians and Muslims believe that they must not ignore causing suffering to others and repair any damage they may have caused.
- ☐ Suffering is an unfortunate part of life that no one can avoid.

Religious attitudes to suffering

Christian beliefs	Muslim beliefs
• Whatever the cause, Christians believe they have a duty to help those who are suffering and recognise that good can come from suffering. • Paul, who suffered greatly at some points in his life, wrote: "We also glory in our sufferings, because we know that suffering produces perseverance; perseverance, character; and character, hope." *Romans 5:3–4* [NIV] • Christians try to follow the example of Jesus. He helped many whom he saw were suffering and told his followers to do the same.	• God allows suffering to happen, often for reasons unknown to people. • Suffering may be a test from God. Iblis (Satan) tempts people to cause suffering. God will never allow a person to suffer more than they can endure. "You are sure to be tested through your possessions and persons; you are sure to hear much that is hurtful … If you are steadfast and mindful of God, that is the best course." *Qur'an 3:186* • Muslims believe they have a duty to help those who are suffering and recognise that good can come from suffering.

Why does a loving God allow people to suffer?

- It is wrong to blame God for suffering resulting from human actions.
- God could control people to stop them from doing wrong.
- Instead, Christians and Muslims believe that God gave humans **free will** (the ability to make decisions for themselves) and has given guidance about how to use free will responsibly.
- This does not mean that humans can do whatever they want, whenever they want to do it because this would certainly not prevent suffering. If anything, it would increase it.
- The role of the law is to give more guidance about the best way to use free will, together with punishments for those who cause suffering by committing crimes.

Religious attitudes to causing suffering to others

Christian beliefs	Muslim beliefs
• Jesus taught that people should love and respect each other and not use violence in self-defence because it may increase suffering. • However, this does not always work and on occasions, maybe accidentally, Christians do cause others to suffer. • If and when this happens, Christians are taught to apologise and to try to repair the damage they have caused in order to restore relationships. E.g. at Jesus' arrest, one disciple cut off the High Priest's servant's ear. Jesus rebuked the disciple and healed the servant. • So Christians can try to heal the wrong that has been done and the suffering that has been caused.	• Muslims share identity with the whole Muslim community (the ummah) and care and provide for those in need. • Because no human is perfect, on occasions, maybe accidentally, Muslims do cause others to suffer. • If and when that happens, Muslims are taught to be honest with themselves and with God and to try to repair the damage they have caused in order to restore relationships. • God will forgive any Muslim who tries to right their wrong and sincerely repents, just as he did with Adam and Haawa (Eve) when they were tempted to eat the forbidden fruit by Iblis.

APPLY

A Explain carefully what Christians and Muslims believe about free will and how it should be used.

B 'Using violence in self-defence only causes more suffering.'

Think carefully about this and **write a developed argument** to support your opinion about it.

RECAP

9.6 The treatment of criminals – prison, corporal punishment and community service

Essential information:

- [ ] You need to know about three forms of punishment: **prison** (a secure building where offenders are kept for a period of time), **corporal punishment** (punishment of an offender by causing them pain, now illegal in the UK) and **community service** (punishing offenders by making them do unpaid work in the community).
- [ ] Christian and Muslim beliefs and attitudes to the treatment of criminals vary.

You might be asked to compare beliefs on corporal punishment between Christianity (the main religious tradition in Great Britain) and another religious tradition.

Forms of punishment for criminals

	Christian beliefs	Muslim beliefs
Prison • A punishment for serious crimes • The punishment is loss of liberty • Prisoners have no real choice about how to spend their time – everything is controlled for them • They are locked in cells, fed and allowed exercise and interaction with other prisoners at set times • They work in the prison for very little money or take part in training or education programmes	Many Christians believe that prisoners should be treated well when in prison and are keen to support them to make their time in prison useful by encouraging positive activity. They believe it is important that conditions within prison are humane and civilised.	In Muslim countries, prison is used less for punishment and more as a place to keep people awaiting trial or punishment such as caning (corporal punishment) or death. Some Muslims argue that prison may be a greater penalty than inflicting pain through corporal punishment.
Corporal punishment • Punishes offenders by inflicting physical pain • Illegal in the UK and many other countries • Some Muslim countries use corporal punishment such as caning for some offences and amputation of the hand for theft • Punishments often take place in public • Considered to be a breach of human rights	Most Christians do not support corporal punishment. It does not seek to reform an offender and it physically harms the person, so it is seen as a negative and harmful punishment.	Corporal punishment is used in some Muslim countries. It is often carried out in public and they believe it serves as a deterrent, persuading others not to break certain laws. It is laid down in Shari'ah law and can be imposed for offences such as gambling, adultery and drinking alcohol (80 lashes).
Community service • A punishment for minor offences • Allows offenders the chance to reform • Includes 'community payback' which involves doing supervised work in the community, such as cleaning graffiti off buildings • Can include treatment for addiction or medical conditions, counselling or educational opportunities • In some cases, and with the agreement of the victim, a meeting may be set up so the victim can give their side of the story and the offender can apologise for their actions	Christians agree with community service for offenders who are likely to benefit from it. It allows them to make up for what they have done wrong (reparation), deters them from committing offences in the future and reforms them by making them realise the consequences of their actions. No harm is done to the offender which is a positive step.	Shari'ah law makes little use of community service because it is not seen as a sufficient deterrent to protect society from future criminal behaviour. Punishments for Ta'azir crimes (community crimes, such as fraud or anti-social behaviour) are not specified in Shari'ah law and can include rehabilitation.

APPLY

A Explain the different beliefs in Christianity and Islam about corporal punishment.

B 'Criminals should not be treated well.'

What **religious arguments** would you include when evaluating this statement?

9.7 Religious attitudes to forgiveness

RECAP

Essential information:

- [ ] Christians and Muslims believe that **forgiveness** (showing mercy and pardoning someone for what they have done wrong) is important for living a peaceful life.
- [ ] Christians and Muslims do not think forgiveness is a replacement for punishment.

You might be asked to compare beliefs on forgiveness between Christianity (the main religious tradition in Great Britain) and another religious tradition.

Christian attitudes to forgiveness

- The Christian interpretation of forgiveness for those who commit crimes is that they should be forgiven as far as possible, but the offender should be punished to ensure that justice is done.
- If the aim of the punishment is to reform, the punishment should benefit the offender.
- When he was being crucified, Jesus forgave those who crucified him after having been found guilty and sentenced to death:

> "Father forgive them, for they do not know what they are doing." *Luke 23:34* [NIV]

- God expects Christians to show forgiveness to others, no matter what they may have done. In turn, they believe that God will forgive them for any sins they may commit. This is emphasised in the Lord's Prayer:

> "Forgive us our sins as we forgive those who sin against us." *The Lord's Prayer*

- Jesus also told his followers that there is no upper limit to the use of forgiveness.

> "'Lord, how many times shall I forgive my brother when he sins against me? Up to seven times?' Jesus answered, 'I tell you, not seven times, but seventy-seven times.'" *Matthew 18:21–22* [NIV]

TIP

Remember that forgiveness is a core belief in Christianity, although many would argue that it is not a replacement for punishment. In the UK, a person convicted of murder will receive a lengthy prison sentence regardless of whether friends and family of the victim have forgiven them.

In Islam, punishment must satisfy the demands of God and society. However, Muslims can show forgiveness by taking compensation from an offender rather than insisting on the death penalty.

Muslim attitudes to forgiveness

There are two types of forgiveness in Islam:

- **Forgiveness from God** – Only God can truly forgive and will only forgive those he knows are truly sorry and intend to follow the faith properly in the future. This is in line with the compassionate and merciful nature of God.

> "Let them pardon and forgive. Do you not wish that God should forgive you? God is most forgiving and merciful." *Qur'an 24:22*

- **Forgiveness from humans** – People should forgive each other in order to allow goodness to be established over evil. The offender should seek the forgiveness of the victim before expecting God to forgive. If the forgiven act is unknowingly repeated, it should be forgiven again.

> "Pardon each other's faults and [God] will grant you honour." *Hadith*

APPLY

A Show how Christian beliefs about forgiveness are different from Muslim ones.

B 'Nobody should expect to be forgiven more than once.'

Write a logical chain of reasoning that agrees with this statement and one that gives a different point of view.

TIP

Knowing and using an example of someone who has forgiven may assist you in this unit.

RECAP

9.8 Religious attitudes to the death penalty

Essential information:

The **death penalty** is a form of punishment in which a prisoner is put to death for their crimes. Arguments about the death penalty are often based on:

- **the principle of utility** – the idea that an action is right if it promotes maximum happiness for the maximum number of people
- **the sanctity of life** – the idea that all life is holy as it is created and loved by God; human life should not be misused or abused.

You might be asked to compare beliefs on the death penalty between Christianity (the main religious tradition in Great Britain) and another religious tradition.

The debate about the death penalty

The death penalty was abolished in the UK in 1969 so since then, no criminal has been executed in the UK. It is also illegal in the European Community but still exists in some states in the USA, China and in some Muslim countries, such as Saudi Arabia.

Innocent people may die	Principle of utility	Sanctity of life
• Several people executed in the UK in the 1950s have since been pardoned because new evidence has cast serious doubt over their guilt. • There are several people who would have faced the death penalty who were later freed from prison because they were innocent.	• It seems likely that the principle of utility should support the death penalty. • However, if the death penalty is used as retribution, it is wrong. • If it is proven to protect society, it can be justified because many people will benefit.	• The sanctity of life suggests that the death penalty is wrong. • However, some religious believers think that justice overrides the sanctity of life. • The Old Testament teaching of 'eye for eye' can be used to support this view.

Christian attitudes to the death penalty

Christians across many denominations have different views about the death penalty. Some of the arguments they use are based on Bible passages and others relate to general Christian and social principles.

Agree	Disagree
• Genesis 9:6 and Exodus 21:23–24 teach retribution. • Retribution is justified for people who commit the worst possible crimes. • It deters people from committing horrific crimes because they know what will happen to them. • It protects society by removing the worst criminals so they cannot cause harm again.	• Ezekiel 33:11 teaches that wrongdoers should be reformed. • The best aim of punishment is reformation. A dead criminal cannot be reformed and given a second chance. • There is little evidence that the death penalty is a deterrent. The UK murder rate is no higher than in countries that have the death penalty. • Many murders are done on the spur of the moment. The threat of punishment doesn't enter into the murderer's thinking. • God gave life and only God has the right and authority to take it.

Muslim attitudes to the death penalty

> "Do not take life, which God has made sacred, except by right." *Qur'an 6:151*

- Muslim teachings favour the death penalty and Shari'ah law suggests that it should be used for some crimes including murder and rape. This is seen as a deterrent and fair retribution.
- However, the victim is encouraged to show mercy by accepting money from the offender to save their life.

> "But if the culprit is pardoned by his aggrieved brother, this shall be adhered to fairly, and the culprit shall pay what is due in a good way." *Qur'an 2:178*

- Not all Muslims agree with the death penalty. Some see it as a misinterpretation of the Qur'an's teaching.

APPLY

A Identify **two** religious teachings about the death penalty.

B **Write a paragraph to support the statement**, 'No religious believer should support the death penalty.' Include religious teachings.

9 Exam practice

Test the 1 mark multiple-choice question

1 Which **one** of the following punishments is illegal in the UK?

A Corporal punishment B Prison C Paying a fine D Community service **[1 mark]**

2 Which **one** of the following is correct? An action is right if it follows the principle of utility and promotes the maximum...?

A Pain B Sadness C Happiness D Profit **[1 mark]**

Test the 1 mark question

3 Give **one** aim of punishment. **[1 mark]**

____

4 Give **one** reason why some people commit crimes. **[1 mark]**

____

Test the 4 mark question

5 Explain **two** different beliefs in contemporary British society about whether the death penalty should be restored in the UK.

In your answer you should refer to the main religious tradition of Great Britain and one or more other religious traditions. **[4 marks]**

• **Explain one belief.**	*Some Christians believe that the death penalty is correct because it follows the Old Testament teaching of 'eye for eye, tooth for tooth'.*
• Develop your explanation with more detail/an example/ reference to a religious teaching or quotation.	*'Eye for eye, tooth for tooth' means that an offender should receive back the same as he or she has done, so if he has murdered someone, he should be killed.*
• **Explain a second belief.**	*Muslims also believe that although the death penalty is justified for murder, the family of the victim can accept payment from the murderer in order to save his life.*
• Develop your explanation with more detail/an example/ reference to a religious teaching or quotation.	*If they accept payment, their merciful action is considered to be a good deed and will help them to gain a place in paradise. The murderer is likely to face spending the rest of their life in prison.*

6 Explain **two** different beliefs about community service.

In your answer you must refer to one or more religious traditions. **[4 marks]**

• **Explain one belief.**	
• Develop your explanation with more detail/an example/ reference to a religious teaching or quotation.	
• **Explain a second belief.**	
• Develop your explanation with more detail/an example/ reference to a religious teaching or quotation.	

7 Explain **two** similar religious beliefs that support retribution as an aim of punishment.
In your answer you must refer to one or more religious traditions. **[4 marks]**

Test the 6 mark question

8 Explain **two** religious beliefs about reformation as an aim of punishment.
Refer to sacred writings or another source of religious belief and teaching in your answer. **[6 marks]**

• **Explain one belief.**	*One Christian belief is that reformation is a preferable aim of punishment because it seeks to help offenders change their behaviour.*
• Develop your explanation with more detail/an example.	*This means they are less likely to commit any further offences, so they won't hurt anybody else or need to be punished again.*
• **Explain a second belief.**	*A second Christian belief is that reformation is a compassionate response towards wrongdoing.*
• Develop your explanation with more detail/an example.	*Christians believe that to show compassion for others is to follow the teachings of Jesus, who told his disciples to turn the other cheek.*
• **Add a reference to sacred writings or another source of religious belief and teaching.** If you prefer, you can add the reference to your first belief instead.	*The words of Paul in Romans 12:21 support this idea: 'do not be overcome by evil, but overcome evil with good.'*
• Apply the reference by explaining how it links to the question.	*This suggests that retribution should not be used to get back at someone, and helping them to reform is a good action.*

TIP
When using scripture, you must show the examiner that you understand its relevance to the question.

9 Explain **two** religious beliefs about forgiveness.
Refer to sacred writings or another source of religious belief and teaching in your answer. **[6 marks]**

• **Explain one belief.**	
• Develop your explanation with more detail/an example.	
• **Explain a second belief.**	
• Develop your explanation with more detail/an example.	
• **Add a reference to sacred writings or another source of religious belief and teaching.** If you prefer, you can add the reference to your first belief instead.	
• Apply the reference by explaining how it links to the question.	

10 Explain **two** religious beliefs about hate crimes.
Refer to sacred writings or another source of religious belief and teaching in your answer. **[6 marks]**

Test the 12 mark question

11 'It is right to forgive all offenders whoever they are and whatever they have done.'

Evaluate this statement. In your answer you:

- should give reasoned arguments in support of this statement
- should give reasoned arguments to support a different point of view
- should refer to religious arguments
- may refer to non-religious arguments
- should reach a justified conclusion.

[12 marks]

Plus SPaG 3

REASONED ARGUMENTS IN SUPPORT OF THE STATEMENT ● **Explain why some people would agree with the statement.** ● Develop your explanation with more detail and examples, which may include non-religious ideas. ● Refer to religious teaching. Use a quote or paraphrase or refer to a religious authority. ● **Evaluate the arguments.** Is this a good argument or not? Explain why you think this.	*Christians should always forgive anybody who wants to be forgiven. When the disciples asked Jesus how many times they should forgive, suggesting that seven was a fair number, Jesus told them it should be seventy-seven times. In other words, there should be no maximum. Jesus even asked God to forgive the people who crucified him because they didn't know what they were doing. So it should not matter how many times, whoever is asking to be forgiven or what they have done to be forgiven for.* *If someone is forgiven, there is a better chance that they will be reformed and try hard to make sure that whatever they have done is never repeated. This is what repentance is about and forgiveness and repentance are closely linked. No sin is unforgiveable and so people, especially religious people, should always forgive, especially as this does not mean that the sinner is not punished because they have been forgiven.*
REASONED ARGUMENTS SUPPORTING A DIFFERENT VIEW ● **Explain why some people would support a different view.** ● Develop your explanation with more detail and examples, which may include non-religious ideas. ● Refer to religious teaching. Use a quote or paraphrase or refer to a religious authority. ● **Evaluate the arguments.** Is this a good argument or not? Explain why you think this.	*Some people who are victims of serious crimes find it very difficult to forgive. They cannot imagine how they can ever feel anything but hatred for someone who has wronged them so horribly. A victim of a serious crime may find it hard to forgive and they are highly unlikely to ever forget it. Time is a great healer and maybe forgiveness is more easily given some years later. The line in the Lord's Prayer that says: 'Forgive us our sins, as we forgive those who sin against us' is unrealistic because there are some awful things that should never be forgiven unless the offender shows they are truly sorry and remorseful, and even then, it is almost impossible. Many Jews find it impossible to forgive the Nazis for the Holocaust and why should they be expected to?*
CONCLUSION ● **Give a justified conclusion.** ● Include your own opinion together with your own reasoning. ● **Include evaluation.** Explain why you think one viewpoint is stronger than the other or why they are equally strong. ● Do not just repeat arguments you have already used without explaining how they apply to your reasoned opinion/conclusion.	*In my opinion, forgiveness is an ideal that religions want people to work towards. I think if they become the victims themselves, they may change their mind. We are only human. Maybe Muslims have it right because they teach that offenders should seek forgiveness from their victim before expecting God to forgive them. To me, this seems fair.*

TIP

The first paragraph no only shows good knowle of the Bible's teaching forgiveness but also ma its meaning clear. The r paragraph develops the argument by relating t teaching directly to th statement being evaluated.

TIP

In this case the student has used reli perspectives throughout the answer. is important to use religious argume in the answer to reach the higher lev but you may also use non-religious arguments. For example, non-religio people would see no reason to forgiv all offenders, because they would no be guided by religious teachings about forgiveness.

12 'The idea of the sanctity of life shows the death penalty is wrong.'

Evaluate this statement. In your answer you:

- should give reasoned arguments in support of this statement
- should give reasoned arguments to support a different point of view
- should refer to religious arguments
- may refer to non-religious arguments
- should reach a justified conclusion.

TIP Don't forget that the focus of the statement is on the sanctity of life and the death penalty, not just whether the death penalty is wrong.

[12 marks]
Plus SPaG 3 marks

REASONED ARGUMENTS IN SUPPORT OF THE STATEMENT ● **Explain why some people would agree with the statement.** ● Develop your explanation with more detail and examples, which may include non-religious ideas. ● Refer to religious teaching. Use a quote or paraphrase or refer to a religious authority. ● **Evaluate the arguments.** Is this a good argument or not? Explain why you think this.	
REASONED ARGUMENTS SUPPORTING A DIFFERENT VIEW ● **Explain why some people would support a different view.** ● Develop your explanation with more detail and examples, which may include non-religious ideas. ● Refer to religious teaching. Use a quote or paraphrase or refer to a religious authority. ● **Evaluate the arguments.** Is this a good argument or not? Explain why you think this.	
CONCLUSION ● **Give a justified conclusion.** ● Include your own opinion together with your own reasoning. ● **Include evaluation.** Explain why you think one viewpoint is stronger than the other or why they are equally strong. ● Do not just repeat arguments you have already used without explaining how they apply to your reasoned opinion/conclusion.	

13 'There is no good reason why anyone should commit a crime.'

Evaluate this statement. In your answer you:

- should give reasoned arguments in support of this statement
- should give reasoned arguments to support a different point of view
- should refer to religious arguments
- may refer to non-religious arguments
- should reach a justified conclusion.

TIP Don't forget to include a logical chain of reasoning.

[12 marks]
Plus SPaG 3 marks

Check your answers using the mark scheme on page 157. How did you do?
To feel more secure in the content you need to remember, re-read pages 122–129.
To remind yourself of what the examiner is looking for, go to pages 6–11.

10 Religion, human rights and social justice

10.1 Social justice and human rights

RECAP

Essential information:

- [ ] **Social justice** is ensuring that society treats people fairly whether they are living in poverty or wealthy, and protects people's **human rights** – the basic rights and freedoms to which all humans should be entitled.
- [ ] All people have a **responsibility** (a duty of care) not to harm the rights of others.

Christian and Muslim beliefs

Working for justice is a religious and social responsibility for Muslims and Christians.

Christians promote social justice by:	Muslims promote social justice by:
• following Jesus' teaching as in the parable of the Sheep and the Goats (Matthew 25:31-46). • campaigning to improve the lives of the less fortunate in society.	• giving Zakah (alms). This is a compulsory payment of 2.5% of their savings to good causes every year. • becoming involved in social and community projects such as working with people experiencing homelessness or living in poverty.

The Universal Declaration of Human Rights (UDHR)

- The UDHR, which the UK signed, was adopted by the United Nations in **1948**. It states:

> "All human beings are born free and equal in dignity and rights. They are endowed with reason and conscience and should act towards one another in a spirit of brotherhood." *The Universal Declaration of Human Rights*

- In **1998**, the UK government passed the Human Rights Act that reinforces the UDHR. It prohibits slavery, torture and forced labour and includes the rights to life, liberty, security, education, privacy, a fair trial, family life, free elections and to get married.

Cairo Declaration of Human Rights (CDHR) and Muslim teachings

In **1990** the 57 states in the Organisation of the Islamic Conference adopted the CDHR based on the Qur'an, Sunnah and Islamic legal tradition. All the rights and freedoms included in the CDHR are subject to Shari'ah law.

> "All men are equal in terms of basic human dignity and basic obligations and responsibilities, without any discrimination on the basis of race, colour, language, belief, sex, religion, political affiliation, social status or other considerations." *Cairo Declaration of Human Rights*

Responsibilities

- Humans have the right to freedom of speech but the responsibility not to say something that causes offence to someone else.
- Children have the right to protection from cruelty and neglect but the responsibility not to harm each other.
- This applies to individuals, as well as countries and their governments.

APPLY

A Explain how social justice may influence the way a religious person lives.

B 'Everybody's human rights should be protected.'

Write a detailed argument agreeing with this statement and one for a different opinion.

TIP

If you are including scripture in your answer, don't worry if you can't remember the quote exactly. Summarize or paraphrase it instead.

10.2 Prejudice and discrimination

RECAP

Essential information:

- [ ] Christians and Muslims believe in **equality** – that humans are of equal value and status.
- [ ] **Prejudice** (holding biased opinions about an individual or group without knowing all the facts) and **discrimination** (the actions or behaviour that result from prejudice) go against Christian and Muslim teaching.

TIP
Remember:
attitudes (thinking) = prejudice
actions and behaviour (doing) = discrimination.

Equality

- Christians and Muslims both believe that being created in God's image makes people very special and precious.
- Whatever their status, religion or gender, they are equally valuable and can have the same relationship with God.
- People should only be judged on how well they live their lives in obedience to God, not on wealth or status.

> "There is neither Jew nor Gentile [non-Jew], neither slave nor free, nor is there male or female for you are all one in Christ Jesus." *Galatians 3:28* [NIV]

> "People are equal as the teeth of a comb." *Hadith*

- Jesus taught people to treat everyone as having equal value when he said, 'love your neighbour as yourself' (Mark 12:31 [NIV]).

Christian and Muslim views on prejudice based on sexuality

- Following the example and teaching in Genesis and the Qur'an about Adam and Eve, opposite-sex sexual relationships (between a man and a woman) became considered to be natural and what God intended.
- Same-sex sexual relationships (between man and man, or woman and woman) are more controversial.

Christian views	Muslim views
• Some Christians see same-sex sexual relationships as sinful whilst others see them as morally acceptable. • Those who oppose same-sex sexual relationships believe that the purpose of a sexual relationship is to create children, something that same-sex couples cannot do.	• Many Muslims see same-sex sexual relationships as sinful and against Shari'ah law, whilst others see them as acceptable and loving. • In some countries, same-sex sexual relationships are punishable by death. In others, people who are attracted to people of the same sex are encouraged to repent rather than confess.

- Those who think same-sex sexual relationships are acceptable focus more on the love between people, rather than on the sexual act which is of lower importance.
- Recent changes in British legislation have given equality to everybody regardless of sexuality and same-sex couples can now legally marry.
- Some Muslim countries, e.g. Lebanon and Turkey, are debating whether to allow same-sex marriage.

TIP
For more religious beliefs about human sexuality go to page 74.

APPLY

A Explain the difference between prejudice and discrimination.

B **Write a developed reason** for agreeing that all people are born equal and one for a different opinion.

TIP
In a question such as this, there is no need for you to express your opinion.

10.3 Religious freedom

RECAP

Essential information:

Religions believe that people have **freedom of religion** (the right to believe or practise whatever religion one chooses) and **freedom of religious expression** (the right to worship, preach or practise one's faith in whatever way one chooses).

> You might be asked to compare beliefs on freedom of religious expression between Christianity (the main religious tradition in Great Britain) and another religious tradition.

Religious freedom

- Christianity is currently the main religious tradition in Great Britain.
- The reigning monarch is the official Head of the Church of England and has been referred to as the 'defender of the faith' since 1521.
- The government protects the freedom of religious expression which gives all individuals the right to follow whichever faith they choose or none.
- Laws forbid the persecution of members of any faith, and any person can encourage anybody else to follow their faith, provided they do not preach hatred and intolerance.
- These freedoms are protected in both the Universal and the Cairo Declaration of Human Rights.

> "Everyone has the right to freedom of thought, conscience and religion; this right includes freedom to change his religion and belief, and freedom … to manifest his religion or belief in teaching, practice, worship and observance." *UDHR*

- In some parts of the world governments do not allow their citizens such freedoms.
- In Britain there are still some who discriminate against members of particular religious traditions.
- Those found guilty of such behaviour in Britain can be punished by a court.
- Conflict based on politics and a divide between Protestants and Catholics in Northern Ireland during the second half of the twentieth century has largely been ended.

Religious teachings on freedom of religion

Christian beliefs	Muslim beliefs
• Christian teaching encourages tolerance and harmony. • Different Christian denominations fighting each other or against other religions are not following Paul's words in the New Testament: "If it is possible, as far as it depends on you, live at peace with everyone." *Romans 12:18* [NIV] "Watch out for those who cause divisions and put obstacles in your way that are contrary to the teaching you have learned. Keep away from them." *Romans 16:17* [NIV]	• Muslims believe that religious freedom is part of God's design and freedom of belief is taught in the Qur'an. "Now the truth has come from your Lord: let those who wish to believe in it do so and let those who wish to reject it do so." *Qur'an 18:29* • The whole of a believer's life can be seen as religious expression if it is lived according to God's will. • Shari'ah law does have provisions to punish people who convert from Islam to another faith, although these are only strongly enforced in a few countries. • Some Muslim countries have strict blasphemy laws that stop people criticising the Qur'an, Muhammad, Jesus or any of the prophets.

In Britain, Christians and Muslims join followers of other faiths in interfaith organisations. They promote constructive dialogue that highlights what faiths have in common and promote harmony not division.

APPLY

A Explain the attitudes to freedom of religion from the main religious tradition of Great Britain and one or more other religious traditions.

B **Explain, with reference to religion**, whether you think people should be free to follow any religion they choose without any interference from anybody else.

10.4 Prejudice and discrimination – race

RECAP

Essential information:

- ☐ Christians and Muslims oppose racial prejudice and other forms of discrimination.
- ☐ **Positive discrimination** (treating people more favourably because they have been discriminated against in the past) can help to ensure equality of opportunity.

Racism

- **Racism** means showing prejudice against someone because of their ethnic group or nationality.
- In Britain, racism was made illegal in the 1976 Race Relations Act.

Christian beliefs

- Christians oppose racism. It denies equality of opportunity to people purely because of where they come from or the colour of their skin.

> "There is neither Jew nor Gentile, neither slave nor free, nor is there male and female for you are one in Christ Jesus." *Galatians 3:28* [NIV]

- At the time this was a revolutionary way of thinking and the fact that discrimination is still a problem in some parts of the world shows Paul's vision is still not completely accepted.
- In the twentieth century, races were kept apart with black people being discriminated against in countries such as South Africa and the USA.
- The actions of Christians such as Archbishop Desmond Tutu (South Africa) and Dr Martin Luther King (USA), with the help of others, persuaded their respective governments that racist policies were unfair and needed to be changed.

Muslim beliefs

- The Qur'an does not support the idea that differences of race or skin colour justify treating people unfairly.
- It also teaches equality and that differences in the way people look shows God's creativity and variety.

> "People, We created you all from a single man and a single woman, and made you into races and tribes so that you should get to know each other." *Qur'an 49:13*

> "An Arab is not better than a non-Arab and a non-Arab is not better than an Arab; a white person is not better than a black person, nor is a black person better than a white person…" *Muhammad*

- The Muslim brotherhood (ummah) makes no distinction between people of different races.

Positive discrimination

The use of positive discrimination can help groups that have previously been discriminated against gain equal access to opportunities.

- For example, people with disabilities sometimes experience discrimination and often do not have equal access to physical spaces. Many people support the use of positive discrimination, e.g. giving wheelchair users front-row positions at a football ground so they can see the match.
- Some political parties in Britain may use positive discrimination to give more women the chance to be elected to Parliament, because there have always been many more male MPs than female.

APPLY

A Explain why religious believers disagree with racial prejudice.

B 'All discrimination is wrong.'

Write a chain of reasoning in support of this statement and also for a different point of view. Give your opinion with a reason, then develop and elaborate it with some religious teaching.

TIP

A statement such as this is difficult to argue against. In this instance, positive discrimination could help you to come up with such an argument.

10.5 The status and roles of women

RECAP

Essential information:

- Both Christians and Muslims believe that women and men have equal status in the eyes of God. They are of equal value and will be held equally accountable for their actions.
- The roles of women within religions vary as attitudes have changed through the years.

TIP
Being equal does not mean everybody is the same.

Christian views on the roles of women in religion

- At the time of the early Christians (first century CE), attitudes to women were very different from today. Paul wrote:

> " Women should remain silent in the churches. They are not allowed to speak […] for it is disgraceful for a woman to speak in the church. " *1 Corinthians 14:34–35* [NIV]

- He also wrote that just as Christ is the head of man, so a man is head of a woman.
- Many Christians believe that Paul's writings are a reflection of the times he lived in. Society has now changed and what 2000 years ago seemed right and normal is not so now.
- Some Christian non-conformist Churches have ordained women as ministers for nearly 100 years.
- The Catholic and Orthodox Churches do not allow women to be priests.
- In 1993 women were allowed to become priests in the Church of England and in 2014, Rev Libby Lane became the first female bishop.

You might be asked to compare beliefs on the status of women in religion between Christianity (the main religious tradition in Great Britain) and another religious tradition.

Muslim views on the roles of women in religion

Muslims believe that men and women were designed for different purposes.

- Traditionally men are the providers and women bring up children and look after the home.
- Women have the responsibility to teach their children the basics of Islam.
- Mothers teach their children about their future roles as husband and father or wife and mother.
- Many women now have a paid job. The money they earn is for themselves.
- Men are also expected to take a role in the home.

Although all Muslims have a duty to obey and worship God, women have a different role from men.

- As mothers, women do not have to attend mosque five times a day for prayers, nor for Jummah (Friday) prayer. If they choose to attend, they worship separately from men.
- Even though Muslim women can become scholars, teachers and in some cases preachers, they cannot become an imam unless no man is present at the worship.

TIP
For more about religious views on sexuality and gender equality, go to pages 74 and 81.

APPLY

A Explain **two** religious beliefs about the role of women in religion.

B 'It is unfair to treat people differently due to their gender or sexuality.'

Give reasoned arguments to support this statement. Include religious teaching in your answer.

10.6 Teachings about wealth

Essential information:

Christians and Muslims both believe that wealth is a gift from God and should be used responsibly.

You might be asked to compare beliefs on the uses of wealth between Christianity (the main religious tradition in Great Britain) and another religious tradition.

What does the Bible say about wealth?

- The Old Testament says that to thank God, people should pay a **tithe** (one-tenth of annual produce or earnings) to God, to be shared among people living in poverty. (Deuteronomy 14:22) Today some Christians choose to pay a tithe to the Church.
- The focus of the New Testament teaching on wealth is on the dangers associated with it such as greed and selfishness.
- It is easy to become so involved with money that you neglect your spiritual life and forget to love God and love your neighbour. (Matthew 6:24 and 33)
- God's wish is for people to set their hearts on him rather than things on earth which are temporary. (1 Timothy 6:17)

> "Be sure to set aside a tenth of all that your fields produce each year." *Deuteronomy 14:22* [NIV]

> "For the love of money is a root of all sorts of evil." *1 Timothy 6:10* [NIV]

TIP
If you use the quotation from 1 Timothy 6:10, you must include 'for the love of' at the beginning otherwise you change its meaning.

Muslim principles

- Wealth is a blessing from God and should be used to benefit everybody. It should not be gained from gambling, fraud, deception and producing or selling alcohol.
- The value of money is only in the good it can do, especially helping people living in poverty.
- Having wealth is not wrong but hoarding excessive wealth is discouraged.

> "Tell those who hoard gold and silver instead of giving in God's cause that they will have a grievous punishment." *Qur'an 9:34*

- A Muslim's first responsibility is to serve God and too much wealth can be a distraction.
- Greed and selfishness must be avoided and exploitation of others is wrong.

> "Beware of greed for it is ready poverty." *Hadith*

- Islam teaches that **usury** – the act of loaning money with interest – is forbidden.

> "God blights usury, but blesses charitable deeds with multiple increase." *Qur'an 2:27*

What is the responsible use of wealth?

Christian views	Muslim views
• Everybody needs money to live but Christians believe that those with excess money should give it to the Church for its upkeep and mission, including providing for people living in poverty. • The Parable of the Rich Man and Lazarus ended with a rich man in hell for not helping Lazarus the beggar (Luke 16:19–31). • The Parable of the Sheep and Goats states that those who help people living in poverty are rewarded with a place in heaven.	• The first duty of a husband is to provide for his wife and children. • It is a duty to consider others and to use any remaining money for them. • Muslims are required to give 2.5% of their savings to the mosque every year for people living in poverty (**Zakah**). This purifies the remainder of what they have. • They are encouraged to choose to make any additional voluntary contributions to charity (**Sadaqah**).

APPLY

A Explain **two** religious teachings about wealth.

B 'Giving to charity should be compulsory.'

Write a developed argument in support of the statement.

TIP
You do not have to believe any teachings you use. If they are relevant and help you to develop your answer, you should use them.

10.7 Exploitation of people living in poverty

RECAP

Essential information:

- [ ] There is **exploitation** (misuse of power or money to get others to do things for unfair reward) of people living in poverty worldwide.
- [ ] They are exploited by being paid unfairly, excessive interest on loans and **people trafficking** – the illegal movement of people, typically for the purposes of forced labour or sexual exploitation.

Fair pay

- Most Christians and Muslims would agree with the Organisation of the Islamic Conference (OIC) 1990 statement:

> “All workers shall be entitled – without any discrimination between males and females – to fair wages for his work without delay, as well as to the holidays, allowances and promotions which he deserves. On his part, he shall be required to be dedicated and meticulous in his work.” *Organisation of the Islamic Conference*

- In 2025, the National Living Wage in Britain was £12.21 per hour for workers aged 21 or over; it is less for younger workers.
- The majority of people in Britain earn more than the National Living Wage. In many low-income countries, the National Living Wage does not exist and many workers are paid a small fraction of the minimum in Britain.
- Some are so desperate that they are forced into work in textiles factories where they work hard for little reward, making clothes for wealthy countries such as Britain. Conditions in the factories are often unsafe. Labour rights such as fair pay, working conditions and hours worked are ignored.
- As long as companies are prepared to buy goods cheaply and sell them for a large profit, people will continue to be exploited.

Excessive interest on loans

For those living in poverty:

- Cheap loans are not available, so there is often little choice but to go to a loan company that offers small short-term loans with massive interest rates (sometimes over 1000%).
- These unsecured 'payday loans' are legal in Britain but end up costing people living in poverty vastly more than they borrow, especially if they cannot repay quickly.
- They are unlikely to be able to afford a mortgage so cannot buy a house, missing out on it increasing in value and providing them with a profit.

- The Christian Church does not oppose in principle the charging of interest but does oppose the charging of excessive interest on loans.
- Charging interest (**usury**) on loans is against Shari'ah law. It can lead to injustice and exploitation of people living in poverty.

People trafficking

- Moving to high-income countries is attractive to those in low-income countries because the quality of life is better.
- However, they may be restricted by immigration rules preventing them from settling or working in their target country.
- Many are forced into paying a people trafficker to transport them illegally.
- If they arrive, they may be found work by the trafficker with very low pay and in unsafe conditions, often in 'sweatshop' factories or in the sex industry as prostitutes.
- As they are working and living illegally, they cannot report this exploitation to the authorities.
- Some are kidnapped and trafficked to work against their will.
- The Qur'an 2:177 says that to 'liberate those in bondage' is a worthy act. Because trafficking exploits the vulnerable, it is against Islamic principles. Christians have similar beliefs.

TIP
When including religious teaching try to make it relevant and include your thoughts about it.

APPLY

A Explain why some people use people traffickers.

B 'High-income countries requiring cheap goods are to blame for exploitation.'

Write two chains of reasoning, one supporting the statement and one supporting a different opinion. Give your opinion with a reason, develop it and elaborate it with religious teaching.

10.8 Giving money to people living in poverty

RECAP

Essential information:

- Christians and Muslims have a religious duty to help people living in poverty.
- Those in need should also use their talents to provide for themselves by working.

Giving aid

- There are occasions when people need help to provide basic needs; for example, when a disaster strikes, **emergency aid** (short-term aid; help given in a time of crisis) is needed.
- Voluntary aid organisations such as **Christian Aid** and **Islamic Relief** immediately mobilise their workers, many of whom are volunteers, to provide emergency supplies such as food, water, blankets, basic shelter and medical supplies.
- The money for supplies and transport comes from charitable donations.
- Providing emergency aid is just a part of the work of charitable organisations.
- **Long-term aid** is assistance given to a low-income community over a long period of time that has a lasting effect. It consists of development work designed to help those who receive it to look after their own welfare.
- An old saying, used to illustrate the meaning of long-term aid is: 'Give a man a fish and feed him for one day, teach a man to fish and feed him for life.'
- The aim is to help people to become less dependent on outside aid and be more self-reliant.

Justice

Christians and Muslims believe strongly in fairness and justice. One way that justice is shown is through the **Fairtrade** movement, which provides long-term development opportunities based on trade, not charity.

- Fairtrade products are guaranteed to be grown and traded justly. Workers are paid fairly and work in good conditions.
- The price paid for the goods is a little higher than some non-Fairtrade goods, but consumers know that they are buying a product which has not been produced by workers who are exploited.
- Profits from the sale of Fairtrade products are used to further develop communities overseas.
- Fairtrade reduces the reliance on aid and gives people in low-income countries self-respect.
- Fairtrade allows Christians and Muslims to exercise the concept of **stewardship (khalifah)** – looking after the earth and people living on it on behalf of God – and show their love of God and their neighbour.

In Britain, people of all faiths support those in need by helping in soup kitchens and food banks and by helping the charities that support people living in poverty to find work so they can support themselves in future.

Responsibilities of those living in poverty

- Everybody has talents and abilities to help themselves out of poverty if they have the opportunity to do so.
- Providing opportunities is an important part of helping people to provide for themselves.
- Both Christians and Muslims encourage people living in poverty to help themselves by working, but there are some who are unable to do so. This may be because there are few jobs available in their area, they lack the qualifications required and training is not available, they are badly suited to certain jobs – possibly through disability – or their domestic arrangements make full-time work impossible.
- Muslims use Zakah payments to help people living in poverty in the community.
- However, Muslims are encouraged to work, if possible, so that they do not have to rely on the generosity of others.
- The same applies to Christians. Paul wrote 'If a man will not work, he shall not eat.' (2 Thessalonians 3:10 [NIV])
- Although the harshness of this reflects the situation and time in which it was written, it does stress that wherever possible, people should provide for themselves and their families by working.

APPLY

A Explain **two** ways that long-term aid enables people in low-income countries to provide for themselves.

B 'Religious believers don't do enough to help people living in poverty.'

Write one paragraph supporting this view and another which expresses a different point of view.

TIP

If writing about long-term aid, Fairtrade is a good example.

10 Exam practice

Test the 1 mark multiple-choice question

1 Which **one** of the following best describes prejudice?

A Doing something to someone which is unfair
B Misusing power to get people to do things
C Unfairly judging someone before knowing the facts
D Using violent action to harm someone **[1 mark]**

2 Which **one** of the following is **not** an action which goes against human rights?

A People trafficking
B Promoting tolerance
C Racial prejudice
D Exploiting people living in poverty **[1 mark]**

Test the 1 mark question

3 Give a definition of 'discrimination'. **[1 mark]**

____

4 Give **one** way in which a religious person should use their wealth. **[1 mark]**

____

Test the 4 mark question

5 Explain **two** different beliefs in contemporary British society about what role women should be allowed in worship.

In your answer you should refer to the main religious tradition of Great Britain and one or more other religious traditions. **[4 marks]**

• **Explain one belief.**	*The main religious tradition of Great Britain is Christianity and in many denominations women are allowed to take a full and active role in leading worship.*
• Develop your explanation with more detail/an example/reference to a religious teaching or quotation.	*For example, Libby Lane became an Anglican bishop, and in the United Reformed and Methodist denominations, women are also allowed to be preachers and ministers.*
• **Explain a second belief.**	*In contrast in Islam, although men and women are seen as equals they are believed to have been given different roles by God.*
• Develop your explanation with more detail/an example/reference to a religious teaching or quotation.	*A woman's duty is to teach the children about Islam in the home. The imam who leads the prayers at the mosque is usually a man.*

TIP
This is a good start to the answer. It immediately identifies Christianity as the main religious tradition of Great Britain.

6 Explain **two** different religious beliefs about prejudice based on sexuality.
In your answer you must refer to one or more religious traditions. **[4 marks]**

• **Explain one belief.**	
• Develop your explanation with more detail/an example/reference to a religious teaching or quotation.	
• **Explain a second belief.**	
• Develop your explanation with more detail/an example/reference to a religious teaching or quotation.	

TIP
Do not confuse prejudice based on sexuality with gender prejudice.

7 Explain **two** similar religious beliefs about the importance of human rights.
In your answer you must refer to one or more religious traditions. **[4 marks]**

10 Exam practice

Test the 6 mark question

8 Explain **two** religious beliefs about social justice.

Refer to sacred writings or another source of religious belief and teaching in your answer. **[6 marks]**

• **Explain one belief.**	*Muslims believe social justice is important because people should be treated as equals.*
• Develop your explanation with more detail/an example.	*All Muslims who can afford it have to give Zakah (alms). This is a compulsory payment of 2.5% of their savings to good causes every year.*
• **Explain a second belief.**	*Christians believe that working to promote social justice brings them closer to God.*
• Develop your explanation with more detail/an example.	*So, many Christians have campaigned to improve human rights, for example Martin Luther King Jr, who led a peaceful movement to achieve social justice for black people who were discriminated against in America.*
• **Add a reference to sacred writings or another source of religious belief and teaching.** If you prefer, you can add the reference to your first belief instead.	*The parable of the Sheep and Goats supports this Christian belief: 'Take your inheritance, the kingdom prepared for you since the salvation of the world. For I was hungry and you gave me something to drink, I was a stranger and you invited me in…' (Matthew 25:34–36)*
• Apply the reference by explaining how it links to the question.	*This supports the idea of social justice because it shows Christians how they should behave towards those in need.*

TIP

The parable of the Sheep and Goats is a useful story to quote when dealing with issues of justice, poverty or helping those in need.

9 Explain **two** religious beliefs about the duty to tackle poverty.

Refer to sacred writings or another source of religious belief and teaching in your answer. **[6 marks]**

• **Explain one belief.**	
• Develop your explanation with more detail/an example.	
• **Explain a second belief.**	
• Develop your explanation with more detail/an example.	
• **Add a reference to sacred writings or another source of religious belief and teaching.** If you prefer, you can add the reference to your first belief instead.	
• Apply the reference by explaining how it links to the question.	

10 Explain **two** religious beliefs about the dangers of wealth.

Refer to sacred writings or another source of religious belief and teaching in your answer. **[6 marks]**

Test the 12 mark question

11 'All religious believers should give to charities that help people living in poverty.'

Evaluate this statement. In your answer you:

- should give reasoned arguments in support of this statement
- should give reasoned arguments to support a different point of view
- should refer to religious arguments
- may refer to non-religious arguments
- should reach a justified conclusion.

[12 marks]

Plus SPaG 3 m

REASONED ARGUMENTS IN SUPPORT OF THE STATEMENT ● **Explain why some people would agree with the statement.** ● Develop your explanation with more detail and examples, which may include non-religious ideas. ● Refer to religious teaching. Use a quote or paraphrase or refer to a religious authority. ● **Evaluate the arguments.** Is this a good argument or not? Explain why you think this.	*If all religious believers gave to charities it would go a long way to ending a lot of poverty in the world. So many people are suffering because they do not have enough money to buy food, clothes and provide a home for themselves. While a lot of food is thrown away in countries, some people struggle to have one meal a day. Thousands have to survive on less than £1 a day. So if all religious believers were generous in their giving it would make life a lot more bearable for people living in poverty. Some people are living in poverty because of natural disasters or are refugees from war. They need emergency aid and religious believers should respond and it should be their duty to give to charities that are helping.*
REASONED ARGUMENTS SUPPORTING A DIFFERENT VIEW ● **Explain why some people would support a different view.** ● Develop your explanation with more detail and examples, which may include non-religious ideas. ● Refer to religious teaching. Use a quote or paraphrase or refer to a religious authority. ● **Evaluate the arguments.** Is this a good argument or not? Explain why you think this.	*However, some religious believers are living in poverty themselves, so will not be able to afford to help others. They are struggling to survive and have no extra money to give to charity. So you can't expect those religious believers to starve in order to give to people living in poverty. Some may prefer to do work to help the charities like distributing and collecting envelopes for Christian Aid. Not all religious believers have to give money; they can help in other ways.*
CONCLUSION ● **Give a justified conclusion.** ● Include your own opinion together with your own reasoning. ● **Include evaluation.** Explain why you think one viewpoint is stronger than the other or why they are equally strong. ● Do not just repeat arguments you have already used without explaining how they apply to your reasoned opinion/conclusion.	*It is true that charities do a lot of good in helping people living in poverty. However, it is unfair just to expect religious believers to donate money to the charities. Everyone should try and help if they can whether they are religious or not. Not all religious believers are able to donate money but they can pray or give their time to help charities.*

TIP

A key word in this statement is 'all'. It hints that some religious believers might not have a duty to give to charities. The student explains that not all believers can afford to help as some are living in poverty themselves. The question doesn't mention money, it just says 'give to charities', so the student has rightly explained other ways people could help, for example by helping raise money for the charity.

TIP

The conclusion is good because the student widens the debate to all people, not just religious believers. They also include a new way that believers could help – through prayer.

12 'Discrimination is always wrong.'

Evaluate this statement. In your answer you:

- should give reasoned arguments in support of this statement
- should give reasoned arguments to support a different point of view
- should refer to religious arguments
- may refer to non-religious arguments
- should reach a justified conclusion.

[12 marks]
Plus SPaG 3 marks

REASONED ARGUMENTS IN SUPPORT OF THE STATEMENT ● **Explain why some people would agree with the statement.** ● Develop your explanation with more detail and examples, which may include non-religious ideas. ● Refer to religious teaching. Use a quote or paraphrase or refer to a religious authority. ● **Evaluate the arguments.** Is this a good argument or not? Explain why you think this.	
REASONED ARGUMENTS SUPPORTING A DIFFERENT VIEW ● **Explain why some people would support a different view.** ● Develop your explanation with more detail and examples, which may include non-religious ideas. ● Refer to religious teaching. Use a quote or paraphrase or refer to a religious authority. ● **Evaluate the arguments.** Is this a good argument or not? Explain why you think this.	
CONCLUSION ● **Give a justified conclusion.** ● Include your own opinion together with your own reasoning. ● **Include evaluation.** Explain why you think one viewpoint is stronger than the other or why they are equally strong. ● Do not just repeat arguments you have already used without explaining how they apply to your reasoned opinion/conclusion.	

TIP
Don't forget that your spelling, punctuation and grammar are assessed in 12 mark questions.

13 'Everybody should have the freedom to follow whichever religion they wish to.'

Evaluate this statement. In your answer you:

- should give reasoned arguments in support of this statement
- should give reasoned arguments to support a different point of view
- should refer to religious arguments
- may refer to non-religious arguments
- should reach a justified conclusion.

[12 marks]
Plus SPaG 3 marks

Check your answers using the mark scheme on page 158. How did you do?
To feel more secure in the content you need to remember, re-read pages 134–141.
To remind yourself of what the examiner is looking for, go to pages 6–11.

Apply answers

1 Christianity: Beliefs and teachings

Please note that these are suggested answers to the Apply questions, designed to give you guidance, rather than being definitive answers.

Where questions have been taken from AQA specimen papers, these suggested answers have neither been provided nor approved by AQA, nor do they constitute the only possible solutions.

1.1 **A** 'We believe in one God' (the Nicene Creed)/ first of the Ten Commandments. **B** *You might include*: Christians are inspired to follow the teaching of the Bible/ believe they have a relationship with God/ communicate with God through prayer/ find comfort in God in challenging times/ pray and worship/ try to follow Jesus' example.

1.2 **A** Creating humans/ caring for humans/ sending his son, Jesus, to live among humans/requiring justice. **B** Suffering was brought into God's perfect world by Adam and Eve's disobedience/ the result of human free will/ a test of faith/ without suffering people can't show positive human qualities such as compassion/ by overcoming suffering humans learn to be strong and appreciative of good in the world. *Remember to develop each point with more detail.*

1.3 **A** 1: These persons are God the Father, the Son (Jesus) and the Holy Spirit/ these three persons are named in the Apostles Creed and the Nicene Creed. 2: God the Father is the creator of all life/ acts as a good father towards humankind, who are his children/ is omnipotent, omnibenevolent, omniscient and omnipresent. **B** *Arguments for:* 1, 2, 4, 6, 7. *Arguments against*: 3, 5, 8. *In your justified conclusion you should weigh up both sides of the argument and then say which side you personally find more convincing and why.*

1.4 **A** They value every human being as created by God/ they believe people should look after the natural world. **B** *You might conclude that this is a strong argument because it is true that Christians believe in God's omnipotence and the truth of the Bible. But you might think it is a weak argument because theories of evolution and the Big Bang are widely accepted by many Christians despite not being 'proved'. It doesn't matter whether you think the argument is weak or strong, the important thing is to carefully explain* why *you think it is weak or strong.*

1.5 **A** Jesus was God in human form/ 'The Word became flesh and made his dwelling among us' (John 1:14 [NIV])/ Jesus was born of a virgin, Mary. **B** *E.g. 'The belief that Jesus was conceived by the Holy Spirit is given in Matthew's Gospel which says, 'His mother Mary was pledged to be married to Joseph, but before they came together, she was found to be pregnant by the Holy Spirit.'*

1.6 **A** 1: Jesus' death restored the relationship between people and God. 2: God understands human suffering because Jesus, who is God, experienced it. **B** When Jesus died he took the sins of everyone on himself (the atonement)/ if Jesus had not died he would not have risen from the dead. *The answer could be improved by developing reasons why the crucifixion is an important belief rather than merely describing what took place.*

1.7 **A** The women were told by angels that Jesus had risen/ Jesus appeared to the disciples. **B** Paul wrote, 'And if Christ has not been raised, our preaching is useless and so is your faith' (1 Corinthians 15:14 [NIV])/ 'He rose again according to the scriptures' (the Nicene Creed)/ the resurrection shows the power of good over evil and life over death/ Christians will be resurrected if they accept Jesus/ 'I look for the resurrection of the dead and the life of the world to come' (the Nicene Creed).

1.8 **A** Gives hope of life after death with Jesus/ inspires Christians to live in the way God wants. **B** *In your paragraph you should weigh up both sides of the argument and then say which side you personally find more convincing and why.*

1.9 **A** Christians believe that when they die God will judge them on their behaviour and actions during their lifetime/ their faith in Jesus/ how they serve others unselfishly. *Refer to the Parable of the Sheep and the Goats to support your points. Apply the Parable to the question:* The Parable shows how people will be judged on their behaviour towards people in need. **B** *You might include*: the promise of heaven inspires people to be kind to others/ people want to be with Jesus when they die so they follow his teachings/ on the other hand, no one can be sure there is an afterlife, so it is not a good way to get people to behave/ an atheist would question how a loving God could punish people forever in hell. *In your justified conclusion you should weigh up both sides of the argument and then say which side you personally find more convincing.*

1.10 **A** A loving God would not condemn people to hell/ God is forgiving so would offer everyone a second chance to repent. **B** *Arguments in support might include*: the promise of heaven would encourage good behaviour/ the threat of hell would prevent bad behaviour/ belief in heaven takes away the fear of death/ gives hope that people will experience eternal happiness even if their life on earth has been hard. *Other views might include*: atheists don't believe in heaven or hell but still have moral principles/ most people do not consider belief in the afterlife when deciding how to behave/ morality is formed in childhood by parental teaching/ if heaven and hell were made up to encourage good behaviour, it hasn't worked.

1.11 **A** Salvation by grace of God freely given through faith in Jesus/ 'For it is by grace you have been saved' (Ephesians 2:8 [NIV]), which supports the belief that humans are saved by God's grace / Salvation by doing good works/ 'In the same way, faith by itself, if it is not accompanied by action, is dead' (James 2:17 [NIV]), which suggests that salvation isn't achieved through belief alone but by following God's laws and doing good deeds. **B** *In deciding whether you find this argument convincing, try to think of what others might say against it.*

1.12 **A** Jesus' death made up for the original sin of Adam and Eve/ Jesus' resurrection was proof that his sacrifice was accepted by God. **B** *There is no 'right' order, but suggested arguments in support*: 4, 5, 2, 8. *Arguments against*: 1, 6, 7, 3. *Missing from this evaluation is any reference to specific Christian teaching, for example a reference to sacred writing. A justified conclusion is also needed.*

2 Christianity: Practices

Please note that these are suggested answers to the Apply questions, designed to give you guidance, rather than being definitive answers.

Where questions have been taken from AQA specimen papers, these suggested answers have neither been provided nor approved by AQA, nor do they constitute the only possible solutions.

2.1 **A** Private prayer/ singing hymns of praise in church. **B** *Arguments in support might include:* a set ritual is familiar to people/ provides a powerful emotional bond/ liturgical worship may be more formal, so more dramatic/ give a powerful sense of tradition. *Arguments in support of other views might include:* spontaneous worship is more powerful as it comes from the heart/ charismatic worship involves speaking in tongues so is a powerful emotional experience/ the silence of a Quaker service may be more powerful than one that uses words and hymns/ it depends on an individual Christian's point of view whether one type of service is more powerful than another.

2.2 **A** It is the prayer Jesus taught his disciples/ it is a model of good prayer as it combines praise to God with asking for one's needs. **B** *You might include an example*: a Christian may wish to pray for something personal using their own words, such as the strength to overcome an illness. *Or add a religious teaching*: Jesus said to pray in your room with the door closed so that God who sees in secret will reward you (Matthew 6:6).

2.3 **A** 1: Believers' baptism: full immersion in a pool/ person is old enough to make a mature decision about their faith. 2: Infant baptism: blessed water is poured over the baby's head/ parents and godparents make promises of faith on behalf of the child. **B** *Arguments in support might include*: at baptism the parents promise to bring up the child as a Christian so they would be lying/ it is hypocritical/ the symbolic actions have no meaning for them. *Arguments against might include*: they may not be religious themselves but that doesn't mean they should not give their child a chance to be a member of the Church/ the child receives grace at baptism regardless of their parents' future actions/ the child is cleansed from sin.

2.4 **A** 1: Christians receive God's grace/ by joining in the sacrifice of Jesus/ their faith is strengthened/ they become closer to God. 2: Communion brings the community of believers together in unity by sharing the bread and wine/ this provides support and encouragement for those going through a difficult time/ encourages church members to love others in practical ways. **B** *In your paragraph you should weigh up both sides of the argument and then say which side you personally find more convincing and why.*

2.5 **A** 1: An Orthodox Holy Communion is mainly held behind the iconostasis/ the priest distributes the consecrated bread and wine on a spoon. 2: Holy Communion in the United Reformed Church has an 'open table' so anyone can receive communion/ bread is broken and passed around the congregation/ wine is distributed in small cups. **B** *Arguments for the statement might include:* the ministry of the Word is very important because it focuses on the life and teaching of Jesus/ reminds people of sacred writing in the Old Testament/ provides spiritual education for the congregation through the sermon given by the priest/ allows the community to pray for themselves and others. *Arguments against might include*: Holy Communion services should focus on the consecration and sharing of bread and wine because that is the most important part of the service/ people receive the body and blood of Jesus/ recall Jesus' death and resurrection which saved them from sin.

2.6 1: Lourdes: pilgrims go there to seek healing, both spiritual and physical/ to help the sick bathe in the waters/ to strengthen their faith/ to take part in services with people speaking many different languages from many countries/ it is a busy place with crowds of people, unlike Iona which is quieter and more remote. 2: Iona: pilgrims wish to spend time in quiet prayer, reading the Bible or meditating/ to enjoy the natural beauty of the place so they feel closer to God who created nature/ to worship with others who are like-minded/ some prefer to feel God's presence in silence and solitude rather than in a busy place like Lourdes. **B** On a pilgrimage there are many opportunities for prayer and meditation/ for reading the scriptures/ for reflecting on one's life/ whereas on a holiday people usually spend time enjoying themselves and reading novels rather than scriptures, etc. *A Christian teaching that supports pilgrimage might include*: Jesus withdrew to a lonely place when he wanted to pray/ Bernadette was told by Mary in a vision to build a church in Lourdes and pray for sinners, so Christians are following their traditional teaching by going there.

2.7 **A** By attending services which emphasise Jesus is risen/ by celebrating with family and friends/ giving Easter eggs to children to symbolise new life. **B** *Arguments for might include*: Christmas is very commercialised/ many people think about food, presents and seeing their relatives, not about Jesus/ not many people go to church at Christmas/ some think that in multicultural Britain, celebrating Christmas as a religious festival might offend others. *Arguments against might include*: Christmas is still a religious holiday in Britain/ the royal family go to church on Christmas Day and many Christians attend Midnight Mass/ carol services are held to prepare for the coming of Jesus into the world/ schools have nativity plays about Jesus' birth and often collect presents to give to children who are less fortunate.

2.8 **A** 1: The community of Christians/ holy people of God/ Body of Christ. 2: A building in which Christians worship. **B** The Church is the Body of Christ and as such has a duty to help the needy/ Christians are taught to love their neighbour/ the Parable of the Sheep and the Goats/ the Parable of the Good Samaritan.

2.9 **A** Patrol streets in urban areas to support vulnerable people/ challenge gang and knife crime/ listen to people's problems/ help young people who have had too much to drink and may end up in trouble/ try to stop anti-social behaviour/ in this way they show love of neighbour/ 'Faith by itself, if it is not accompanied by action, is dead' (James 2:17 [NIV]), which supports the work that Street Pastors do because they are active in the local community as part of their Christian duty and do not just believe in God. **B** *Two religious arguments might include*: Jesus taught that Christians should help others by showing agape love towards them/ this means being unselfish, caring and putting others' needs before your own, including praying for your neighbours' needs/ Jesus taught Christians should give practical help to others in the Parable of the Sheep and the Goats/ he said to feed the hungry, clothe the naked, etc. *Non-religious arguments against the statement might include*: praying is pointless/ not a practical action/ no one will know if prayer works to help them/ Christians should not have to be Street Pastors or social workers/ it is the police and social services' responsibility, not the Church's responsibility.

2.10 **A** By telling non-believers that Jesus Christ, the Son of God, came into the world as its saviour/ by spreading the Christian faith through evangelism. **B** *Arguments for*: 1, 3, 5. *Arguments against*: 2, 4, 6. *You should weigh up both sides of the argument and then say which side you personally find more convincing.*

2.11 **A** Through organisations that promote evangelism, such as Christ for all Nations/ through personal witness and example. **B** *You should weigh up the argument and suggest how it could be improved – e.g. by referring to the Great Commission (which suggests all Christians have a duty to spread the gospel), or by considering arguments for the statement.*

2.12 **A** The Church works on a personal level to try to restore relationships between individuals or between conflicting groups in the community / the Church has sponsored different organisations that work for reconciliation, such as the Irish Churches Peace Project. **B** Jesus taught, 'Love the Lord your God with all your heart and with all your soul and with all your mind. This is the great and first commandment.' (Matthew 22: 37–38 [NIV])/ therefore reconciliation to God is most important/ reconciliation to one's neighbour is second: 'Love your neighbour as yourself' (Matthew 22:39 [NIV]).

2.13 **A** Smuggling Bibles into the USSR to give comfort to persecuted Christians/ sending money to projects that support persecuted Christians. **B** *A religious argument might include*: it is possible for a Christian to be happy even in times of persecution because they believe they are sharing in the sufferings of Jesus/ their courage can inspire others to become Christians/ persecution strengthens their faith. *A non-religious argument might include*: no one can be happy while being persecuted/ they may be angry at the injustice of their treatment and turn to violence or stop believing in God.

2.14 **A** 1: Emergency relief includes food, shelter and water to people suffering from a natural disaster or sudden war/ parables such as the Good Samaritan show that helping those who are in need even if they are strangers is a good thing to do and this is the foundation of the work of overseas relief missions. 2: Long-term aid may include education or new farming equipment that helps to make people independent of aid/ 'If anyone has material possessions and sees a brother or sister in need but has no pity on them, how can the love of God be in that person?' (1 John 3:17 [NIV]), which supports the idea that Christians should work to support those who do not have what they need and this applies to the work of overseas relief missions. **B** *Arguments for the statement might include*: religious charities can respond quickly to emergencies but it is not their role to provide long-term aid/ the countries themselves should be helping their own people/ long-term aid might make people dependent on religious charities. *Arguments against might include*: religious charities should provide long-term aid because people are still in need/ it will give independence eventually/ it is better to teach people how to make a living for themselves than merely to feed them for a short period of time/ the Parable of the Sheep and the Goats teaches that God will judge people on whether they have helped their fellow humans because helping them is helping Jesus Christ.

3 Islam: Beliefs and teachings

Please note that these are suggested answers to the Apply questions, designed to give you guidance, rather than being definitive answers.

3.1 **A** 'He is God the One'/ there is only one God/ God is a unified, indivisible being/ God does not consist of different Persons/ 'God the eternal'/ God has always existed/ 'He begot no one nor was He begotten'/ God was not born or came into being out of something else/ God does not have any children/ 'No one is comparable to him'/ God is unique/ no other person or thing has God's qualities. **B** *Arguments in support of the statement*: Tawhid is the belief in one, indivisible God, so Muslims should only worship one God/ also means there is nothing comparable to God, so Muslims should never make anything in their lives more important than God – this influences Muslims to prioritise God in their lives/ e.g. by praying to God five times a day/ e.g. by putting God before their family or jobs/ means everything they do should be centred around pleasing or obeying God. *Arguments in support of other views*: belief in the prophets is more important because this means accepting that God's revelations through the prophets are true and the Qur'an is the word of God/ the Qur'an is the source of authority for all matters of doctrine, practice and law, so has a huge influence on the way Muslims live and worship/ belief in God's judgement is more important/ motivates Muslims to take responsibility for their actions/ to live good lives/ avoid sin in their daily lives.

3.2 **A** God is immanent/ present everywhere in the world and the universe/ God is also transcendent/ beyond and outside the universe/ God can be both because he created the universe (so is outside it) but is also able to act within it/ God is merciful/ shows compassion, mercy and forgiveness/ God is just/ will punish people who act badly or make bad choices. **B** *Arguments agreeing with the statement*: Sunni and Shi'a Muslims share the same fundamental beliefs/ e.g. they both believe in the same God/ acknowledge the importance of the prophets/ so both groups agree with the core beliefs in the Shahadah ('There is no God but Allah and Muhammad is the Prophet of Allah')/ differences in leadership are not as important as differences in belief, and many of the beliefs are the same. *Arguments disagreeing with the statement:* tensions and conflict between Sunni and Shi'a Muslims in the world today suggest the differences are more important than the similarities/ the rightful leader of a religion is very important, as this is the person that everyone follows/ looks to for guidance and advice/ Sunni and Shi'a Muslims not only disagree about who the rightful leader is, but how much authority they should have/ Sunni and Shi'a Muslims emphasise different beliefs/ e.g. Sunni Muslims are more likely to believe that God has already determined everything that will happen in the universe/ all of these differences are important enough to split Islam into two distinct groups.

3.3 **A** God is transcendent because he created the universe, so is beyond and outside it, but he is also immanent because he is able to act within the universe, and is within all things. **B** *Fairness and justice*: it is more important for Muslims to know that God will judge people fairly and equally on the Day of Judgement/ motivates them to do good during their lives/ accept responsibility for their actions/ accept God's judgement as being fair/ teaches them the importance of justice/ encourages them to act fairly and justly towards others. *Immanence*: it is more important to know that God is present in and involved with life on earth/ helps Muslims to form a closer relationship with God/ suggests that God cares about the world and what happens in it. *Omnipotence*: it is most important to know that God is all powerful/ explains how God is able to create and sustain the universe/ contributes to belief in the supremacy of God's will/ helps Muslims to accept God's will. *Your conclusion should explain whether or not you agree with the statement and why, by referring to some of the points above.*

3.4 **A** Angels serve God/ pass on God's words to people through the prophets/ take care of people throughout their lives/ record everything a person does during their lives/ take people's souls to God after they die/ escort people into paradise or hell/ send rain, thunder and lightning to earth. **B** *Agree*: angels are how God communicates with people/ by passing on his messages perfectly to the prophets/ the Qur'an is the source of authority for all matters of doctrine, practice and law/ without the angel Jibril this may not have been passed on to Muhammad, or passed on imperfectly, so Islam would be very different/ if God was not able to communicate with Muslims, then they would not really know how to worship, obey or please him/ the existence of Islam is based on revelations to the prophets that have come through the angels. *Disagree:* it is impossible to know how Islam would have developed without angels, but if God wanted to communicate with people, he would have found a way regardless/ e.g. by speaking to them directly/ through visions or miracles/ there are examples of this in the history of Islam/ e.g. when Ibrahim had a dream in which God asked him to sacrifice his son.

3.5 **A** Many Muslims believe they will be judged by God for their actions on the Day of Judgement and rewarded or punished as a result/ so they have the responsibility to make sure their actions are good enough to be rewarded by God. **B** *Arguments in support of the statement could include*: some Muslims believe God has already determined everything that will happen in the universe/ has written down everything that will happen in a 'book of decrees'/ because God created people and because his will is so powerful, Muslims must act according to his will/ some Muslims believe they are not able to change their destiny or the overall plan that God has set for them as a result. *Arguments in support of other views:* even Muslims who believe they cannot change their overall destiny still believe they do have some choice over how they behave/ many Muslims believe predestination means God knows everything that is going to happen, but does not decide everything that is going to happen/ so they have the free will to make their own choices, which is why God's judgement is an important aspect in Islam/ 'God does not change the condition of a people [for the worse] unless they change what is in themselves' (Qur'an 13:11).

3.6 **A** Barzakh. **B** *Some Muslims would agree because*: they believe where they spend the afterlife is determined by their actions and faith during their lifetime/ God will judge all people on the Day of Judgement and send those who have kept their faith in God and done good deeds to heaven/ heaven is a state of eternal happiness in the presence of God/ this reward should encourage Muslims to live a good life through which they show their faith in God. *Some people might disagree because*: they believe it is best to live in the present/ an approach to life should not be based on beliefs in something for which there is no proof/ faith in God should not be dependent on the reward of heaven/ there are other reasons for doing good deeds/ e.g. out of a sense of kindness and compassion.

3.7 **A** Prophets help Muslims to understand God's message/ to stay on the right path/ act as good role models/ teach Muslims how to live a good life in obedience to God. **B** *Reasons why Muslims would disagree might include*: Muhammad is more important because he received the final revelation of Islam/ received the Qur'an, which is the source of authority for all matters of doctrine, practice and law/ 'he is God's Messenger and the seal of the prophets' (Qur'an 33:40)/ he helped to fully establish Islam by conquering Makkah and converting the city to Islam. *Arguments to support the statement could include:* Adam is the father of the human race – all of the human race (including Muhammad) is descended from Adam/ God gave Adam knowledge and understanding, which Adam passed on to the rest of the human race/ so the knowledge of how to live a good life in obedience to God stems from Adam.

3.8 **A** The Ka'aba is a small, cube-shaped building in the centre of the Grand Mosque in Makkah/ it is important to Muslims because it is considered to be the house of God/ the holiest place in Islam. **B** *Arguments in support of the statement*: Ibrahim showed total dedication to God/ fulfilled all the tests and commands given to him by God/ e.g. he refused to worship idols and preached that there is only one God/ he followed God's command to rebuild the Ka'aba/ he was willing to sacrifice his son to God/ he left his wife and son in the desert on God's command/ these events show he had complete faith in God/ was willing to put God before his family. *Arguments in support of other views:* Ibrahim tried to stop idol worship by using an axe to destroy all the idols in his town temple/ some people might say this could encourage Muslims to respond with violence to something they think is wrong/ some people might say that Ibrahim should not have been so willing to sacrifice his own son/ so does not provide a good role model for Muslim families.

3.9 **A** The Imams are the leaders of Shi'a Islam/ descendants of Muhammad/ chosen by God/ able to interpret the Qur'an and Islamic law without fault/ important for helping to preserve and explain the law/ for guiding Muslims in how to live correctly/ the twelfth Imam will return in the future to bring justice and equality to all. **B** *Arguments to support the statement*: Muhammad received the Qur'an from God, which has a huge influence on how Muslims live and worship God/ he converted the city of Makkah to Islam without which Islam might not exist today/ he agreed with God that Muslims should pray five times a day/ Sunni Muslims still follow this practice. *Arguments to support other views*: the knowledge of how to live a good life in obedience to God originally stems from Adam, so he has had a greater impact/ Ibrahim's actions influence Muslims when they go on Hajj, as the pilgrimage recounts events in his life, so Ibrahim has a stronger impact on this pillar of Islam/ Ibrahim's willingness to sacrifice his son to God is a strong message to Muslims to put God first, which may have significantly impacted individual Muslims in their lives and decision-making.

3.10 **A** The Psalms. **B** The Qur'an was revealed by the angel Jibril/ who directly passed on God's words to Muhammad/ Muhammad learned these words by heart and scribes wrote them down/ an official version of the Qur'an was compiled to make sure God's words were not distorted/ because the Qur'an contains accurate transcriptions of God's words, it is the highest authority in Islam/ other holy books do not have the same authority because they have been lost/distorted/corrupted over time.

4 Islam: Practices

Please note that these are suggested answers to the Apply questions, designed to give you guidance, rather than being definitive answers.

4.1 **A** Salah – Muslims are expected to pray three or five times a day/ sawm – Muslims are expected to fast during the month of Ramadan/ Zakah – Muslims are expected to give 2.5% of their savings to charity every year/ Khums – a 20% tax, half of which goes to charity and half to religious leaders/ Hajj – Muslims are expected to undertake the Hajj pilgrimage once in their lifetime/ jihad – the struggle to maintain the faith and defend Islam/ amr-bil-maruf – encouraging people to do what is good/ nahi anil munkar – discouraging people from doing wrong/ tawallah – showing love for God and people who follow him/ tabarra – not associating with the enemies of God. **B** The Shahadah states there is only one God (Allah)/ Islam is founded on this belief/ it influences Muslims to worship God as the creator of everything/ to never make anything in their lives more important than God/ the Shahadah also states that 'Muhammad is the Prophet of Allah'/ this reflects how important Muhammad is as the person who received the final revelation of Islam/ belief in Muhammad means belief in the Qur'an as the word of God/ this influences Muslims to take the Qur'an seriously and follow its teachings/ e.g. by praying a number of times a day/ giving Zakah/ fasting/ going on pilgrimage.

4.2 **A** Muslims perform ritual washing (wudu)/ wash their faces, hands and feet under running water/ or sand or dust if water is not available/ to make themselves spiritually clean. **B** *Arguments for:* prayer has to be done three or five times a day, every day/ this means Muslims have to set aside time for prayer regardless of what else they are doing during the day/ they also have to get up before sunrise every day to pray, which is very early in the summer months. *Arguments against:* some Muslims might find fasting for a whole month harder, as this requires more discipline and commitment/ some might find going on Hajj harder if they are physically weak or do not have the money to travel to Makkah.

4.3 **A** Sunni Muslims pray five times a day/ Shi'a Muslims pray three times a day by combining the midday and afternoon prayers, and sunset and night prayers/ unlike Sunni Muslims, Shi'a Muslims rest their foreheads on a clay tablet when prostrating in prayer/ because they believe in only using natural elements/ in a mosque the mihrab indicates the direction to pray/ outside the mosque Muslims may use a special compass to find the right direction/ in a mosque the prayers are led by an imam/ at home prayers may not be led by anyone. **B** *Arguments which agree:* structured prayers mean people know exactly what to do when they pray/ do not have to come up with the right words to use/ they unite a religious community/ provide comfort because of the familiarity. *Arguments which disagree:* structured prayers are too restrictive/ spontaneous prayers allow a person to pray about their own personal concerns/ allow a person to develop a closer relationship with God/ are more meaningful.

4.4 **A** The Night of Power is when Jibril first appeared to Muhammad and started revealing the Qur'an/ Qur'an 96:1–5 contains the words that Jibril spoke/ Jibril instructed Muhammad to start reciting his words/ the Night of Power happened on one of the odd-numbered dates in the second half of Ramadan/ observing the Night of Power gives Muslims the benefits of worshipping for a thousand months/ 'The Night of Glory is better than a thousand months' (Qur'an 97:3). **B** *Arguments which agree:* the Qur'an is the word of God/ the source of Muslim beliefs and practices, so Muslims should know it as well as possible/ studying the Qur'an during Ramadan is a way of thanking God for revealing the Qur'an/ Muslims study the Qur'an during the Night of Power, which is thought to give them the benefits of worshipping for a thousand months. *Arguments which disagree:* fasting shows greater discipline and commitment/ this shows obedience and dedication to God/ Muslims are obligated to fast/ 'So any one of you who is present that month should fast' (Qur'an 2:18)/ fasting reminds Muslims why it is important to help those in poverty.

4.5 **A** Zakah is 2.5% of savings; Khums is 20% of savings/ Zakah goes to charity; Khums also goes to Shi'a religious leaders/ Zakah is given by Sunni and Shi'a Muslims; Khums is only given by Shi'a Muslims. **B** *Arguments which agree:* giving Zakah or Khums helps to remove selfishness and greed/ teaches Muslims to use their money to help others/ this pleases God/ if Muslims develop a good attitude towards money, this will have a lasting effect all year round, not just when Zakah or Khums is given. *Arguments which disagree:* the most important reason is because it is a requirement for Muslims/ helps Muslims to purify their souls and so become closer to God/ helps those in need/ strengthens the Muslim community. *Your answer should also explain why someone else might agree with the statement when you have disagreed with it, or vice versa, by referring to some of the points made above.*

4.6 **A** It is the holiest place in Islam/ the house of God/ it was rebuilt by the prophet Ibrahim/ it is where Hajj begins. **B** *Arguments for:* Hajj requires Muslims to take at least five days out of work/ and to save up the money to travel to Makkah/ it is physically demanding/ e.g. requires Muslims to pray for a whole afternoon in the hot summer sun/ it shows commitment to Islam because it is centred around Muslim beliefs/ the actions of Muslim prophets. *Arguments against:* sincerely reciting the Shadahah in front of Muslim witnesses is the best way as this makes a person a Muslim/ expresses the core beliefs of Islam/ praying is the best way as this demonstrates commitment to God every day/ fasting is the best way as requires the most discipline.

4.7 **A** Pilgrims must enter a state of purity called ihram/ this involves ritual washing, praying and putting on ihram clothing/ it symbolises purity, unity and equality. **B** *Arguments which agree:* the main actions of Hajj recall the actions of the prophets/ e.g. walking between the two hills recalls Hajira's search for water after she was left in the desert by Ibrahim/ standing at Arafat recalls Muhammad's last sermon/ sacrificing an animal recalls Ibrahim's willingness to sacrifice his own son/ remembering the good examples set by the prophets is an important part of Hajj. *Arguments which disagree:* there is more to Hajj that just remembering the actions of the prophets/ e.g. it is about showing dedication and commitment to God/ feeling a part of the Muslim community/ receiving forgiveness for sins/ rejecting evil and the temptation to sin.

4.8 **A** A belief in greater jihad motivates Muslims to live according to the teachings of Islam/ 'This is My path, leading straight, so follow it, and do not follow other ways' (Qur'an 6:153)/ e.g. by observing the Five Pillars/ studying the Qur'an/ putting God above all else/ avoiding temptations/ helping those in need/ a belief in greater jihad encourages Muslims to constantly try to improve themselves/ helps Muslims to acknowledge that this is sometimes a struggle. **B** *Arguments for:* greater jihad is a constant, daily struggle/ many Muslims today are unlikely to take part in lesser jihad in their lives/ greater jihad requires more from Muslims, e.g. observing the Five Pillars/ putting God above everything else/ avoiding temptations and negative traits. *Arguments against:* some Muslims who have pacifist leanings might struggle to take part in a war to defend the faith/ a Muslim might have to sacrifice their own life in combat/ other countries or faiths might be very resistant to a holy war and respond aggressively/ this would make following lesser jihad in today's world potentially devastating for those involved.

4.9 **A** The festivals were started by Muhammad in Madinah, after he fled from persecution in Makkah/ he told the people in Madinah that God had set aside two days for festivities. **B** Id-ul-Fitr celebrates the end of a month of fasting, which requires huge amounts of discipline and commitment, so Muslims should be able to have fun/ Id-ul-Fitr allows Muslims to thank God/ Muslims pray and listen to a sermon as part of the festivals/ for Id-ul-Fitr, Muslims visit their local cemetery to remember the dead/ for Id-ul-Adha, Muslims donate money to people living in poverty/ Ibrahim's willingness to sacrifice his son is relevant today as it reminds Muslims to show complete obedience to God/ festivals help to strengthen the Muslim community.

4.10 **A** By performing plays that tell the story of Husayn's death/ by taking part in public expressions of mourning/ by beating themselves on their chests/ by visiting Husayn's tomb. **B** *Points could include:* for Shi'a Muslims, Ashura is a solemn festival/ day of great sorrow/ as it commemorates the death of Husayn/ which is seen as a symbol of the struggle against injustice, tyranny and oppression/ it is observed with public expressions of grief and mourning/ Muslims might harm themselves to connect with Husayn's suffering.

5 Relationships and families

Please note that these are suggested answers to the Apply questions, designed to give you guidance, rather than being definitive answers.

5.1 **A** 1: Some Christians believe it is the quality of the relationship between the two people, not their gender that is important/ same-sex sexual relationships should show Christian qualities of love, commitment, faithfulness, etc. 2: Opposite-sex sexual relationships are part of God's plan for humanity/ the Qur'an teaches that same-sex sexual relationships are wrong (Qur'an 26:165–166). **B** *Examples of religious arguments*: Christians believe sex expresses a deep, lifelong union and casual sex does not represent this/ Muslims believe the only place for a sexual relationship is within marriage, which is a blessing from God. *Examples of non-religious arguments*: the acceptance of contraception and legal abortion has made casual sex more common/ sex has not been devalued in British society except by those who use it irresponsibly.

5.2 **A** 1: 'You shall not commit adultery' (Exodus 20:14 [NIV]). This can be interpreted to mean that adultery breaks one of the Ten Commandments, which is a sin against God. 2: 'And do not go anywhere near adultery: it is an outrage, and an evil path' (Qur'an 17:32). It can be argued this shows that adultery is unacceptable and takes a person away from God. **B** *In support:* it can be a valid expression of love for each other/ the couple may intend to marry but just can't afford it at the time. *Against:* 'your bodies are temples of the Holy Spirit' (1 Corinthians 6:19 [NIV])/ Islam teaches that sex is a gift from God which should always be reserved for marriage. *A development may be:* the Qur'an forbids sex before marriage/ it is considered to be a serious sin, like adultery or rape.

5.3 **A** Catholic and Orthodox Churches believe the use of contraception within marriage goes against the natural law/ Muslims accept the use of contraception within marriage to help with family planning, but not to avoid having children altogether. **B** *Arguments for might include*: the decision of whether or when to have children is up to the couple/ no one else knows their particular circumstances/ it is wrong to bring a baby into deprivation/ contraception prevents unwanted pregnancies and the spread of sexually transmitted infections. *Arguments against might include*: religious authorities have a duty to guide their followers to carry out God's will/ it is a Catholic and Muslim belief that God intended married couples to have a family/ children are a blessing from God/ so guidance about the proper use of contraception is needed to help people make correct choices.

5.4 **A** Marriage is God's gift to humans at creation/ a lifelong union blessed by God/ a covenant before God/ the proper place to enjoy a sexual relationship/ to raise children. **B** Marriage is a legal contract/ society is more stable if the rights of all people are protected/ cohabitation does not protect the children or remaining parent if one partner decides to leave the relationship/ 'The Church sees marriage between a man and a woman, as central to the stability and health of human society' (House of Bishops of the General Synod of the Church of England)/ the Qur'an teaches that a sexual relationship should only take place within marriage, so cohabitation is considered sinful.

5.5 **A** Catholic Church teaches that marriage is permanent/ a sacrament/ cannot be dissolved by civil divorce/ vows made before God must be kept/ therefore oppose remarriage while a partner is still alive/ other Christians believe that sometimes divorce is the lesser of two evils/ the Church should reflect God's forgiveness/ people should have a second chance for happiness/ approve of remarriage as long as the couple take the vows seriously/ Muslims can remarry after divorce, particularly if there are children/ they see the family as a most important part of society. **B** *For*: children are badly affected by divorce and parents have a duty to their children/ marriage is a sacrament and reflects the love Christ has for his Church/ Jesus taught that anyone who divorced and remarried was committing adultery (Mark 10:11–12)/ divorce is 'hateful to Allah' (Hadith). *Against*: continual arguments or abuse can damage children more than divorce/ atheists and humanists do not believe vows are made before God/ some Christians think the Church should reflect God's forgiveness and allow couples a second chance for happiness/ Islam allows divorce although with certain conditions.

5.6 **A** Members of a Christian family should 'love one another', as it is in the family that a child learns to love/ a nuclear family allows Christians to follow God's plan for humanity/ the extended family is the basis of Islamic society, and part of God's plan for humanity/ a Christian family is where a child learns faith in God and Jesus/ Muslims believe the family shapes the moral values and character of their children. **B** *For*: many non-religious people and some Christians agree the gender of the parents makes no difference to a child's upbringing/ a same-sex couple that gives love and security to their children will make just as good parents as an opposite-sex couple/ it is the quality of their parenting that matters. *Against*: all religions agree children should grow up in a loving, secure family, but not all would agree the gender of the parents makes no difference/ some people think children should have male and female role models as they grow up/ Christians and Muslims who oppose same-sex sexual relationships would disagree with same-sex parents for the same reasons, they might argue that same-sex parents would not provide a good example for their children.

5.7 **A** 1: E.g. children are taught to 'love your neighbour as yourself'/ to follow commandments such as 'Honour your father and your mother...' (Exodus 20:12 [NIV]). This can be interpreted to mean that being kind to others, even people you don't know, supports Christian teaching. 2: Muslim parents, particularly mothers, teach their children how to pray/ how to follow the teachings in the Qur'an/ 'Honour your children and perfect their manners' (Hadith). This can be interpreted to mean that, as part of a Muslim upbringing, parents should teach their children how to behave with good manners. **B** *For the statement*: children should do more for their parents when they get older, as their parents cared for them when they were younger/ many elderly relatives today live alone and need the extra support/ Christians and Muslims are taught to respect their elderly parents/ 'Listen to your father, who gave you life, and do not despise your mother when she is old' (Proverbs 23:22)/ 'Lower your wing in humility towards [your parents] in kindness and say, "Lord, have mercy on them, just as they cared for me when I was little"' (Qur'an 17:24). *Against the statement*: families in the UK are already doing a lot for their elderly relatives/ e.g. even if they live far away, children might contribute to their care or contact them regularly/ many Muslims have elderly relatives living with them/ Christians and Muslims already support their elderly relatives because of teachings such as, 'Honour your father and mother' (Exodus 20:12 [NIV]). *You should weigh up both sides of the argument and then say which side you personally find more convincing.*

5.8 **A** Prejudice is unfairly judging someone before the facts are known / holding biased opinions about people based on their gender or race etc./discrimination is acting on the prejudice/ doing something which treats someone unfairly, e.g. not giving a job to a woman who has children. **B** Despite the Sex Discrimination Act making gender discrimination illegal, women still get paid less than men for similar jobs/ there are still more men than women in senior positions/ some areas of employment are considered inappropriate for women or men/ Paul taught that this was wrong when he said, 'There is neither... male nor female, for you are all one in Christ Jesus' (Galatians 3:28 [NIV])/ Islam also teaches that men and women are equal.

6 Religion and life

Please note that these are suggested answers to the Apply questions, designed to give you guidance, rather than being definitive answers.

6.1 **A** It provides greater understanding of God/ of God's creation/ it is within the scope of the Qur'an/ science explains how things happen, and the Qur'an explains why they happen/ *reference to similarities between science and the Qur'an*. **B** *Agree*: God has the power to do anything so creation through the Big Bang is possible/ if religious creation stories are not read literally then it is possible for the Big Bang to be the method through which God created the universe. *Disagree*: religious creation stories must be literally true, so it is not possible to believe the Big Bang theory/ the Big Bang was triggered by random chance, not God.

6.2 **A** Looking after something on behalf of somebody else, e.g. looking after the earth for God. **B** This must be true because God would or could not create anything that is not wonderful and valuable/ the earth inspires awe and wonder/ provides everything needed to live/ people learn about God through creation, so it must be wonderful and valuable to achieve this learning/ the earth must be valuable if God has made humans stewards of it.

6.3 **A** Air – fumes from transport, industry etc./ land – poor disposal of waste products, overdevelopment/ water – dumping waste into water courses and the sea, including plastic waste and micro plastics. **B** E.g. *'I agree because many are still using vehicles that cause a lot of pollution and they don't always dispose of their waste in a way that does not harm the earth. It is important for religious believers to do as much as they can to help the environment, not only to protect it for future generations, but also because the teachings of their religion require it (such as the teaching of stewardship) and because it shows respect for God's creation. So they should try to do things like recycle more and use their cars less.'*

6.4 **A** It is cruel because it harms animals/ it is unnecessary because scientists can use other methods to test products/ experimenting on animals is not good stewardship / Muslims are taught that taking any life without just cause will result in them being held accountable at judgement/ some Christians believe humans have dominion over animals, so can use them for their own needs. **B** All killing of living beings is cruel/ animals bred for experimentation have no freedom in their lives/ experimenting on animals is not good stewardship/ there are alternatives that are not harmful to animals/ Muslims believe they will be held accountable to God for taking any life without just cause/ Christians believe in dominion which some interpret as meaning humans can use living things for their own purposes.

6.5 **A** The origins of human life are exactly as recorded in scripture/ evolution is a biological principle and not opposed to Christianity or Islam/ God created original life which has evolved naturally as science teaches/ evolution is correct for all creatures except humans/ God continues to preside over evolution/ evolution is false because God made humans as descendants of Adam and Eve (Hawwa). **B** *E.g. for the statement: 'The story of Adam and Eve is more important than evolution because it teaches religious believers valuable lessons. For example, that humans are equally created in God's image, that opposite-sex sexual relationships are part of God's plan, and that misusing God's free will has serious consequences. In order to follow God it is more important to understand these lessons than to know how life began.' E.g. against the statement: 'The belief that life evolved on earth is more important than the story of Adam and Eve because this story cannot be proved. It is likely the story was made up to help people believe in God, as it seems difficult to believe human life simply started with a man and woman created by God. It is more important to understand how life really developed than to know about a story that is probably not true.'*

6.6 **A** The pregnancy endangers the woman's life/ the woman's physical or mental health is endangered/ there is a strong risk the baby will be born with a severe disability/ an additional child may endanger the health of other children in the family/ within the first 24 weeks of pregnancy/ must be decided by at least two doctors. **B** *For*: being brought up with a poor quality of life is not loving/ cruel/ possibly not the child's preferred option had they been able to choose/ abortion removes the possibility of a life of suffering. *Against*: preventing life is never the best option/ the sanctity of life/ 'You shall not murder.' (Exodus 20:13 [NIV])/ the family should be supported to improve the child's quality of life/ better a poor quality of life than no life/ abortion is not permitted in Islam for financial reasons.

6.7 **A** *An argument in favour*: drugs used to end life are God-given/ people should have the choice to end their own life/ most loving and compassionate thing to do/ may allow a painless death. *How religious beliefs disagree*: against the sanctity of life/ murder/ suffering may be for a purpose/ against predestination/ not a right reason for killing/ a sin against God. **B** It is murder/ sinful/ interferes with God's plan/ open to abuse/ disrespects the sanctity of life/ only God should take life/ may be against the will of the person suffering/ suffering can bring a person closer to God/ *see 6.7 A for other reasons.*

6.8 **A** The dead are resurrected into new bodies/ everybody is brought before God/ the book of life is opened and deeds weighed to enable God's judgement/ non-believers and those who did insufficient good go to hell/ believers who did good go to heaven to be with God. **B** *E.g. I agree with this statement. Some people believe that human life is valuable but are more concerned about their own destiny than other people. They want to go to heaven rather than hell because they believe that eternity with the possibility of God is the best option. Because the Bible says that God made life in his image, they feel that valuing human life by helping people living in poverty will be rewarded with a better life after death. The sacrifice they make by helping others is worth it.*
Others take their responsibilities to God more seriously. They also recognise that God made all humans in his image and so see it as their duty to God to value life. This means that if they do all they can to help others maintain and improve their valuable life, they are serving God. This is their main motivation rather than doing what they think God wants in order to get into heaven. However, being granted a place in heaven isn't just about helping others. God knows people's thoughts and reasoning and his decision is final.

7 The existence of God and revelation

Please note that these are suggested answers to the Apply questions, designed to give you guidance, rather than being definitive answers.

7.1 **A** *Muslim Design argument*: God created humans to serve him and be in charge of creation/ the world is well ordered and balanced to sustain life/ the world is beautiful and made up of complex, independent parts/ it must have been designed and only God can do this. *William Paley*: the intricacy and complexity of earth shows it cannot have appeared by chance. *Isaac Newton*: the thumb is evidence of design because it allows precise delicate movement. *Thomas Aquinas*: only an intelligent being could keep everything in the universe in a regular order. *F.R. Tennant*: everything in the universe is perfect to sustain life. **B** *See the answers to 5.1 A for arguments to agree with the statement. Arguments against could include*: natural selection happens by chance/ species are developed by evolution, not a designer/ suffering proves there is no designer God/ order and structure in nature is imposed by humans, not God.

7.2 **A** If everything has a cause, what caused God?/ the universe could be eternal/ the universe may not need a cause/ the Big Bang was random chance/ religious creation stories are myths and not actually true. **B** *For the statement*: everything (including the universe) has a cause to explain its existence/ to cause everything to exist there must be something existing that is eternal and without a cause/ this can only be God, so God must exist/ this means God caused everything to exist, possibly by causing the Big Bang. *Against the statement: see the answers to 5.2 A.*

7.3 **A** E.g. the revelation of the Qur'an: Muhammad received revelations from the angel Jibril/ these began at Mount Hira on the Night of Power/ they continued for over 20 years/ they were written down to form the Qur'an/ the incarnation of Jesus: an angel appeared to Mary and Joseph telling them that they would have a child/ Mary became pregnant by virgin conception and gave birth to Jesus/ predicted and explained as being direct action from God/ recorded in the Gospels of Matthew and Luke. **B** *E.g. 'There is never enough evidence to prove that miracles are the work of God, instead of having a (perhaps unknown) scientific explanation. People who claim to have witnessed miracles are making them up or mistaken about what they have experienced. On the other hand, anyone who has witnessed a miracle is unlikely to remember it wrongly and there are 69 recorded miracles at Lourdes alone. They cannot all have been remembered wrongly. If Jesus had not performed miracles, they wouldn't have been written down in the Bible, and people who were there at the time would have spoken out if they thought the miracles were made up.'*

7.4 **A** If God was loving, he would not allow suffering/ evil exists because God does not/ an all-knowing and all-powerful God would know about suffering and do something to prevent it/ God would not have created an earth that causes suffering through natural disasters. **B** *E.g. 'Science challenges the existence of God because it gives explanations for things that used to be explained with God, which means God is no longer needed as the answer to these things. For example, some people would say the Big Bang theory removes the need to believe that God created the universe. Science also challenges the accuracy of religious creation stories. However, others believe science can help to* *explain God's creation. For example, the Big Bang theory explains how God created the universe, and the theory of evolution explains how God brought life to earth and developed it to what it is like now. Science does not have to challenge religious creation stories if these are not interpreted literally.'*

7.5 **A** A specific experience of God such as a dream, vision, prophecy or miracle. *Any example from scripture, tradition, history or the present day can be given.* **B** *E.g. 'I disagree with this statement because visions can have a profound effect on people's lives, which would be unlikely to happen if they were not real. For example, Saul converted to Christianity after he saw a blinding light and heard Jesus' voice. The way he changed his life as a result of this vision means it probably did happen. Also, he certainly did not expect to experience God in this way because he was very opposed to Christianity.'*

7.6 **A** God's presence in nature/ reason, conscience or morality/ worship/ reading scriptures/ the lives of religious leaders. *Include examples.* **B** *E.g. 'Over the centuries, what was originally written is unlikely to have been changed, because believers were not prepared to change what they thought was the word of God. Even though the world has changed over time, people believe that scripture is still relevant nowadays because God's words are timeless, and can still help people to believe in God.'*

7.7 **A** *Drawing of a symbol for each of the seven ideas about God.* **B** *E.g. 'I agree it is not possible to properly express God's nature in words because God's nature is outside the comprehension of any other being, because nobody but God is all-powerful, knows everything or is eternal. Humans are subject to limits, God is not. God is infinite, humans are finite. Because language is finite, there are no words to fully express God. However, some people might argue it is possible to express God's nature in words because the Bible does a good job of telling Christians what God is like, and Muslims have 99 names for God to describe his nature. Although these words may not fully express God's nature, they certainly help people to understand God.'*

7.8 **A** Drugs or alcohol can make a person lose touch with reality/ wishful thinking means people can persuade themselves that something has happened purely because they want it to/ hallucinations can be symptoms of some illnesses/ some people might lie to become famous or rich, as it is hard to disprove their lies/ some may genuinely believe they have had a revelation but there may be a perfectly normal explanation that they do not know about. **B** *E.g. 'There is no way to prove that a revelation means God does exist. There are perfectly normal explanations for what people say are revelations, so they cannot be considered as evidence for God. For example, they might just be hallucinations caused by illness, or made up by someone to get attention. There is no way to know if a person's 'revelation' is genuine or not, so it cannot act as proof that God exists.'*

8 Religion, peace and conflict

Please note that these are suggested answers to the Apply questions, designed to give you guidance, rather than being definitive answers.

8.1 **A** Christians believe God sent Jesus to save people from sin, so Jesus' sacrifice on the cross gives hope to Christians that their sins will be forgiven if they sincerely repent/ Christians should forgive others as Jesus forgave his enemies on the cross/ Muslims believe God is 'compassionate' and 'merciful'/ God alone can forgive but people must be truly sorry and intend to follow the faith properly in the future/ both Muslims and Christians believe God offers forgiveness to all who ask in faith. **B** *Arguments for*: the Christian Church teaches that killing is wrong/ Jesus' teaching does not support war/ Jesus told people to love their enemies/ Islam means 'peace'/ the Qur'an emphasises peace (e.g. Qur'an 25:63). *Arguments against*: Christians believe in the just war theory/ it is sometimes necessary to take part in war for self-defence/ Muslims believe fighting in self-defence or in defence of the faith can be justified.

8.2 **A** There is an injustice/ they believe in loving their neighbours/ defending the faith if it is attacked. **B** *You might wish to use recent terrorist attacks as examples*/ 'You shall not murder' (Exodus 20:13 [NIV])/ 'Do not take life, which God has made sacred' (Qur'an 17:33).

8.3 **A** d) Forgiveness. **B** *Agree*: if attacked, a country has the right to retaliate/ the enemy started the conflict so they should expect a response/ the Bible teaches, 'An eye for an eye, a tooth for a tooth'/ justice must prevail/ Islam teaches that retaliation is justified in order to guard people against injustice and to protect human lives. *Disagree*: retaliation is wrong because it is just getting back at someone, which is likely to prolong rather than resolve the conflict/ Jesus taught retaliation was wrong when he told people to 'turn the other cheek'/ Jesus taught forgiveness and reconciliation were needed to bring about peace/ the Qur'an says that although retaliation may seem right, if a person is patient and forgives, this is one of the greatest things.

8.4 **A** *Beliefs must be different*. All religions are against the use of weapons of mass destruction/ Christians believe life is sacred (sanctity of life)/ only God has the right to end life/ God created the earth and it should not be destroyed with WMD/ nothing can justify the use of WMDs which target innocent people/ some Christians and Muslims agree with the possession of nuclear weapons as a deterrent/ to maintain peace and prevent attack/ some people think the use of nuclear weapons in war can be justified/ e.g. they ended the Second World War. **B** 'You shall not murder' (Exodus 20:13 [NIV])/ only God has the right to end life (sanctity of life)/ 'Do not contribute to your destruction with your own hands' (Qur'an 2:195).

8.5 **A** If the cause of the war is just/ if the war is fought in self-defence/ if the faith is under attack. **B** Quakers believe war is never justified/ Jesus taught that even the anger that leads to violence is wrong (Matthew 5: 21–22)/ Jesus did not try to resist arrest and told Peter to put his sword away/ although Islam agrees with a just war, Muslims believe it is better to avoid war if possible/ 'Know that the evil of war is swift, and its taste bitter' (Hadith).

8.6 **A** Fighting for God or a religious cause/ authorised by a high religious authority. **B** *The argument is very brief. It could be supported by points such as*: in a democracy people are entitled to freedom of speech/ there is no need to turn to violence to defend religion/ religious freedoms are guaranteed by Human Rights legislation/ God does not want people to fight each other/ Jesus taught people to 'turn the other cheek'. *A different point of view might be*: if a particular religious group is constantly attacked, they may feel justified in using violent means to respond/ although this is not what is really meant by 'holy war'.

8.7 **A** The Anglican Pacifist Fellowship works to overcome the inequality and injustice that lead to war by sponsoring the Week of Prayer for World Peace, contributing to peace-related events and religious services, and raising awareness of the issue of pacifism/ the Muslim Peace Fellowship works against injustice and for peace by trying to deepen people's understanding of Muslim teachings about peace, through publications, conferences, and developing non-violent strategies for issues in society. **B** Conflict is often caused by injustice/ if people feel their rights are being denied they may wish to take violent action to achieve equality of opportunity/ e.g. racist laws in some countries have provoked violent clashes with the authorities/ it is better to make sure people are treated with equal dignity and respect so that conflict is avoided/ Christians and Muslims believe all human beings are created by God so should be treated fairly/ Christian charities like Christian Aid and Caritas campaign to establish human rights in the hope that wars will not be necessary to bring about justice/ Muslim organisations such as Muslim Aid and the Muslim Peace Fellowship work to find non-violent ways of addressing social imbalance.

8.8 **A** By raising money to help refugees through organisations such as Caritas and Muslim Aid/ by going to war-torn areas to deliver emergency supplies to victims. **B** *Agree*: if a country has taken the serious decision to go to war, it should try to defeat the enemy as quickly as possible to prevent more loss of innocent life/ it is sometimes not practical to take the enemy prisoner to help them survive. *Disagree*: according to the conditions of a just war, only appropriate force should be used, so if the enemy tries to surrender they should not be killed/ Muslim rules for a just war state that innocent civilians on the enemy side must be protected and helped to survive/ St Paul teaches, 'Do not repay anyone evil for evil … If it is possible … live at peace with everyone' (Romans 12:17–18 [NIV]).

9 Religion, crime and punishment

Please note that these are suggested answers to the Apply questions, designed to give you guidance, rather than being definitive answers.

9.1 **A** Evil actions are wicked things some people do which usually cause serious harm to other living creatures/ evil intentions are what the offenders hope to achieve by behaving in a wicked or destructive way. **B** *For the statement*: intentions are the reasons for actions/ loving and compassionate intentions usually bring about good actions/ 'But I tell you that anyone who looks at a woman lustfully has already committed adultery with her in his heart' (Matthew 5:28 [NIV]). *Against the statement*: nobody is helped or harmed by intentions but they may be by actions / 'faith by itself, if it is not accompanied by action, is dead' (James 2:17 [NIV]).

9.2 **A** Poverty can lead people to steal food/ a person's upbringing may lead them to view crime as acceptable/ people may break a law in order to protest against it/ greed may prompt someone to steal something they want. **B** *Arguments for the statement could include*: addiction takes away choice/ a person may need to commit crimes to fund their addiction/ addiction may cause illegal actions because the offender doesn't realise what they are doing. *Arguments against the statement could include*: addicts should be helped to defeat their addiction so they do not commit crimes/ Islam forbids the consumption of addictive drugs/ there is no good reason for committing crimes/ there are other reasons (e.g. poverty and mental health problems) for committing crimes.

9.3 **A** Hate crimes usually involve violence and possibly killing/ murder is unlawful killing/ hate crimes result from prejudice, murder can have other reasons/ murder is generally considered to be worse/ some murders are classed as hate crimes. **B** *For*: hatred of a criminal is not constructive/ reasons why the criminal committed the crime should be considered/ love and compassion are religious teachings that should extend even to criminals. *Against*: criminal actions can cause great harm and upset/ some victims never fully recover from a criminal action/ 'let everyone be subject to the governing authorities, for there is no authority except that which God established' (Romans 13:1 [NIV])/ crimes break Christian and Islamic teachings and morality/ Shari'ah law focuses on deterrence by making an example of some criminals.

9.4 **A** *Retribution*: getting your own back/ the offender should receive the same (not greater) injuries and harm that their actions caused. *Deterrence*: putting people off from committing crimes/ the punishment should be severe enough to prevent repetition of the offence. *Reformation*: changing someone's behaviour for the better/ offenders are helped to change so they do not reoffend. **B** *For*: severe punishment can help prevent future crimes/ Shari'ah law supports severe punishment as a deterrent/ 'Cut off the hands of thieves … a deterrent from God' (Qur'an 5:38)/ the criminal deserves severe punishment for what they have done/ 'eye for an eye' means punishment should equal harm caused, so more serious crimes deserve severe punishment. *Against*: less severe punishment may lead more easily to repentance and change/ positive methods (e.g. reformation) are more likely to have a lasting effect/ 'Do not take revenge, my dear friends' (Romans 12:19 [NIV]).

9.5 **A** Free will is given by God to allow humans to make their own choices and decisions/ it does not mean humans can choose to do whatever they want; there are good or bad consequences to every action/ temptation makes free will harder to use properly/ religious beliefs and teachings encourage the responsible use of free will, as does the law and human conscience. **B** *For*: all violence causes suffering/ violence is not loving and doesn't show respect, even in self-defence/ better to try to repair damage that has been done rather than responding with further violence/ Jesus gave an example during his arrest when he healed the High Priest's servant/ there is a duty in Christianity and Islam to help relieve suffering, not cause and increase it. *Against*: using violence in self-defence may cause less harm than allowing an attack to continue/ e.g. the use of atom bombs helped to end the Second World War.

9.6 **A** Christians oppose all punishment that causes harm to offenders/ corporal punishment has no element of reform/ Muslim Shari'ah law agrees with corporal punishment for some offences/ it is seen as a deterrent and often carried out in public. **B** *Against:* Christians believe in compassion and 'love your neighbour' so criminals should be treated well/ all humans are deserving of respect as they are created by God. *For:* 'eye for an eye' suggests offenders who commit serious crimes should receive severe punishment/ Shari'ah law supports severe punishment in order to deter others/ Shari'ah law supports corporal punishment/ God is sometimes pictured as a harsh but fair judge.

9.7 **A** Christians should forgive a person no matter what they have done/ Jesus said there is no limit to the number of times a person should forgive/ Muslims believe only God can truly forgive, and only when he knows the offender is truly sorry and intends to follow the faith properly/ the offender should seek forgiveness from the victim before expecting God to forgive them. **B** *E.g. 'I agree that nobody should expect to be forgiven more than once because they should have learned from their original mistake. If they were punished on the first occasion they should have used the chance to repent and promised not to offend again. Christians who deliberately reoffend break promises to God. On the other hand, Christians are taught they should forgive again. When asked how many times they should forgive, Jesus said, 'not seven times, but seventy-seven times.' Because of this Christians should forgive as many times as necessary, even if the offender does not expect it. They should also try to help the offender not to commit offences in future.'*

9.8 **A** Some Bible passages agree with retribution (e.g. Genesis 9:6)/ others with reform (e.g. Ezekiel 33:11)/ 'You shall not murder' (Exodus 20:13 [NIV])/ death penalty does not reform the offender, which Christians believe is an important aim/ does not respect the sanctity of life/ Islam sees the death penalty as a fair retribution and deterrent/ although the victim is encouraged to show mercy by accepting payment from the murderer/ some Muslims believe the death penalty misinterprets the Qur'an's teaching. **B** The death penalty is not loving or compassionate/ may kill an innocent person by mistake/ life is sacred and only God has the right to take it/ evidence suggests that it does not deter/ a dead offender cannot be reformed/ the victim's family may not want it to happen.

10 Religion, human rights and social justice

Please note that these are suggested answers to the Apply questions, designed to give you guidance, rather than being definitive answers.

10.1 **A** They might treat others fairly/ make sure people's human rights are protected/ encourage people to act with respect and compassion/ work to create a more equal society. **B** *For:* everyone is entitled to have rights/ they allow the more disadvantaged to be treated with justice and compassion which are both teachings of Christianity and Islam/ supported by the parable of the Sheep and the Goats/ promote equality/ supported by Qur'an 49:13/ allow people freedom to live their lives as they wish/ not protecting human rights goes against responsibilities to others and God. *Against*: some people (e.g. murderers) do not deserve rights/ rights should be earned/ those who do not respect the rights of others should have no rights themselves.

10.2 **A** Prejudice is an attitude that some people are superior to others because of their gender, race, sexuality, etc./ discrimination is acting on prejudiced opinions. **B** *For*: religious creation stories say all people are born equal/ everyone is born in the same way, without possessions and completely dependent/ all have equal value as humans/ all have the same access to God/ 'people are equal as the teeth of a comb' (Hadith)/ 'you are all one in Christ Jesus' (Galatians 3:28 [NIV]). *Against*: some are born into wealthy countries or families and some into low-income countries and families living in poverty, so life opportunities are unequal/ historically certain groups have been seen as dominant, giving better opportunities (e.g. men and women are not always treated equally).

10.3 **A** Nobody is forced to be a Christian/ other faiths are welcomed in Christian countries/ everybody has the right to choose a faith (or none)/ the persecution of members of any faith and preaching religious hatred or intolerance are against mainstream Christian teaching/ Muslims believe religious freedom is part of God's design and agree with Christian attitudes/ 'let those who wish to believe in it do so and let those who wish to reject it do so' (Qur'an 18:29)/ in some Muslim countries, Shari'ah law prohibits changing faith from Islam. **B** *Use of any answers to 10.3 A that are relevant to support an opinion*/ it is a basic human right to be allowed to follow a faith/ following any faith can only be helpful to a person and society as a whole/ some sects and interpretations of major faiths may be harmful and so should be avoided.

10.4 **A** It is unjust/ denies belief in equality/ harmful/ illegal/ 'there is neither Jew nor Gentile, neither slave nor free, nor is there male and female for you are one in Christ Jesus' (Galatians 3:28 [NIV])/ not loving or compassionate/ against the will of God etc./ Qur'an teaches equality (Qur'an 49:13)/ Muhammad said 'a white person is not better than a black person, nor is a black person better than a white person.' **B** *E.g. 'I believe all discrimination is wrong because it can cause great harm to people. It is also completely unjust because Christians and Muslims believe all humans are created by God, in his image, and with equal rights. Behaving in any other way shows no love and respect to others and makes them feel that they are in some way inferior and wrong through no fault of their own. However, positive discrimination is an exception because it is not harmful. This means to treat people of some minority groups better than others, for example by giving disabled people special areas of seating in sports stadiums and theatres. This allows them equal opportunity to see sports or arts performances because it removes problems with access. Some Christians see this as fulfilling the prophecy of Amos: 'Let justice roll on like a river and righteousness like a never-failing stream' (Amos 5:24). Some Muslims also think this displays justice, which God commands (Qur'an 16:90).'*

10.5 **A** Men and women have equal status in the eyes of God/ Catholic and Orthodox Christianity do not allow women to be priests/ women cannot become imams unless no man is present at the worship/ women have the responsibility to teach their children the basics of Islam. **B** It is not treating people equally/ This goes against Christian and Muslim teachings/ Galatians 3:28/'People are equal as the teeth of a comb' (Hadith)/ gender or sexuality is not a choice/ it is based on prejudice, which is a negative attitude/ it goes against justice, love and compassion, which are central values to all faiths.

10.6 **A** Wealth is a blessing from God/ excess wealth should be shared with those who have less/ wealth can be dangerous/ can cause greed and selfishness/ 'Beware of greed for it is ready poverty' (Hadith)/ wealth can cause neglect of the spiritual life/ it is not possible to serve both God and money/ 'For the love of money is the root of all sorts of evil' (1 Timothy 6:10 [NIV])/ usury is forbidden in Islam. **B** *E.g. 'Charities are desperate for money so they can carry out their work. They rely on people's generosity to give them money. If giving to charity was compulsory, it is likely they would receive more than they do at present, so could help more people in need throughout the world. Muslims are required to give 2.5% of their savings to charity each year, so the idea of compulsory giving is not unknown.'*

10.7 **A** They are desperate to start a new life in a safer and more wealthy country/ they cannot cross the sea on their own/ they have no legal right to enter another country so have to do it illegally. **B** *E.g. 'High-income countries that prefer to buy cheap goods do cause exploitation. In order to have cheap goods, the cost of making them has to be reduced to a minimum. This means exploiting workers by paying them next to nothing. If people in high-income countries were prepared to pay a little more, the workers could be paid more. Exploitation goes against religious ideas of justice, compassion and love, and shows that Amos' vision that justice should flow like a river and righteousness like a stream has not yet been reached. However, another opinion is that it is the multinational companies that make the goods, and the shops that sell the goods, who are to blame. Designer goods are often made in low-income countries by people who are exploited, yet they are expensive to buy because the producers and shops are keen to make ever bigger profits because they are so greedy. Islam warns against greed and hoarding money (Qur'an 9:34), and in 1 Timothy it says, 'the love of money is the root of all evil.' So exploitation of low-income countries is caused by the greed of rich people, not people living in poverty who want to buy decent things at prices they can afford.'*

10.8 **A** Long-term aid educates people in skills such as literacy, numeracy and basic training to allow them to access work/ teaches them agricultural methods to grow their own crops/ provides assistance for setting up a small business to earn enough to provide for their needs. **B** *Arguments in support*: The fact that so many people are still living in poverty shows that much more still needs to be done/ some religions do not set a good example to believers because they invest a lot of wealth in places of worship rather than giving it to people living in poverty/ 'If a man will not work, he shall not eat' (2 Thessalonians 3:10 [NIV]). *Arguments for a different point of view*: religions have a history of giving to charity/ have set up charities that work with people living in poverty at home and abroad/ many religious believers do all they can to help people living in poverty/ they may be living in poverty themselves so they don't have the money to spare/ some could help out more in practical ways if they cannot afford to give much.

Exam practice answers

1 Christianity: Beliefs and teachings

Test the 1 mark multiple-choice question

1. B) Incarnation

2. C) Benevolent

Test the 1 mark question

Suggested answers, other relevant answers would be credited. 1 mark for a correct point.

3. Through good works/ through the grace of God/ through faith/ through Jesus' death/ through obeying the Ten Commandments/ through loving one's neighbour/ through prayer/ through worship/ through the Holy Spirit.

4. Christians believe everyone will be raised from the dead (resurrection)/ face judgement of God/ immediately or at the end of time/ Judgement Day/ Second Coming of Christ/ Jesus rose from the dead/ people will be judged on how they lived their lives/ sent to heaven, hell or purgatory/ resurrection of the body/ restoration to glorified bodies.

Test the 4 mark question

Suggested answers, other relevant answers would be credited. 1 mark for each simple point, another mark for developing each point, so a maximum of 4 marks for two developed points.

6. Christians may show respect towards all of God's creation/ actively work for conservation/ show stewardship/ take practical steps like recycling/ be energy efficient.

Christians may treat others with respect/ all are created 'in imago dei' (in God's image)/ work for peace between people/ support charities that help people in need/ reflect God in all they do.

Christians may take care of themselves (both body and soul)/ adopt healthy lifestyles/ develop spiritual practices/ prayer/ worship/ meditation.

7. Christians believe that because God is loving, God wants the best for them/ they accept God's will as being for their benefit, even if it does not appear to be so/ they love others because God loves them.

God's greatest act of love was sending his Son Jesus/ to save people from sin/ to gain eternal life/ so they are grateful to God/ express their thanks through worship or praise.

God is love/ qualities of love described in Paul's letter to the Corinthians/ patient/ kind/ not easily angered/ Christians try to live according to these descriptions of love.

Test the 6 mark question

Suggested answers, other relevant answers would be credited. 1 mark for each simple point, another mark for developing each point, so a maximum of 4 marks for two developed points, plus 1 extra mark for a correct reference to a source of religious belief or teaching, and 1 more extra mark for applying the reference to the question.

9. Christians believe God is omnipotent (all-powerful)/ has supreme authority/ can do all things/ 'Nothing is impossible with God' (Luke 1:37 [NIV]), which illustrates God's omnipotence and can be interpreted to mean that all things are possible for God/ is loving (benevolent)/ wants good for God's creation/ wants people to love God freely in return/ 'God so loved the world that he gave his one and only Son, that whoever believes in him shall not perish but have eternal life' (John 3:16 [NIV])/ is just (fair/righteous)/ wants people to choose good over evil/ punishes wrongdoing/ is the perfect judge of human character.

Christians believe there is only one God/ 'The Lord is our God, the Lord alone' (Deuteronomy 6:4 [NIV])/ but within God there is a Trinity of persons/ Father, Son (Jesus), Holy Spirit/ 'Our Father in heaven' (Lord's Prayer)/ the Spirit's presence at Jesus' baptism.

God is the creator of all that is/ 'In the beginning, God created the heavens and the earth' (Genesis 1:1 [NIV])/ the Spirit was present at creation/ the Word of God (the Son) was involved in creation too.

10. Christians believe Jesus restored the relationship between God and humanity/ Jesus atoned for the sins of humankind/ God accepted his death as atonement for sin by raising Jesus from the dead/ 'Jesus Christ [...] is the atoning sacrifice for our sins, and not only for ours but also for the sins of the whole world' (1 John 2: 1–2 [NIV]), which can be interpreted to mean that atonement is achieved through God sacrificing his son for all to achieve salvation.

Through the atonement of Jesus, humans can receive forgiveness for sin/ be able to get close to God/ gain eternal life/ sin has been defeated/ 'For the wages of sin is death, but the gift of God is eternal life in Christ Jesus our Lord' (Romans 6:23 [NIV]).

Jesus' death atoned for the original sin of Adam and Eve/ Adam chose to disobey God, but Jesus chose to offer his life as a sacrifice/ 'For since death came through a man, the resurrection of the dead also comes through a man. For as in Adam all die, so in Christ all will be made alive' (1 Corinthians 15:21 [NIV]).

Test the 12 mark question

Suggested answers shown here, but see page 10 for guidance on levels of response.

1 Arguments in support

- Hell is not a place/ exploration of the earth and space have not discovered a place where spirits are punished forever/ although hell is shown in paintings as a place of fire and torture ruled by Satan (the devil) somewhere beneath the earth, no such place exists.
- The idea of hell is inconsistent with a benevolent God/ Christians believe God is loving/ a loving God would never send anyone to eternal damnation in hell/ like a loving Father, God will give people another chance if they repent.
- The idea of hell is just a way of comforting those who want to see justice/ some people get away with many bad things and seem not to receive punishment in this life/ the idea of hell ensures the idea of justice being done, but it does not really exist.

Arguments in support of other views

- Today hell is more often thought to be an eternal state of mind being cut off from the possibility of God/ the state of being without God, rather than a place/ a person who did not acknowledge God or follow his teachings would necessarily end up without God in the afterlife.
- Christians believe God is just/ it is only fair that someone who has gone against God's laws should be punished eventually/ it is a just punishment for an immoral life.
- Jesus spoke about hell as a possible consequence for sinners/ 'But I tell you that anyone who is angry with a brother or sister will be subject to judgment [...] And anyone who says, 'You fool!' will be in danger of the fire of hell.' (Matthew 5:22 [NIV])/ 'If your right eye causes you to stumble, gouge it out and throw it away. It is better for you to lose one part of your body than for your whole body to be thrown into hell.' (Matthew 5:29 [NIV])/ 'For if God did not spare angels when they sinned, but sent them to hell, putting them in chains of darkness to be held for judgment' (2 Peter 2:4 [NIV]).

2 Arguments in support

- Salvation means deliverance from sin and admission to heaven brought about by Jesus/ saving one's soul/ sin separates people from God who is holy/ the original sin of Adam and Eve brought suffering and death to humankind/so God gave the law so that people would know how to stay close to him/ Jesus'teaching takes the law even further
- One way of gaining salvation is through good works/ by having faith in God and obeying God's laws/ obeying the Ten Commandments (Exodus 20:1–19); this is the best way of being saved because by doing so the Christian is avoiding sin/ following other Christian teachings such as the Beatitudes (Matthew 5:1–12) helps gain salvation through good works/ being merciful/ a peacemaker.
- Christians believe God gave people free will to make moral choices/ following God's law shows the person is willing to use their free will wisely.

Arguments in support of other views

- The best way of gaining salvation is through grace/ grace is a free gift of God's love and support/ it is not earned by following laws/ faith in Jesus is all a person needs to be saved/ 'For it is by grace you have been saved, through faith – and this is not from yourselves, it is the gift of God – not by works, so that no one can boast.' (Ephesians 2:8–9 [NIV]).
- Merely following the law is a legalistic approach/ it can hide sinfulness inside a person/ Jesus criticised the Pharisees for following the law but having evil hearts/ Jesus said, 'The teachers of the law and the Pharisees sit in Moses' seat. So you must be careful to do everything they tell you. But do not do what they do, for they do not practice what they preach.' (Matthew 23:2–3 [NIV]).
- Most Christians believe both good works and grace (through faith in Jesus) are needed to be saved/ you can't prove you have faith unless you show it in your outward behaviour/ a danger in believing in salvation through grace alone is that people can feel specially chosen so look down on others/ not feel they have to obey God's law as they are already 'saved'.

2 Christianity: Practices

Test the 1 mark multiple-choice question

1. D) Liturgical worship

2. C) Christmas

Test the 1 mark question

Suggested answers, other relevant answers would be credited. 1 mark for a correct point.

3. By setting up charities/ Christian Aid/ CAFOD/ Tearfund/ by raising or donating money/ by working overseas in low-income countries/ by praying for justice for people living in poverty/ by campaigning for people living in poverty.

4. Prayer helps Christians communicate with God/ develop and sustain their relationship with God/ thank God for blessings/ praise God/ ask God for help for oneself or others/ find courage to accept God's will in difficult times.

Test the 4 mark question

Suggested answers, other relevant answers would be credited. 1 mark for each simple point, another mark for developing each point, so a maximum of 4 marks for two developed points.

6. *Ways must be different*:

Infant baptism: Catholic, Orthodox, Anglican, Methodist and United Reformed Churches baptise babies/ 'I baptise you in the name of the Father, and of the Son, and of the Holy Spirit'/ blessed water poured over the baby's head/ sign of cross on baby's forehead/ anointing with oil/ white garment/ candle/ godparents' and parents' promises.

Believers' baptism: others such as Baptist and Pentecostal Christians baptise those who are old enough to make their own decision about baptism/ baptise people who have made a commitment to faith in Jesus/ full immersion in pool/ minister talks about meaning of baptism/ candidates are asked if they are willing to change their lives/ Bible passage/ brief testimony from candidate/ baptised 'in the name of the Father, and of the Son, and of the Holy Spirit'.

7. *Interpretations must be different*:

Catholic, Orthodox and some Anglican Christians believe the bread and wine become the body and blood of Christ/ Jesus is fully present in the bread and wine/ a divine mystery/ those receiving become present in a mystical way at the death and resurrection of Christ/ receive God's grace/ Holy Communion is a sacrament.

Protestant Christians see Holy Communion as a reminder of Jesus' words and actions at the Last Supper/ bread and wine are symbols of Jesus' sacrifice/ they help them reflect on the meaning of Jesus' death and resurrection for their lives today/ it is an act of fellowship.

Test the 6 mark question

Suggested answers, other relevant answers would be credited. 1 mark for each simple point, another mark for developing each point, so a maximum of 4 marks for two developed points, plus 1 extra mark for a correct reference to a source of religious belief or teaching, and 1 more extra mark for applying the reference to the question.

9. Spreading the Christian gospel/ by public preaching/ by personal witness.

Evangelism is considered a duty of Christians because of the Great Commission/ 'Therefore go and make disciples of all nations, baptising them in the name of the Father and of the Son and of the Holy Spirit, and teaching them to obey everything I have commanded you' (Matthew 28:19–20 [NIV]), which describes the instructions Jesus gave to his disciples to evangelise and these are instructions that Christians today follow/people have a desire to share the good news with others because they have experienced it themselves.

Christians believe they are called to do more than just know Jesus in their own lives/ they are called to spread the good news to non-believers that Jesus is the Saviour of the world.

When the early disciples received the Spirit at Pentecost they were given the gifts necessary to carry out the Great Commission/ the Spirit gives some people wisdom/ knowledge/ faith/ gifts of healing/ miraculous powers/ prophecy/ the ability to speak in tongues and understand the message of those who speak in tongues.

10. Christians may work for reconciliation in their own lives by forgiving their enemies/ making up with people they have offended/ going to the sacrament of Reconciliation to be reconciled with God/ 'But I tell you, love your enemies and pray for those who persecute you' (Matthew 5:44 [NIV]), which illustrates a way that reconciliation can be achieved: by being benevolent towards those who might be against you.

Christians may work for reconciliation between political or religious groups through organisations/ e.g. through the Irish Churches Peace Project/ the Corrymeela Community/ which sought to bring Catholic and Protestant communities together in Northern Ireland/ through discussion and working on their differences together.

Christians could work for more global reconciliation through an organisation such as the Community of the Cross of Nails at Coventry Cathedral/ which works with partners in many countries/ to bring about peace and harmony in areas where conflict and violence are present.

Christians do this work because of Jesus' teaching and example/ as Paul says, 'For if, while we were God's enemies, we were reconciled to him through the death of his Son, how much more, having been reconciled, shall we be saved through his life!' (Romans 5:10 [NIV]).

Test the 12 mark question

Suggested answers shown here, but see page 10 for guidance on levels of response.

12. Arguments in support

- Going to a place where Jesus or saints lived and died can inspire people/ it can teach people more about their religion's history/ can strengthen faith as it increases knowledge about holy people/ Christians make pilgrimages to the Holy Land as it is where Jesus lived, preached, died and resurrected from the dead/ Christians can experience for themselves what it was like to live there/ they follow in the footsteps of

Jesus/ meet others who share their faith/ the effort and discipline needed strengthens their faith.

- Some Christians go on pilgrimage to places where miracles are said to have occurred/ e.g. Lourdes in France/ they pray to be healed from sin/ physical illness or mental health problems/ to thank God for a special blessing/ to help others who are disabled or ill, putting into practice love of neighbour.
- Some Christians go on pilgrimage to a remote place/ e.g. Iona in Scotland/ they go to have quiet time to pray/ read scriptures/ connect with God through nature/ reflect on their lives/ particularly if facing a big decision/ refresh their spiritual lives in today's busy world.

Arguments in support of other views

- Pilgrimage does not always bring people closer to God/ some places are very commercialised/ it can disappoint people who had a certain mental image of a place to see that it is touristy/ it can be very crowded so not a place for reflection/ some people on the pilgrimage may just see it as a holiday, making it hard to concentrate on God.
- Pilgrimage can be expensive/ not everyone can afford going abroad/ not everyone has time to make a pilgrimage, e.g. getting time off work/ family commitments.
- Other ways of becoming closer to God are better than pilgrimage/ daily prayer in one's own home can bring the peace of mind and heart the person needs/ receiving Holy Communion brings people closer to God than any journey/ going to the sacrament of Reconciliation can be done locally.

13. Arguments in support

- The Church (meaning all Christians) has a mission to spread the good news/ that Jesus Christ is the Son of God/ came into the world to be its saviour/ the Great Commission/ 'Therefore go and make disciples of all nations, baptising them in the name of the Father and of the Son and of the Holy Spirit, and teaching them to obey everything I have commanded you' (Matthew 28:19–20 [NIV]).
- Christians believe they are called to do more than just know Jesus in their own lives/ they are called to spread the good news to non-believers that Jesus is the Saviour of the world.
- When the early disciples received the Spirit at Pentecost they were given the gifts necessary to carry out the Great Commission/ the Spirit gives some people wisdom/ knowledge/ faith/ gifts of healing/ miraculous powers/ prophecy/ the ability to speak in tongues and understand the message of those who speak in tongues/ Christians today receive the Holy Spirit at their Confirmation/ they are called to be disciples of Jesus, like the first disciples/ so they must spread the faith fearlessly as the disciples did.

Arguments in support of other views

- The main job of a Christian is to believe in Jesus/ follow the commandments/ worship God/ love one's neighbour as oneself/ live a good life in the hope of eternal life in heaven.
- Many Christians do not have the personality to preach to others about their faith/ do not have the time if working/ have family responsibilities/ are not public speakers/ do not want to antagonise people who are unsympathetic non-believers/ cannot go abroad to work as missionaries.
- There are other ways of showing one's faith to others without actually 'telling them'/ being a good neighbour/ helping those in need/ working with charities/ worshipping God/ showing integrity/ having high moral principles that make non-believers notice that faith makes a difference to the Christian believer.

3 Islam: Beliefs and teachings

Test the 1 mark multiple-choice question

1. D) The Torah
2. C) Jibril

Test the 1 mark question

Suggested answers, other relevant answers would be credited. 1 mark for a correct point.

3. Sunni Muslims believe their leader should be elected, whereas Shi'a Muslims believe their leader should be a descendant of Muhammad and chosen by God/ Shi'a Muslims believe their leader has the authority to provide religious guidance, whereas Sunni Muslims don't/ Sunni Muslims believe Abu Bakr was the rightful leader after Muhammad died; Shi'a Muslims believe Ali was/ Sunni Muslims follow the six articles of faith; Shi'a Muslims follow the five roots of 'Usul ad-Din/ Sunni Muslims pray five times a day; Shi'a Muslims three times a day/ Sunni Muslims give Zakah; Shi'a Muslims also give Khums.
4. Everlasting life after death

Test the 4 mark question

Suggested answers, other relevant answers would be credited. 1 mark for each simple point, another mark for developing each point, so a maximum of 4 marks for two developed points.

6. God is immanent/ present everywhere in the world and the universe/ involved with life on earth/ God is transcendent/ beyond and outside the universe/ God is beneficent/ all-loving and all-good/ seen in his gift to humans of everything they need to live on earth/ God is fair and just/ will judge all people equally on the Day of Judgement/ God is merciful/ cares for people and understands their suffering/ forgives people who are truly sorry/ God is omnipotent/ has the power to create and sustain everything in the universe/ is aware of all human actions and thoughts.
7. Encourages Muslims to take responsibility for their actions/ because they know God will hold them accountable and reward or punish them accordingly/ motivates Muslims to follow the teachings in the Qur'an and dedicate their lives to God/ e.g. by following the Five Pillars or Ten Obligatory Acts/ helps Muslims to accept unjust situations/ as they know God will provide justice in the afterlife.

Test the 6 mark question

Suggested answers, other relevant answers would be credited. 1 mark for each simple point, another mark for developing each point, so a maximum of 4 marks for two developed points, plus 1 extra mark for a correct reference to a source of religious belief or teaching, and 1 more extra mark for applying the reference to the question.

9. Muhammad received the final revelation of Islam/the Qur'an from God/ which is the highest source of authority for all matters relating to Muslim teaching, practice and law/ 'he is God's messenger and the seal of the prophets' (Qur'an 33:40), which explains that – as the seal of the prophets – Muhammad is the most important prophet because he finalised the teachings of Islam / helped to fully establish Islam/ by conquering Makkah and converting the city to Islam/ travelled to heaven and met God/ agreed with God that Muslims should pray five times a day.
10. There is only one God/ God is a unified, indivisible being who cannot be divided into different persons/ God is eternal/ has always existed/ God was not born or came into being out of something else/ God does not have any children/ God is unique/ no other person or thing has God's qualities/ 'Say, "He is God the One, God the eternal. He begot no one nor was He begotten. No one is comparable to Him."' (Qur'an 112:1–4), which illustrates Tawhid clearly because being incomparable means there can only be one and there are no others like God.

Test the 12 mark question

Suggested answers shown here, but see page 10 for guidance on levels of response.

12. Arguments in support

- The Qur'an is God's word/ as passed on by the angel Jibril to Muhammad/ so must include everything God wants Muslims to know about how to live a good life in obedience to him.
- The Qur'an is accepted as the highest authority in Islam/ e.g. the authority of the holy books is one of the six articles of faith in Sunni Islam/ so Muslims should always look to the Qur'an for guidance on how to live a perfect Muslim life.
- The Qur'an includes stories about the lives of the prophets/ who were sent to earth to help make sure people followed God's path/ act as good role models to Muslims.
- Major Muslim practices stem from the Qur'an, such as fasting during Ramadan (Qur'an 2:18)/ giving Zakah (Qur'an 2:215)/ undertaking Hajj (Qur'an 3:97).

Arguments in support of other views

- Shi'a Muslims believe the Imams are necessary to help explain the teachings in the Qur'an/ as the Qur'an was written hundreds of years ago so needs interpreting for the modern world/ as the Qur'an can be interpreted in different ways.
- The Sunnah (Muhammad's teachings and actions) also have the authority to provide religious guidance/ help Muslims to live a perfect Muslim life.
- Some Muslim practices are not detailed in the Qur'an/ e.g. giving to charity is mentioned in the Qur'an, but the exact amount that should be given as Zakah is not/ this was worked out at a later date by Muslim scholars.

13. Arguments in support

- God sends prophets to earth to help convey his desires for humanity/ they do this by conveying God's words and setting good examples for how to live a life in obedience to God/ so Muslims should pay attention to the prophets as role models.
- Ibrahim showed total dedication to God/ fulfilled all the tests and commands given to him by God/ e.g. he was willing to sacrifice his son to God/ he left his wife and son in the desert on God's command/ these events show he had complete faith in God/ was willing to put God before his family/ which gives Muslims a strong example of how they should put God before everything else.
- Muhammad dedicated his life to preaching God's word and proclaiming that God is One/ challenged the people of Makkah to give up habits that went against God's word, despite facing persecution as a result/ provides a good example of how Muslims should dedicate their lives to God.

Arguments in support of other views:

- Angels are pure and sinless/ do not ever displease God/ ceaselessly praise and worship God/ always obey God's commands/ these are all traits that Muslims should aspire to.
- Angels take care of people throughout their lives/ this could inspire Muslims to show kindness to others.
- The prophets showed violence in some of their actions/ e.g. Ibrahim smashed the idols in the temple with an axe/ e.g. Muhammad marched on the city of Makkah/ so it could be said they are not good role models from this point of view.

4 Islam: practices

Test the 1 mark multiple-choice question

1. C) Shahadah
2. B) Husayn

Test the 1 mark question

Suggested answers, other relevant answers would be credited. 1 mark for a correct point.

3. Compass/ mihrab/ qiblah wall.
4. By donating directly to a charity/ by giving to a mosque.

Test the 4 mark question

Suggested answers, other relevant answers would be credited. 1 mark for each simple point, another mark for developing each point, so a maximum of 4 marks for two developed points.

6. Muslims circle the Ka'aba/ remembering the shrine God told Ibrahim to build/ Muslims walk seven times between the hills of Safa and Marwah/ this recalls Hajira's search for water/ Muslims collect water from the well of Zamzam/ this recalls when Ishmael struck his foot on the ground and water gushed up from the earth/ Muslims throw pebbles at the Jamarat/ this recalls when Ibrahim threw stones at the devil/ Muslims sacrifice an animal/ this recalls Ibrahim's willingness to sacrifice his own son.

7. It is important to fast during Ramadan because this is a command from God/ revealed to Muhammad via the angel Jibril/ 'So any one of you who is present that month should fast' (Qur'an 2:18)/ it is important to fast because it develops self-discipline/ shows obedience and dedication to God/ reminds Muslims to help those in poverty.

Test the 6 mark question

Suggested answers, other relevant answers would be credited. 1 mark for each simple point, another mark for developing each point, so a maximum of 4 marks for two developed points, plus 1 extra mark for a correct reference to a source of religious belief or teaching, and 1 more extra mark for applying the reference to the question.

9. It is one of the Five Pillars and Ten Obligatory Acts/ Muslims are expected to take part in Hajj at least once during their lifetime/ 'Pilgrimage to the House is a duty owed to God by people who are able to undertake it' (Qur'an 3:97), which tells Muslims that God wants them to visit the Kabah and therefore go on Hajj if they can afford to/ to show commitment to God/ to become closer to God/ to be reminded of the good examples set by the prophets/ e.g. Ibrahim's willingness to sacrifice his own son/ 'Who could be better in religion than those who [...] follow the religion of Abraham, who was true in faith?' (Qur'an 4:125)/ to feel part of the Muslim community.

10. Jihad is the struggle against evil/ greater jihad is the inward, personal struggle to follow the teachings of Islam/ '... this is My path, leading straight, so follow it, and do not follow other ways' (Qur'an 6:153), which supports the belief in greater jihad because greater jihad is the struggle to follow God in everything Muslims do throughout their lives/ it is more important than lesser jihad/ requires Muslims to put God above everything else/ to observe the Five Pillars and study the Qur'an/ lesser jihad is the outward, collective struggle to defend Islam from threat/ it is acceptable to fight in self-defence if all other peaceful methods have been tried first/ it cannot be used to justify terrorist attacks.

Test the 12 mark question

Suggested answers shown here, but see page 10 for guidance on levels of response.

12. Arguments in support

- Giving to charity helps the most vulnerable members of the Muslim community/ e.g. by providing them with food and shelter/ this gives them strength/ it also brings the whole community together, by making wealthy people more aware of people living in poverty.
- Giving Khums helps to fund religious education/ this increases knowledge and understanding in the Muslim community, so making it stronger.
- A strong community is important because this protects the faith from attack/ giving to charity provides support for Muslims/ thus making it easier for Muslims to follow Muslim teachings (e.g. prevents stealing to feed a family)/ so any practice that strengthens the community is important.

Arguments in support of other views

- Other practices also strengthen the Muslim community/ e.g. prayer connects Muslims together (as they all pray facing Makkah/ all use the same prayers and rak'ah)/ Hajj brings Muslims together and creates a strong sense of community/ particularly as Muslims all wear similar ihram clothing (usually white)/ celebrating festivals brings Muslims together.
- Other things are more important than strengthening the Muslim community/ e.g. showing obedience to God/ following the examples of the prophets/ putting God above everything else/ so other practices are more important for these reasons/ e.g. prayer and studying the Qur'an.

13. Arguments in support

- Christian festivals (such as Easter and Christmas) are official public holidays in Britain, so the festivals of other predominant religions should be recognised in the same way.
- Making Id-ul-Fitr an official public holiday would give Muslims time off work to attend special prayers in mosques or large outdoor areas/ visit their local cemetery to pray for the dead/ celebrate with family and friends.
- Id-ul-Fitr allows Muslims to celebrate the end of a month of fasting/ it is an important reward for a difficult month requiring great self-discipline/ this should be recognised officially.
- Id-ul-Fitr allows Muslims to thank God for giving his wisdom and guidance in the Qur'an/ many Muslims would say this is the most important part of their history to remember, as without the Qur'an Islam would not exist in the same way today/ making Id-ul-Fitr an official public holiday would help with this.

Arguments in support of other views

- Christianity is the main religious tradition in Britain/ so only Christian festivals should be recognised as official public holidays/ if Muslim festivals were made official public holidays, Hindu/Sikh/Buddhist festivals would have to be made official public holidays as well.
- If Id-ul-Fitr was made an official public holiday this would dilute the meaning and significance of the festival/ in the same way that Christmas has become commercialised and is celebrated by non-Christians as well as Christians.
- Instead it would be better for businesses to give Muslims time off to celebrate/ some Muslim businesses in Britain already do this.

5 Relationships and families

Test the 1 mark multiple-choice question

3 D) Stability

4 B) A couple and their children

Test the 1 mark question

Suggested answers, other relevant answers would be credited. 1 mark for a correct point.

3 Christians believe all people are created equal by God/ 'love your neighbour' applies to everyone/ Christians follow Jesus' example in treating women with equal value/ 'There is neither Jew nor Gentile, neither slave nor free, nor is there male and female, for you are all one in Christ Jesus' (Galatians 3:28 [NIV])/ men and women can have different roles in the family but this does not mean they are not equal in God's sight.

Muslims believe God created all people equal/ 'People, We created you all from a single man and a single woman, and made you into races and tribes so that you should recognise one another' (Qur'an 49:13)/ God will reward anyone, man or woman, who does a good deed (Qur'an 16:97)/ men and women have the same moral and religious responsibilities/ Muhammad supported equal rights for all in the community.

4 Christians who oppose sex before marriage think cohabitation is wrong/ Catholic and Orthodox Churches believe a sexual relationship should only take place within marriage/ many Anglican and Protestant Christians accept that although marriage is best, people may live together in a faithful, loving, committed way without being married.

Muslims oppose cohabitation as they believe a sexual relationship should only take place within marriage.

Test the 4 mark question

Suggested answers, other relevant answers would be credited. 1 mark for each simple point, another mark for developing each point, so a maximum of 4 marks for two developed points.

6 *Beliefs must be different:*

Christians believe marriage is for life/ vows made in the presence of God should not be broken/ Jesus taught that anyone who divorced and remarried was committing adultery (Mark 10:11–12)/ except in the case of adultery (Matthew 5:32)/ for Catholics marriage is a sacrament that is permanent/ cannot be dissolved by civil divorce/ Catholics can separate but cannot marry someone else while their partner is still alive/ for some Christians divorce is the lesser of two evils/ Protestant Churches accept civil divorce and allow remarriage in church.

Muslims accept divorce as a last resort/ but believe it is hateful to God (Hadith)/ the Qur'an guarantees the rights of men and women to divorce/ reconciliation is encouraged first with the help of family members/ a waiting period of three months is required to establish whether the wife is pregnant and give time for reconciliation.

7 *Beliefs must be different:*

Many Christians believe opposite-sex sexual relationships are part of God's plan for humans/ God created male and female/ told them to 'be fruitful and increase in number' (Genesis 1:28 [NIV])/ sex expresses a deep, life-long union best expressed in marriage/ some Christians oppose same-sex sexual relationships because they go against God's plan/ the Catholic Church teaches that same-sex sexual relationships are sinful/ some Christians think loving, faithful same-sex sexual relationships are just as holy as opposite-sex ones.

Islam teaches opposite-sex sexual relationships are the expected pattern of behaviour/ Muslims are expected to marry and have a family/ the sexual relationship between husband and wife is a blessing from God/ same-sex sexual relationships are forbidden in Islam/ most Muslims believe the Qur'an and Hadith teach that these relationships are against God's will/ will face the judgement of God/ 'Must you, unlike [other] people, lust after males and abandon the wives that God has created for you? You are exceeding all bounds' (Qur'an 26:165–166).

Test the 6 mark question

Suggested answers, other relevant answers would be credited. 1 mark for each simple point, another mark for developing each point, so a maximum of 4 marks for two developed points, plus 1 extra mark for a correct reference to a source of religious belief or teaching, and 1 more extra mark for applying the reference to the question.

9 For Christians, procreation is an important purpose/ procreation is part of God's plan for humanity/ God created man and woman, blessed them and said, 'Be fruitful and increase in number; fill the earth and subdue it' (Genesis 1:28 [NIV]), which supports one purpose of families: to have children/ protection of children is an important purpose/ educating children about Christian values is an important purpose/ 'Children thrive, grow and develop within the love and safeguarding of the family' (The Church of England website)/

For Muslims, protection is an important purpose/ the Qur'an says married people are 'protected' and this protection extends to the family/ raising children to be good Muslims is an important purpose/ 'Honour your children and perfect their manners' (Hadith), which suggests that one important purpose of families is to respect children and bring them up to behave well/ caring for elderly relatives is an important purpose.

10 The Christian Church teaches that both parents and children have responsibilities in a family/ the commandment to 'Honour one's father and mother' (Exodus 20:12 [NIV]) applies to children of all ages, and it suggests that one role of children is to be respectful to their parents because it is a commandment from God/ it includes the respect and care given to the elderly members of the family/ children should obey their parents/ 'Children, obey your parents in everything, for this pleases the Lord' (Colossians 3:20 [NIV]).

Muslims have a duty to respect and care for their parents as they get older/ the Qur'an says that being unkind or disrespectful to one's parents is a great sin (Qur'an 17:23–24), which suggests that one role of children is to be kind and respectful to their parents and not doing this is going against God/ 'It is one of the greatest sins that a man should curse his parents' (Hadith).

Test the 12 mark question

Suggested answers shown here, but see page 10 for guidance on levels of response.

12 Arguments in support

- Most Christians think marriage is the proper place to enjoy a sexual relationship/ sex expresses a deep, loving, lifelong union that first requires the commitment of marriage/ it is one of God's gifts at creation/ 'That is why a man leaves his father and mother and is united to his wife, and they become one flesh' (Genesis 2:24 [NIV]).
- Having sex is part of the trust between partners in marriage/ sex should not be a casual, temporary pleasure/ 'The sexual act must take place exclusively within marriage. Outside of marriage it always constitutes a grave sin.' (Catechism 2390).
- Paul urged sexual restraint: 'Flee from sexual immorality. All other sins a person commits are outside the body, but whoever sins sexually, sins against their own body. Do you not know that your bodies are temples of the Holy Spirit, who is in you, whom you have received from God? You are not your own.' (1 Corinthians 6:18–19 [NIV]).
- Marriage brings security/ protects each partner's rights/ the rights of children/ provides a stable environment in which to raise a family.
- For Muslims, marriage is the foundation of family life/ the only place for a sexual relationship/ a faithful, lifelong partnership where both people take full responsibility for their children/ the best way to have a stable and secure sexual relationship.
- 'There is no institution in Islam more beloved and dearer (to God) than marriage' Hadith

Arguments in support of other views

- Society has changed/ many people do not see sex as requiring the commitment of marriage/ contraception has reduced the risk of pregnancy before marriage/ many people engage in casual sexual relationships.
- The cost of marriage prevents some people from marrying immediately/ some couples want to see if the relationship is going to work before marrying/ some people do not think a marriage certificate makes any difference to their relationship.
- Some Christians accept that for some people sex before marriage is a valid expression of their love for each other/ some Christians may accept cohabitation, particularly if the couple is committed to each other/ more liberal Christians may accept that people may live together in a faithful, loving and committed way without being married.

13 Arguments in support

- The Orthodox and Catholic Churches teach that using artificial contraception within marriage is wrong/ against natural law/ against the purpose of marriage to have children/ having children is God's greatest gift to a married couple/ 'Every sexual act should have the possibility of creating new life' (*Humanae Vitae*, 1968).
- God will not send more children than a couple can care for/ if Catholic couples wish to plan their families they should use a natural method, such as the rhythm method.
- Some Muslims think artificial contraception is wrong/ interferes with God's plans/ God gives people the strength and means to cope with any children/ 'Do not kill your children for fear of poverty … killing them is a great sin' (Qur'an 17:31).

Arguments in support of other views

- Other Christians and Muslims accept the use of artificial contraception provided it is not used to prevent having children altogether/ by mutual consent of the couple.
- Its use may allow a couple to develop their relationship before having children/ prevent sexually transmitted infections/ help reduce the population explosion.
- The Church of England approved the use of artificial contraception at the Lambeth Conference in 1930/ 'The Conference agrees that other methods may be used, provided that this is done in the light of Christian principles.'
- Some Muslims accept artificial methods if the wife's health is at risk/ to avoid serious financial difficulties/ to space pregnancies/ Islam is sympathetic to family planning/ 'God wishes to lighten your burden; man was created weak' (Qur'an 4:28).

6 Religion and life

Test the 1 mark multiple-choice question

1. C) A good or gentle death
2. B) Life is sacred

Test the 1 mark question

Suggested answers, other relevant answers would be credited. 1 mark for a correct point.

3 Can only happen during the first 24 weeks unless the woman's life is in danger/ risk to woman's physical and mental health/ risk the baby will be born with a severe disability/ an additional child may endanger the physical or mental health of other children in the family/ must take place in an authorised clinic/ two doctors must agree.

4 A wonderful place where God resides/ paradise/ beautiful garden of physical and spiritual pleasures/ eternal/ opposite from hell/ no suffering (Revelation 4:2–6)/ for all who live a good life and obey the teachings of the Qur'an or Bible/ a place after death for the faithful/ there are mansions below which flow rivers/ provision of delicious food and drink.

Test the 4 mark question

Suggested answers, other relevant answers would be credited. 1 mark for each simple point, another mark for developing each point, so a maximum of 4 marks for two developed points.

6 *Beliefs must be similar*:

Animal experimentation makes sure products such as medicines and food are safe to use/ most Christians believe it is good stewardship of the earth's resources to use animals in this way/ some Christians believe humans are more important than animals as they have dominion over them/ so animal experimentation is acceptable if it saves human lives/ as long as the animals are treated as kindly as possible.

Most Muslims believe animal experimentation should be allowed for essential human needs/ but the animals should not be made to suffer unnecessarily as this is against Muslim principles.

7 *Beliefs must be different*:

A minority of Christians believe that as God put people in charge of the world they can use the resources as they wish/ God gave humans dominion and created the natural resources so that they may be used/ 'Rule over the fish in the sea and the birds in the sky and over every living creature that moves on the ground.' (Genesis 1:28)/ this has led in some cases to the overuse and abuse of natural resources.

Muslims believe God has given them the role of stewards (khalifah), so natural resources should be used responsibly/ damaging the earth is a serious sin/ 'do not take more from it than what you need' (Hadith)/ on the Day of Judgement, humans will be judged by God for how well they have looked after the earth.

Test the 6 mark question

Suggested answers, other relevant answers would be credited. 1 mark for each simple point, another mark for developing each point, so a maximum of 4 marks for two developed points, plus 1 extra mark for a correct reference to a source of religious belief or teaching, and 1 more extra mark for applying the reference to the question.

9 Christians believe God created the earth for humans to use and look after/ stewardship means humans have a responsibility to look after the earth on behalf of God/ God put Adam into the Garden of Eden 'to work it and take care of it' (Genesis 2:15 [NIV]), which can be interpreted to mean that one duty of humans is to protect the Earth and look after it as a steward/ it is an act of love to protect the earth for future generations.

Muslims believe they have a duty to respect, nurture and care for the environment/ it is a sin to damage the earth/ humans have the role of stewards (khalifah)/ 'Every single Muslim that cultivates or plants anything of which humans, animals or birds may eat is counted as charity towards them on his behalf' (Hadith), which suggests that it is the duty of humans to protect the Earth by looking after plants for the benefit of life on Earth and that this will be rewarded by God.

10 Christians and Muslims believe the universe was designed and made by God out of nothing/ the Bible and the Qur'an say that God made the universe and all life in it in six days/ 'In the beginning God created the heavens and the earth' (Genesis 1:1 [NIV]), which can be used to support the belief that God created the universe at the beginning of time/ 'your Lord is God who created the heavens and earth is six days' (Qur'an 7:54), which can be used to support the belief that God created the universe in six days/ some Christians believe God used the Big Bang to create the universe/ most Christians believe the creation stories are symbolic/ most Muslims believe 'six days' refers to six longer periods of time.

Test the 12 mark question

Suggested answers shown here, but see page 10 for guidance on levels of response.

12 Arguments in support

- It would either make abortion easier (supporting pro-choice) or harder (supporting pro-life).
- Making abortion easier gives more rights to women/ the woman has to experience the pregnancy, give birth to the baby and bring it up, so she should have the right to choose whether to continue with the pregnancy/ life does not begin until birth (or the moment the foetus can survive outside the womb), so abortion is not a form of killing.
- Making abortion stricter gives more rights to the unborn child/ respects the sanctity of life/ makes it harder to take away life given by God/ makes it harder to interfere with God's plan for people (Jeremiah 1:5).
- Some Muslims and Christians would remove the law altogether to make abortion illegal.

Arguments in support of other views

- The current law is the best compromise between groups that support abortion and groups that don't/ there is a reasonable balance between the rights of the woman and the unborn child/ the law respects the quality of life of both the woman and the unborn child.
- Making abortion illegal could endanger the life of the woman/ might prompt women to carry out unsafe abortions by themselves.
- For those who believe life starts at conception, making abortion easier would result in more killing of human life.

13 Arguments in support

- A minority of Christians believe humans were given dominion over the earth so can do what they want with it/ 'Rule over the fish in the sea and the birds in the sky and over every living creature that moves on the ground' (Genesis 1:28 [NIV]).
- If resources are destroyed or used up, scientists will develop alternatives.
- Humans need natural resources to sustain their way of life.

Arguments in support of other views

- Most Christians and Muslims believe humans were put on the earth as stewards to look after it on behalf of God for future generations/ God put Adam into the Garden of Eden 'to work it and take care of it' (Genesis 2:15 [NIV])/ it is wrong to destroy something that belongs to someone else (i.e. God).
- Many of the earth's natural resources are non-renewable so there is only a limited supply of them/ using them up too quickly will probably make life much harder for future generations/ this shows a lack of love and respect for others.

7 The existence of God and revelation

Test the 1 mark multiple-choice question

1. C) Theist

2. B) Mortal

Test the 1 mark question

Suggested answers, other relevant answers would be credited. 1 mark for a correct point.

3. The argument contradicts itself/ it says everything has a cause, but what caused God to exist?/ if God is eternal, why can't the universe be eternal?/ the Big Bang was a random event, not caused/ just because events on earth have causes does not necessarily mean the universe itself has a cause.

4. Misuse of freewill (e.g. war) / natural causes (e.g. earthquakes, floods)/ Disobedience of Adam and Eve (Hawwa).

Test the 4 mark question

Suggested answers, other relevant answers would be credited. 1 mark for each simple point, another mark for developing each point, so a maximum of 4 marks for two developed points.

6 *Beliefs must be different*:

An event performed by God which appears to break the laws of nature/ *an example of such an event*/ for Christians they confirm God's existence/ show God is at work in the world/ are answers to prayer.

Muslims see them more as individual religious experiences, although they may still point towards the existence of God.

They are not real/ they are lucky coincidences that have nothing to do with God/ may be made up for fame or money/ healing miracles may be mind over matter or misdiagnosis/ can be explained scientifically in a way we don't yet know.

7 *Beliefs must be similar*:

Comes through ordinary human experiences/ seeing God's creative work and presence in nature/ through reason or conscience/ through worship or scripture/ the Bible and Qur'an help to reveal what God is like and how he wants people to live/ the power of the words in the Bible and Qur'an are so strong that people can come to believe in God through reading or hearing them/ the Qur'an is the actual word of God as revealed to Muhammad so carries great authority.

People are mistaken in interpreting normal events as general revelation/ nature is special but has nothing to do with revelation/ scriptures are opinions of their writers and not inspired by God/ scripture can be wrongly interpreted.

Test the 6 mark question

Suggested answers, other relevant answers would be credited. 1 mark for each simple point, another mark for developing each point, so a maximum of 4 marks for two developed points, plus 1 extra mark for a correct reference to a source of religious belief or teaching, and 1 more extra mark for applying the reference to the question.

9. For Christians, a way of God revealing something about himself/ direct experience of God in an event, such as a vision or prophecy/ e.g. Moses receiving the Ten Commandments, Mary finding out she is pregnant from the angel Gabriel, Saul's vision/ can have a great influence on people's lives. The Ten Commandments illustrate special revelation because Moses had a direct experience with God when God gave him the Ten Commandments.

Some Muslims would say there is no special revelation/ the revelation of the Qur'an to Muhammad was a divine revelation, given only to prophets and messengers/ Muslims can gain nearness to God and experience dreams, angels, visions or miracles but these are not divine revelation as nobody else can claim to be a prophet/ 'It is not granted to any mortal that God should speak to him except through revelation or from behind a veil' (Qur'an 42:51), which suggests that special revelation in Islam does not occur when humans speak to God but through revelation that happens to the prophets such as Muhammad.

10. Omnipotent/ omniscient/ benevolent/ immanent/ transcendent/ personal/ impersonal/ 'In the beginning God created the heavens and the earth' (Genesis 1:1 [NIV]), which illustrates God's omnipotence because God is powerful enough to complete such an immense action/ creator/ *any ideas in scripture related to creation, possibility of relationship with God through prayer, incarnation of Jesus, work of the Holy Spirit.*

Test the 12 mark question

Suggested answers shown here, but see page 10 for guidance on levels of response.

12 Arguments in support

- Miracles are events with no natural or scientific explanation that only God could perform/ only God is all-powerful and transcendent, so able to perform miracles.
- If they occur as a response to prayer, they are a response to asking God for something/ prove that God is listening and responding to prayers.
- They are usually good and God is the source of all that is good.
- The fact that some people convert to Christianity after experiencing a miracle is proof of God's existence.
- The miracle of the revelation of the Qur'an is hugely important to Muslims.
- 67 healing miracles have officially been recognised as taking place at Lourdes.
- Miracles exist and are caused by God, therefore God exists.

Arguments in support of other views

- Miracles are lucky coincidences and nothing to do with God.
- Whether something counts as a miracle is a matter of interpretation.
- They may have scientific explanations we haven't yet discovered.
- Healings could be mind over matter or misdiagnosis.
- Some miracles are made up for fame or money.
- If God is involved in miracles, this means he is selective and unfair (as only a few people experience them)/ but God cannot be selective and unfair/ therefore he cannot be involved in miracles.
- If miracles don't exist or have other explanations, they are nothing to do with God, so do not prove he exists.

13 Arguments in support

- A loving God would not allow people to suffer.
- God should be aware of evil and suffering because he is omniscient/ if so, he should use his powers to prevent it because he is omnipotent/ because God does not do this, he cannot exist.
- If God made all of creation to be perfect then there would not be earthquakes, droughts, etc./ suffering caused by the natural world is an example of poor design, which no God would be responsible for.

Arguments in support of other views

- It is unfair to blame God for suffering because he doesn't cause it.
- Suffering is a result of the disobedience of Adam and Eve (Hawwa)/ the result of humans misusing their free will.
- If there was no evil, no one would be able to actively choose good over bad/ learn from their mistakes/ show compassion and kindness towards others who are suffering.
- Humans are in charge of looking after the earth and God chooses not to interfere.
- The existence of evil doesn't necessarily prove God does not exist, but could suggest he is not all-loving or all-powerful.

8 Religion, peace and conflict

Test the 1 mark multiple-choice question

1. C) Justice

2. D) Conventional weapons

Test the 1 mark question

Suggested answers, other relevant answers would be credited. 1 mark for a correct point.

3. Just cause/ correct authority/ good intention/ last resort/ reasonable chance of success/ proportional methods used.

4. For Christians violent protest goes against Jesus' teachings not to use violence/ goes against the commandment 'You shall not murder.' (Exodus 20:13 [NIV])/ does not show 'love of neighbour'/ goes against the sanctity of life/ goes against 'So in everything, do to others what you would have them do to you, for this sums up the Law and the Prophets' (Matthew 7:12 [NIV]).

For Muslims, violence is only allowed in self-defence/ 'Do not kill each other, for God is merciful to you' (Qur'an 4:29).

Test the 4 mark question

Suggested answers, other relevant answers would be credited. 1 mark for each simple point, another mark for developing each point, so a maximum of 4 marks for two developed points.

6. *Beliefs must be different*:

Christians who support pacifism (e.g. The Religious Society of Friends/Quakers) believe that war can never be justified/ all killing is wrong/ it breaks the commandment 'You shall not murder' (Exodus 20:13 [NIV])/ Jesus taught 'Blessed are the peacemakers, for they shall be called children of God' (Matthew 5:9 [NIV])/ conflicts should be settled peacefully.

Christians who do not support pacifism believe that war is sometimes necessary as a last resort/ they would fight in a 'just war'/ to stop genocide taking place/ to defend one's country or way of life/ to help a weaker country defend itself from attack.

Most Muslims believe in peace but are not pacifists/ accept fighting in self-defence/ to defend their faith and family from attack/ lesser jihad has similar strict rules to the just war theory/ 'Fighting has been ordained for you, though it is hard for you' (Qur'an 49:9).

7. *Beliefs must be similar*:

Forgiveness is showing grace and mercy/ pardoning someone for what they have done wrong/ Christians believe forgiveness is important as in the Lord's Prayer it says 'Forgive us our sins as we forgive those who sin against us'/ this means God will not forgive if Christians do not forgive others/ Christians believe God sets the example by offering forgiveness to all who ask for it in faith/ some Christians believe repentance is needed for forgiveness/ forgiveness does not mean accepting wrongdoing.

In Islam forgiveness is important for living peacefully/ Allah is merciful and the source of all forgiveness/ repentance is a virtue/ forgiveness between believers is encouraged, with a promise of reward from Allah/ however, some sins such as the sin of shirk (associating partners with God) is unforgivable.

Test the 6 mark question

Suggested answers, other relevant answers would be credited. 1 mark for each simple point, another mark for developing each point, so a maximum of 4 marks for two developed points, plus 1 extra mark for a correct reference to a source of religious belief or teaching, and 1 more extra mark for applying the reference to the question.

9. Some Christians believe in the just war theory/ it is right to fight in a war if the cause is just/ war can be the lesser of two evils/ it can be justified if its purpose is to stop atrocities/ people have a right to self-defence/ 'If there is a serious injury, you are to take life for life, eye for eye, tooth for tooth' (Exodus 21:23–24 [NIV]), which some people interpret to mean that it is right to fight a war in retaliation against injury and death/ 'Love your neighbour as yourself' (Matthew 22:39 [NIV]) demands protection of weaker allies through war.

Lesser jihad obliges Muslims to fight under certain conditions/ Muslims must not damage the environment/ kill innocent people/ treat prisoners unfairly/ 'Let those of you who are willing to trade the life of this world for the life to come, fight in God's way' (Qur'an 4:74), which can be interpreted to mean that it is right to fight a war and die for God.

10. It is when individuals or groups restore friendly relations after conflict or disagreement/ it is important to build good relationships after a war so conflict does not break out again/ justice and peace must be restored to prevent further conflict/ to create a world which reflects God's intention in creation/ Christians believe they must be reconciled to others before they can worship God properly/ 'Therefore, if you are offering your gift at the altar and there remember that your brother or sister has something against you, leave your gift there in front of the altar. First go and be reconciled to them; then come and offer your gift.' (Matthew 5:23–24 [NIV]), which suggests that before worshipping God you should reconcile with anyone you are in conflict with and only after you have done that should you worship God.

Reconciliation is a sacrament in the Catholic Church/ Christians believe it is important to ask God for forgiveness for sins/ reconciliation restores a Christian's relationship with God and other people.

Muslims believe God sets the example for reconciliation, as God forgives anyone who asks sincerely in faith/ the Qur'an teaches that those who are humble and reply to aggressive people with words of peace will be considered servants of God, which suggests that God favours people who reconcile with and are kind to people who are against them/ peace and harmony is the main message of Islam.

Test the 12 mark question

Suggested answers shown here, but see page 10 for guidance on levels of response.

12. Arguments in support

- Some religious people believe in the concept of a holy war/ a holy war is fighting for a religious cause or God/ probably controlled by a religious leader/ these believers think that it is justifiable to defend their faith from attack.
- Religion has been a cause of such wars in the past/ e.g. the Crusades, wars between Christians and Muslims, were fought over rights to the Holy Land/ in the Old Testament there are many references to God helping the Jewish people settle in the Promised Land.
- There are many examples of conflicts that involve different religious groups/ e.g. Catholics and Protestants in Northern Ireland during the 'Troubles'/ Israeli–Palestinian conflict/ conflict in India and Pakistan between Muslims and Hindus.
- Some atheists claim that without religion, many conflicts could be avoided/ religiously motivated terrorism would cease.

Arguments in support of other views

- Religion is not the main cause of wars: greed, self-defence and retaliation are all more common causes/ academic studies have found that religion plays a minor role in the majority of conflicts/ most wars have many causes/ e.g. opposition to a government, economic reasons, objection to ideological, political or social systems/ e.g. political differences played a greater role in the conflict in Northern Ireland than religion.
- Christians today believe they should defend their faith by reasoned argument, not violence/ many Christians think no war can be considered 'holy' when there is great loss of life/ '"Put your sword back in its place," Jesus said, "for all who draw the sword die by the sword"' (Matthew 26:52 [NIV])/ 'You have heard that it was said to the people long ago, '"You shall not murder [...]" But I tell you that anyone who is angry with a brother or sister will be subject to judgement' (Matthew 5:21–22 [NIV]).
- The majority of Muslims defend their faith today without violence/ condemn terrorism by groups such as ISIS/ 'Know that the evil of war is swift, and its taste bitter' (Hadith).

13. Arguments in support

- Religious people should be the main peacemakers because of their beliefs/ e.g. Christians believe in 'love your neighbour'/ the sanctity of life/ peace/ forgiveness/ reconciliation/ Jesus taught 'Blessed are the peacemakers'/ there is an emphasis on peace in the Qur'an/ 'Islam' in Arabic comes from 'salam', meaning peace or safety.
- Prayer and meditation can bring inner peace to individuals/ this helps avoid quarrels with others/ peacemaking begins with each person.
- Many religious people are engaged in peacemaking in today's world/ e.g. the Anglican Pacifist Fellowship works to raise awareness of the issue of pacifism/ the 'Peace People' (Mairead Corrigan, Betty Williams and Ciaran McKeown) in Northern Ireland work to bring Catholic and Protestant communities together to stop violence/ the Muslim Peace Fellowship works for greater understanding of Islamic teachings about peace/ works for justice through non-violent strategies.

Arguments in support of other views

- Religious people should be peacemakers, but not the main ones/ the problems of global conflict require global solutions that are beyond any individual to solve/ the United Nations should be the main peacekeeping organisation/ only large organisations or governments with powerful resources can hope to affect peacemaking in the world.
- Religious people can be peacemakers in their own families and support justice and peace groups locally, but they cannot take the lead as peacemakers/ their main duty is to their family/ people have jobs that do not allow them to stop violence across the world/ the most they can do is contribute to organisations which help.
- Everyone should take equal responsibility for helping to contribute towards peace, whether they are religious or not/ some situations might benefit from peacemakers who are not religious.

9 Religion, crime and punishment

Test the 1 mark multiple-choice question

1. A) Corporal punishment

2. C) Happiness

Test the 1 mark question

Suggested answers, other relevant answers would be credited. 1 mark for a correct point.

3. Retribution/ deterrence/ reformation/ protection.

4. Poverty/ upbringing/ mental health problem/ addiction/ greed/ hate/ opposition to an unjust law.

Test the 4 mark question

Suggested answers, other relevant answers would be credited. 1 mark for each simple point, another mark for developing each point, so a maximum of 4 marks for two developed points.

6. *Beliefs must be different*:

Approved of by most Christians/ as allows offenders to make up for what they have done wrong/ helps to reform and rehabilitate offenders/ may involve counselling, treatment or education/ may include an opportunity to apologise to the victim/ no harm is done to the offender.

Not approved of by some Muslims as it is not a sufficient deterrent/ there is no element of retribution/ it is too soft a punishment/ not used much in Shari'ah law.

7. *Beliefs must be similar:*

It makes reoffending unlikely/ it brings justice as the punishment matches the fate of the victim/ it deters others from committing serious crimes/ 'life for life, eye for eye, tooth for tooth' (Exodus 21:23–24 [NIV])/ 'We prescribed for them a life for a life, an eye for an eye' (Qur'an 5:45)/ Muslims believe actions against Shari'ah law are actions against God, so should be punished severely.

Test the 6 mark question

Suggested answers, other relevant answers would be credited. 1 mark for each simple point, another mark for developing each point, so a maximum of 4 marks for two developed points, plus 1 extra mark for a correct reference to a source of religious belief or teaching, and 1 more extra mark for applying the reference to the question.

9. Christians are expected to forgive those who offend against them and if they do God will forgive them/ forgiveness is not a replacement for punishment/ it should be unlimited/ 'not seven times, but seventy-seven times' (Matthew 18:22 [NIV]), which suggests that forgiveness should be complete and not limited/ Jesus forgave those who crucified him and Christians should follow his example/ 'Father forgive them, for they do not know what they are doing' (Luke 23:34 [NIV]).

Muslims believe only God can truly forgive and only for those who are truly sorry/ 'God is most forgiving and merciful' (Qur'an 24:22), which is one of the 99 names for God/ humans should forgive to allow goodness to be established/ offenders should seek forgiveness from their victim before they can expect God to forgive/ 'Pardon each other's faults and [God] will grant you honour' (Hadith).

10. Hate crimes are condemned by Christianity and Islam/ hate crimes target individuals and groups perceived to be different/ Christians believe God created all humans equal in his image/ 'There is neither Jew nor Gentile, slave nor free man, male nor female, for you are all one in Christ Jesus' (Galatians 3:28 [NIV]), which can be interpreted to mean that hate crimes are wrong because they victimise individuals and the Bible says we are all equal in the eyes of Jesus/ hate crimes are not loving ('love your neighbour')/ hate crimes are not just/ 'God commands justice … and prohibits wrongdoing and injustice' (Qur'an 16:90), which can be interpreted to mean that hate crimes are wrong because they are unjust behaviours towards other people which God forbids.

Test the 12 mark question

Suggested answers shown here, but see page 10 for guidance on levels of response.

12. Arguments in support

- Sanctity of life means life is sacred and special to God/ should be valued and respected/ the life of an offender has equal value to any other life/ the use of the death penalty does not respect life.
- Sanctity of life also suggests that only God has the right to take life/ this means it is not right to take another person's life/ this interferes with God's plan for a person's life.

Arguments in support of other views

- Murderers have already taken the life of someone else so their life should not be respected.
- Executing a murderer ensures they don't go on to kill again, thus preserving the sanctity of life/ the death penalty may deter others from killing and breaking the sanctity of life.
- 'Do not take life that God has made sacred, except by right' (Qur'an) overrides the sanctity of life where necessary according to Shari'ah law.
- For those who don't believe in God, sanctity of life does not show that the death penalty is wrong/ there are other reasons for why the death penalty is wrong/ e.g. it is not an effective deterrent/ it does not allow for the possibility of reformation/ it may kill innocent people.

13. Arguments in support

- Committing crime is wrong whatever the reason/ all crime causes someone to suffer.
- People should obey the law/ God put the system of government in place to rule every citizen so it is his law that is being broken (Romans 13:31).
- Christians and Muslims believe it is wrong to commit crime because of poverty/ people should focus on creating a fairer society where the need to steal because of poverty is removed.
- Those who commit crime through illness or addiction should be provided with treatment so they have no reason to commit crimes.
- People who want to protest against an unjust law can do so legally, e.g. through a peaceful protest.

Arguments in support of other views

- Society is not fair so crimes because of need/poverty are justified in some circumstances/ e.g. it may be better to steal food than allow a child to starve.
- Some laws are unjust and the only way to change them is to break them/ peaceful protest is not always powerful enough to change the law.
- All humans have a tendency to do bad things, including crime, because of original sin.
- Those who commit crime because of addiction/mental health problems cannot help it.

10 Religion, human rights and social justice

Test the 1 mark multiple-choice question

1. C) Unfairly judging someone before knowing the facts

2. B) Promoting tolerance

Test the 1 mark question

Suggested answers, other relevant answers would be credited. 1 mark for a correct point.

3. Actions or behaviour that result from prejudice.

4. Christians give money to the Church/ to people living in poverty/ Muslims give Zakah (2.5 per cent of savings) to the mosque for people living in poverty/ Shi'a Muslims give Khums (20% – half of which goes to charity)/ make voluntary contributions to charities/ support food banks.

Test the 4 mark question

Suggested answers, other relevant answers would be credited. 1 mark for each simple point, another mark for developing each point, so a maximum of 4 marks for two developed points.

6. *Beliefs must be different*:

Prejudice is always wrong because it is unjust to single out individuals or groups for inferior treatment/ some Christians and Muslims believe any relationship based on love should be cherished.

Some Christians and many Muslims think same-sex sexual relationships are unnatural and against God/ cannot lead to the 'natural' creation of a child/ goes against God's plan for humans/ same-sex relationships are forbidden in Shari'ah law and punishable by death.

7. *Beliefs must be similar*:

The Bible stresses the importance of providing human rights to all people/ which includes creating a more just society/ 'Let justice roll on like a river' (Amos 5:24 [NIV])/ Christians believe it is not loving to deny people their rights/ rights are written into law, and the law is inspired by God so must be obeyed/ Christians have a responsibility to help provide human rights/ 'faith without deeds is useless' (James 2:20 [NIV]).

Shari'ah law ensures human rights are protected/ working for justice (which includes creating access to human rights) is a religious duty for Muslims/ 'God commands justice, doing good and generosity towards relatives' (Qur'an 16:90).

Test the 6 mark question

Suggested answers, other relevant answers would be credited. 1 mark for each simple point, another mark for developing each point, so a maximum of 4 marks for two developed points, plus 1 extra mark for a correct reference to a source of religious belief or teaching, and 1 more extra mark for applying the reference to the question.

9. Poverty is sometimes caused by injustice and Christians must combat injustice/ poverty involves suffering and Christians are expected to help relieve suffering/ e.g. the Parable of the Sheep and Goats, which suggests that Christians should follow the behaviour of the sheep and help those in need and this can help tackle poverty/ people have God-given talents that they should use to help overcome poverty/ e.g. the Parable of the Talents/ tackling poverty is good stewardship/ Jesus' teaching to 'love your neighbour' encourages Christians to help those in poverty.

Muslims must also combat injustice/ 'Adhere to justice, for that is closer to awareness of God' (Qur'an 5:8), which can be interpreted to mean that Muslims should help tackle poverty because doing so supports justice which is what God wants/ tackling poverty is good stewardship (khalifah)/ Muslims are expected to show kindness to people living in poverty/ partly by giving Zakah and Khums/ 'be compassionate towards the destitute' (Hadith).

10. Christianity teaches that wealth can lead to traits such as greed and selfishness/ 'the love of money is a root of all sorts of evil' (1 Timothy 6:10 [NIV]), which suggests that it is dangerous to be attached to money because money causes issues that take people away from God/ focusing on wealth brings the danger of ignoring God and neglecting the spiritual life/ 'You cannot serve both God and money' (Matthew 6:24 [NIV]).

Islam teaches that wealth can lead to greed and craving for even more/ 'Beware of greed for it is ready poverty' (Hadith)/ hoarding money is wrong because it should be used for people living in poverty/ 'Tell those who hoard gold and silver instead of giving in God's cause that they will have a grievous punishment' (Qur'an 9:34), which can be interpreted to mean that keeping excessive wealth unnecessarily will lead to punishment from God/ money can distract from God, who is the most important thing in life.

Test the 12 mark question

Suggested answers shown here, but see page 10 for guidance on levels of response.

12. Arguments in support

- Discrimination is an action that can cause physical and psychological harm/ goes against the ideas of equality and justice/ which are central to Christian and Muslim ethics/ 'God commands justice' (Qur'an 39:6).
- Christianity and Islam teach that all people should be treated equally because they are all made in God's image/ 'There is neither Jew nor Gentile, neither slave nor free, nor is there male and female, for you are all one in Christ Jesus' (Galatians 3:28 [NIV]).
- Positive discrimination is still a form of discrimination/ it would be better to treat all people equally.

Arguments in support of other views

- Positive discrimination helps to make up for centuries of negative discrimination against minority groups/ helps to make people aware of the need to rectify negative discrimination against minority groups.
- Positive discrimination shows love and compassion to people who are suffering/ so it can be supported by Christian and Muslim teachings.
- It is important to differentiate between the needs of different people/ not everyone is the same/ some people are better suited to certain roles than others.

13. Arguments in support

- Freedom of religion is a basic human right/ 'Everyone has the right to freedom of thought, conscience and religion' (The United Declaration of Human Rights)/ in the UK the law allows people to follow whichever faith they choose.
- It is wrong to try to force someone to follow a religion/ or to prevent them from following a religion/ it should be a matter of personal choice/ this makes choosing to follow a particular religion more significant/meaningful.
- Forcing people to follow a religion or preventing them from following a religion could lead to more conflict and fighting between different religions.
- Being a Christian or Muslim is a choice that any person can make/ 'Now the truth has come from your Lord: let those who wish to believe in it do so, and let those who wish to reject it do so' (Qur'an 18:29)/ Jesus taught people to show tolerance and harmony.

Arguments in support of other views

- If a religion teaches hatred and intolerance, there should be limits on how it can be taught or practised/ people should not be allowed to join it for the wrong reasons.
- Some people might argue that to show patriotism, a person should follow the main religion in their country.
- Some people might argue that when people are allowed to join any religion, this can lead to conflict and tension between different religious groups, whereas if everyone followed the same religion then there would be more harmony between people.
- Some people might unintentionally harm/upset others through choosing a particular religion/ e.g. by choosing a religion that is different to their parents'/ so perhaps it should not be so easy to switch from one religion to another.
- In some countries blasphemy laws prevent people from criticising Islam/ giving up Islam or changing from Islam to another faith is considered wrong in Shari'ah law.